Accounting
for Derivatives

Accounting for Derivatives

RAYMOND E. PERRY, EDITOR

IRWIN
Professional Publishing®
Chicago • London • Singapore

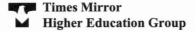 **Times Mirror**
Higher Education Group

Library of Congress Cataloging-in-Publication Data

Accounting for derivatives / Raymond E. Perry, editor.
    p.   cm.
    Includes bibliographical references and index.
    ISBN 0-7863-0541-X
    1. Derivative securities — Accounting. I. Perry, Raymond E.
HF5686.B65A27   1997
657'.48 — dc20   96–20963

Printed in the United States of America
1 2 3 4 5 6 7 8 9 0 DO 3 2 1 0 9 8 7 6

Raymond J. Beier

Raymond J. Beier is a partner in Coopers & Lybrand, LLP's Corporate Finance Practice and leads a unit that advises investment bankers, equity investment firms, and corporate clients on financial accounting and reporting, regulatory aspects, and income tax matters of consummating complex financial transactions. He deals in all forms of mergers and acquisitions, leveraged buyout transactions, joint ventures, and recapitalization transactions. Mr. Beier is also a leading adviser on designing financial products and structuring corporate finance transactions that involve managing interest rate, foreign currency, and commodity price risks. In addition, he advises clients on financing transactions involving special-purpose entities and securitized financing structures. He is also involved with advising Coopers & Lybrand's major industrial and manufacturing clients on structuring acquisitions and financing transactions, including use of derivatives.

Mr. Beier has authored numerous chapters and articles dealing with financial accounting on the structuring of mergers, acquisitions, derivatives, and financing transactions that have appeared in, among others, *The Valuation of Mortgage-Backed Securities, Financial Executive, Handbook of Accounting and Auditing,* and *Mergers and Acquisitions.*

Mr. Beier, a CPA, received his BA and MBA in Finance from the University of Minnesota.

Robert H. Herz

Robert H. Herz is Coopers & Lybrand, LLP's Associate National Director of Accounting and SEC Services. Mr. Herz is C & L's leading partner in the area of accounting for derivatives and financial instruments, and has authored numerous publications on the topic. His works include the chapter "Accounting and Financial Reporting for Derivatives and Synthetics" in the recently published *Handbook of Derivatives and Synthetics — Innovations, Technologies and Strategies in the Global Markets,* as well as Coopers & Lybrand's *Guide to Financial Instruments* and *Foreign Currency Translation and Hedging.* He is also a frequent speaker on this topic and has been widely quoted in the press regarding accounting developments relating to derivatives.

Mr. Herz has served as an engagement partner on a number of Coopers & Lybrand's major securities and derivatives products dealer clients. He has also been heavily involved in advising Coopers & Lybrand's major industrial and manufacturing clients on the use of derivatives in financial risk management. Mr. Herz is Chairman of the Financial Accounting Standards Board's Financial Instruments Task Force, as well as a member of FASB's Emerging Issues Task Force, the American Institute of Certified Public Accountants' Securities and Exchange Commission Regulations Committee, and the New York Stock Exchange's International Capital

Markets Committee. He is both a U.S. certified public accountant (having won the gold medal on the CPA exam) as well as a U.K. chartered accountant.

James A. Johnson

James A. Johnson serves as a Deloitte & Touche, LLP, National Audit Partner in the firm's Capital Markets Group. The group provides accounting, tax, and risk management advice to dealers and users of innovative financial instruments, including complex structured asset sales, derivatives transactions, and hedging strategies. Mr. Johnson's clients include major investment and commercial banks. Mr. Johnson is Chairman of the American Institute of Certified Public Accountants (AICPA) Financial Instruments Task Force, and a former member of both the AICPA's Accounting Standards Executive Committee and the AICPA Committee on Banking. In addition, he serves on the advisory board of the Institute for International Research and on the editorial advisory board of *Derivatives, Tax, Regulatory and Accounting*. Mr. Johnson speaks and publishes extensively in the area of financial instruments. He holds an MBA (University of California at Los Angeles) and is a CPA (New York and California).

Michael A. Moran

Michael A. Moran is a partner in the Financial Services Practice of the New York Office of KPMG Peat Marwick LLP. He has concentrated his efforts on serving the needs of financial services clients during most of his 34 years with the firm. He has dealt with a broad range of accounting and auditing issues related to multinational banking, bank holding companies, trading activities, financial instruments, mergers and acquisitions, risk management, and information systems. He is a member of the firm's SEC Reviewing Partners' Committee and in this capacity, as well as on client engagements, he has dealt with a wide range of domestic and international securities and regulatory filings. He is a member of the Financial Instruments Task Force of the Financial Accounting Standards Board and has served on the Banking Committee of the American Institute of Certified Public Accountants. Mr. Moran is a frequent speaker and lecturer at industry and professional conferences including the Bank Administration Institute, the Institute of Internal Auditors, the American Institute of Certified Public Accountants, and the banking conferences of several state CPA societies. He also serves as an instructor at the KPMG Peat Marwick Executive Education conferences. He has been a speaker at seminars sponsored by the Practicing Law Institute and Executive Enterprises, as well as at conferences and examiner training programs of federal banking regulators. He is an honors graduate of Lehigh University and is a member of both the American Institute of Certified Public Accountants and the New York State Society of Certified Public Accountants.

Benjamin S. Neuhausen

Mr. Neuhausen is a partner with the Professional Standards Group of Arthur Andersen & Co. His principal areas of specialization include compensation and employee benefits, financial instruments, insurance, health care, and leasing. His responsibilities include advising clients and engagement personnel on the accounting issues, and preparing the firm's responses to proposals from the FASB, SEC, AICPA, and other standards-setting bodies. Before joining the Accounting Principles Group, Mr. Neuhausen worked in the audit practice of Arthur Andersen in New York with clients in a variety of industries. From 1979 to 1981, he was an FASB Fellow.

Mr. Neuhausen is a member of the FASB Task Force on Stock-based Compensation. In addition, he was a member of the AICPA Task Force on Employers' Accounting for ESOP

Transactions and a special adviser to the FASB Task Force on Employers' Accounting for Postretirement Benefits.

Mr. Neuhausen earned a B.A. in Economics from Michigan State University and an M.B.A. in Accounting from New York University.

Raymond E. Perry, Editor

Raymond E. Perry retired as a partner in the firm of Deloitte & Touche, LLP, after 38 years with that firm. He subsequently served for three years as a Senior Accounting Fellow on the staff of the Financial Accounting Standards Board. He is currently a member of the FASB's Financial Instruments Advisory Task Force. Mr. Perry's responsibilities with Deloitte & Touche included heading a consultation group in the firm's national office that focused on accounting and auditing issues relating to financial institutions and financial instruments. During his time at the Financial Accounting Standards Board he focused on accounting for financial instruments including heading a project dealing with securitizations and related issues.

John T. Smith

John T. Smith is a partner in the national office of Deloitte & Touche, LLP. He is the partner in charge of policies and standards. Mr. Smith provides accounting consultation and technical support to Deloitte & Touche personnel and clients nationwide on financial instruments including securitizations, hedging and risk management strategies, off-balance-sheet instruments, derivative products, and valuation techniques.

Mr. Smith serves as a member of the Financial Instruments Task Force of the Financial Accounting Standards Board (FASB) and the Working Group on hedging issues. He has served as a member of the FASB's Interest Methods Task Force and has made presentations on financial instruments to various groups, including FASB, the Securities and Exchange Commission, and FASB's Emerging Issues Task Force. He published an article entitled "Complications in Accounting for Hedges against Interest Rate Fluctuations," in the March 1989 issue of *Financial Managers Statement*. He is the primary author of the Deloitte & Touche publication *Financial Instruments: Fair Value Considerations, Implementing SFAS 107*. He is the principal contributor to the publication authored by Deloitte & Touche entitled, *Internal Control Issues in Derivatives Usage, An Information Tool for Considering the COSO Internal Control-Integrated Framework in Derivatives Applications*. In addition, he is a contributing author of an article entitled, "Using Derivatives: What Senior Managers Must Know," published in the January–February issue of *Harvard Business Review*.

Charles W. Smithson

Charles W. Smithson is a Managing Director and head of the CIBC Wood Gundy School of Financial Products. His career has spanned the gamut, with positions in the private sector, in academe, and in government. Prior to joining CIBC, Mr. Smithson was a Senior Vice President of the Chase Manhattan Bank, where he was responsible for risk management research. He was also a Managing Director of the Continental Bank, where he directed research for the global trading and distribution sector. Mr. Smithson taught for nine years at Texas A&M University and later directed the Ph.D. program in finance at the University of North Texas. In government, he served with both the Federal Trade Commission and the Consumer Products Safety Commission. Charles Smithson is the author of numerous articles in academic journals on subjects ranging from regulation to labor market discrimination to financial engineering. He is the author of three books, *The Doomsday Myth, Managerial Economics,* and *The*

Economics of Mineral Extraction, is coauthor of *Managing Financial Risk,* and is one of the editors of *The Handbook of Financial Engineering.* He has been cited in newspapers from the *Des Moines Register* to the *Wall Street Journal.* Charles Smithson served as a member of the working group for the Global Derivatives Project sponsored by the Group of Thirty.

CONTENTS

CHAPTER 3

Accounting for "Free Standing" Interest Rate, Commodity, and Currency Derivatives—Futures, Forwards, Swaps, and Options   25

Raymond J. Beier
Robert H. Herz

CHAPTER 4

Accounting for Embedded Derivatives   93
James A. Johnson

CHAPTER 8

Valuation—Specific Types of Instruments   327
John T. Smith

CHAPTER 9

Management Control of Derivative Operations 359
Michael A. Moran

CHAPTER 1

Introduction: What Is a Derivative?

Raymond E. Perry

The proliferation of financial derivatives during the past 15 years has led to great interest in all aspects of those often complex instruments. The novelty, variety, and complexity of derivatives have overwhelmed traditional accounting practices for financial instruments, which had evolved in earlier years when nonderivative type instruments prevailed. The development of accounting standards directed toward derivatives has lagged and, as a result, present accounting practices for derivatives are often confusing and contradictory. Similar derivatives can have widely different accounting. The purpose of this volume is to put in one place the presently accepted accounting for various types of derivatives. Each chapter is written by an expert in the field.

What is a financial derivative? In the financial press, the term *derivatives* is bandied about daily and either is not defined or is defined simply as "financial instruments that derive their value from some other instrument or index." That description is rarely enlightening and the financial writer probably repeats it by rote with only a vague notion about its meaning. Further, no generally agreed upon or authoritative definition of derivatives exists. Recent documents by the Financial Accounting Standards Board (FASB) describe derivatives as "forwards, futures, swaps or options or financial instruments with similar characteristics." But what are those similar characteristics?

Financial derivatives, like all other financial instruments, are contracts between two parties under which they agree to an exchange: Party A pays cash to Party B on one or more dates and receives from Party B (on one or more dates) cash, another financial instrument, or a commodity. Often the exchange involves cash flows or another financial instrument, the value of which may vary during the term of the contract. Some derivatives, often described as *commodity derivatives,* are not purely financial but involve the exchange of cash for a commodity such as precious metals, minerals, or agricultural commodities. Still other derivatives represent an undivided interest in a pool of financial instruments; for example, residential mortgage loans. Those derivatives derive their value from the underlying residential mortgages usually held in special purpose trusts. The underlying mortgage notes are also derivatives because they contain embedded prepayment options.

Perhaps the best way to understand financial derivatives is to start with financial instruments that are *not* derivatives to see how the two differ. The most common nonderivative financial instruments are U.S. Treasury obligations.[1] The investor (Party A) pays a fixed amount of cash to the government (or to a previous holder) for a U.S. Treasury obligation and the Treasury agrees to pay a fixed amount of cash— interest and principal repayment—on fixed dates to the holder. The amount and dates of payments (cash flows) are fixed in the contract. For financial derivatives, by contrast, the dates

---

1. The only exceptions are Treasuries with a call option. The reason for that exception will become clear later in the discussion.

or amounts or both are variable for at least some of the cash payments or deliveries of other financial instruments, the values of which vary over time.

Interest rate swaps, exchange traded futures contracts, and financial options are common examples of financial derivatives.

Interest Rate Swaps   Parties to an interest rate swap agree to exchange cash flows on specified dates. Party A is obligated to pay a fixed amount of cash, and Party B is obligated to pay a variable amount of cash based on some price index such as the London InterBank Offer Rate (LIBOR).

Exchange Traded Futures Contracts   The parties to an exchange traded futures contract agree to exchange a fixed amount of cash for a specified financial instrument on a fixed future date. The cash amount and the date of exchange are fixed, but the value of the financial instrument is variable; its value will depend on the prevailing market prices at the date of exchange.

Financial Options Contracts   Financial option contracts— puts and calls—are also common derivatives. The writer of a *put* agrees to purchase a defined financial instrument from the holder of the put, at the holder's option, for a fixed price on a future date. The writer of a *call* agrees to sell a defined financial instrument to the holder of the call, at the holder's option, for a fixed price on a future date. The market price of the underlying financial instrument at the exercise date determines whether the holder chooses to exercise the option and which party gains or loses.

Financial forwards (of which exchange traded futures are one example), swaps, and options are referred to as *freestanding derivatives*. Those types of derivatives and their characteristics are discussed by Charles W. Smithson in Chapter 2, A Building-Block Approach to Forwards, Futures,

Swaps, Options, and Hybrid Securities. The accounting standards relating to those derivatives are covered by Robert H. Herz and Raymond J. Beier in Chapter 3, Accounting for Free-Standing Interest Rate, Commodity, and Currency Derivatives—Futures, Forwards, Swaps, and Options.

Many complex financial instruments contain an option or other derivative element embedded in a nonfinancial instrument. Also several different derivatives may be combined in a single financial instrument. The most common types of such instruments and the prevailing accounting standards are discussed by James A. Johnson in Chapter 4, Accounting for Embedded Derivatives.

Securitization and similar transactions that lead to the creation of embedded derivatives are covered by Benjamin S. Neuhausen in Chapter 5, Accounting for Securitization Transactions.

The FASB has been studying the basic accounting for derivatives. Under present accounting many derivatives are off-balance-sheet, and accordingly the only information presented in financial statements may be in the footnotes. The FASB requires extensive disclosure in notes to financial statements, and those requirements are discussed in Chapter 6, Financial Statement Disclosures.

Because accounting measurement and recognition, disclosure, and control of derivatives requires determining their fair values, discussion of valuation is presented by John T. Smith in Chapter 7, Valuation—Concepts, and Chapter 8, Valuation—Specific Types of Instruments.

A number of large prominent public companies have recently reported huge losses from using financial derivatives, thus raising questions as to the adequacy of controls over derivative operations. Those concerns are addressed by Michael A. Moran in Chapter 9, Management Control of Derivative Operations.

CHAPTER 2

A Building-Block Approach to Forwards, Futures, Swaps, Options, and Hybrid Securities

Charles W. Smithson

The increased economic uncertainty first evident in the 1970s has altered the way financial markets function. As foreign exchange rates, interest rates, and commodity prices have become more volatile, corporations have discovered that their value is subject to various financial price risks in addition to the risk inherent in their core business.

To illustrate the effect of changes in a given financial price on the value of a firm, we use the concept of a *risk profile*. Figure 2–1 presents a case in which an unexpected increase in financial price P (that is, the T-bill rate, the price of oil, or the dollar price of a yen) decreases the value of the firm (V). In Figure 2–1, the difference between the actual price and the expected price is shown as ΔP, while ΔV measures the resulting change in the value of the firm. Had ΔP remained small, as it did before the 1970s, the indexed changes in firm

Reprinted from *Managing Financial Risk* by Charles W. Smithson, Clifford W. Smith, Jr., with D. Sykes Wilford (Chicago: Irwin Professional Publishing, 1995), 30–44.

FIGURE 2-1

A Risk Profile Relating the Expected Change in Firm Value (ΔV) to Unexpected Changes in Financial Price (ΔP)

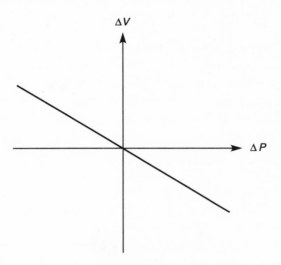

value would have been correspondingly small. But for many companies, the increased volatility of exchange rates, interest rates, and commodity prices (large ΔPs) in the 1970s and 1980s has been a major cause of sharp fluctuations in share prices (large ΔVs). With this greater potential for large swings in value, companies have begun exploring new methods for dealing with financial risks.

Confronted with the increased volatility of financial prices, companies found that the first and most obvious approach was to try to forecast future prices more accurately. If changes in exchange rates, interest rates, and commodity prices could be predicted with confidence, companies could avoid unexpected swings in value. In the context of Figure 2–1, if the actual price could be completely anticipated, ΔP would equal zero and the value of the firm thus would be unchanged. However, economists were generally unsuccessful in predicting changes in interest rates, foreign exchange rates, and commodity prices.

This shouldn't be surprising; attempts to outpredict markets as efficient as the financial markets are unlikely to succeed. Because forecasting cannot be relied on to eliminate risk, the remaining alternative is to *manage* the risks. Financial risk management can be accomplished by using on-balance-sheet transactions. For example, a company can manage a foreign exchange exposure resulting from foreign competition by borrowing in the competitors' currency or by moving production abroad. But such on-balance-sheet methods can be costly and, as firms like Caterpillar have discovered, inflexible.[1]

Alternatively, financial risks can be managed with the use of off-balance-sheet instruments: forwards, futures, swaps, and options. When you first begin to examine these financial instruments, you are confronted by what seems an insurmountable barrier to entry: Participants in the various market and the trade publications seem to possess specialized expertise applicable in only one market to the exclusion of all the others. Adding to the complexities of the individual markets themselves is a welter of jargon—ticks, collars, strike prices, straddles, and so forth. Indeed, it appears to the novice like a Wall Street version of the Tower of Babel, with each group of market specialists speaking a different language.

In marked contrast to this specialist approach, this chapter presents a generalist approach. We treat forwards, futures, swaps, and options not as four unique instruments but rather as four closely related instruments to deal with a single problem—managing financial risk. Indeed, we are going to show how the off-balance-sheet instruments are like those plastic building blocks children snap together. You can build the instruments from one another (or combine the basic instruments into larger creations).

---

1. See "Caterpillar's Triple Whammy," *Fortune,* October 27, 1986.

FORWARD CONTRACTS

Of the four instruments we consider in this chapter, the *forward contract* is the most straightforward and, perhaps for this reason, the oldest. A forward contract obligates its owner to buy a given asset on a specified date at a price (known as the *exercise* or *forward price*) specified at the origination of the contract. If, at maturity, the actual price is higher than the exercise price, the contract owner makes a profit; if the price is lower, the owner suffers a loss.

In Figure 2–2, the payoff from buying a forward contract is superimposed on the original risk profile. If the actual price at contract maturity is higher than the expected price, the firm's inherent risk will lead to a decline in the value of the firm, but this decline will be offset by the profit on the forward contract. Hence, for the risk profile illustrated, this forward contract provides a perfect hedge. (If the risk profile were sloped positively instead of negatively, this risk would be managed by selling instead of buying a forward contract.)

F I G U R E   2 – 2

Payoff Profile for Forward Contracts

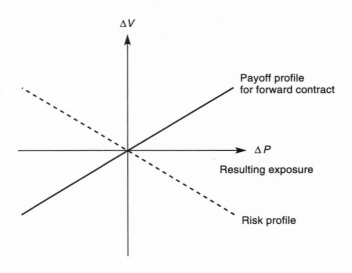

In addition to its payoff profile, two features of a forward contract should be noted. First, the default (or credit) risk of the contract is two-sided. The contract owner either receives or makes a payment, depending on the price movement of the underlying asset. Second, the value of the forward contract is conveyed only at the contract's maturity; no payment is made either at origination or during the term of the contract.

FUTURES CONTRACTS

Although futures contracts on commodities have been traded on organized exchanges since the 1860s, financial futures are relatively new, dating from the introduction of foreign currency futures in 1972. The basic form of the futures contract is identical to that of the forward contract: A *futures contract* obligates its owner to purchase a specified asset at a specified exercise price on the contract maturity date. Thus, the payoff profile for the purchaser of a forward contract as presented in Figure 2–2 could illustrate equally well the payoff to the holder of a futures contract.

Like the forward contract, the futures contract also has two-sided risk. But in marked contrast to forwards, futures markets use two devices that virtually eliminate credit risk. First, instead of conveying the value of a contract through a single payment at maturity, changes in the value of a futures contract are conveyed at the end of the day in which they are realized. Look again at Figure 2–2. Suppose that on the day after origination the financial price rises and, consequently, the contract has a positive value. In the case of a forward contract, this value change would not be received until contract maturity. With a futures contract, this change in value is received at the end of the day. In the language of the futures markets, the futures contract is *cash settled,* or *marked-to-market,* daily.

Because the performance period of a futures contract is reduced by marking-to-market, the risk of default declines accordingly. Indeed, since the value of the futures contract is paid or received at the end of each day, it is not hard to see why Fischer Black likened a futures contract to "a series of forward contracts. Each day, yesterday's contract is settled, and today's contract is written."[2] That is, a futures contract is like a sequence of forwards in which the "forward" contract written on day 0 is settled on day 1 and is replaced, in effect, with a new "forward" contract reflecting the new day-1 expectations. This new contract is then itself settled on day 2 and replaced, and so on until the day the contract ends.

The second feature of futures contracts that reduces default risk is the requirement that all market participants— sellers and buyers alike[3]—post a performance bond called *margin*. If your futures contract increases in value during the trading day, this gain is added to your margin account at the day's end. Conversely, if your contract loses value, this loss is deducted. And if your margin account balance falls below some agreed-upon minimum, you are required to post an additional bond—your margin account must be replenished or your position will be closed out.[4] Because this process generally closes any position before the margin account is depleted, performance risk is materially reduced.[5]

---

2. Fischer Black, "The Pricing of Commodity Contracts," *Journal of Financial Economics 3,* (1976).

3. Keep in mind that if you buy a futures contract, you are taking a long position in the underlying asset—that is, the value of the futures position appreciates with increases in the value of the asset. Conversely, selling a futures contract is equivalent to taking a short position.

4. When the contract is originated on the U.S. exchanges, an "initial margin" is required. Subsequently, the margin account balance must remain above the "maintenance margin." If the margin account balance falls below the maintenance level, the balance must be restored to the initial level.

5. Note that this discussion has ignored daily limits. If there are daily limits on the movement of futures prices, large changes in expectations about the underlying asset can effectively close the market. (The market opens, immediately moves the limit, and then is effectively closed until the next day.) Hence, there could exist an instance in which the broker desires to close out a customer's position but is not able to do so immediately because the market is experiencing limit moves. In such a case, the statement that performance risk is "eliminated" is too strong.

Note that the exchange itself limits the default risk exposure of its customers. Yet while daily settlement and the requirement of a bond reduce default risk, the existence of an exchange (or clearinghouse) primarily transforms risk. More specifically, the exchange deals with the two-sided risk inherent in forwards and futures by serving as the counterparty to all transactions. If you wish to buy or sell a futures contract, you buy from or sell to the exchange. Hence, you need only evaluate the credit risk of the exchange, not the credit risk of some specific counterparty.

From the point of view of the market, the exchange does not reduce default risk; the expected default rate is not affected by the existence of the exchange. However, the existence of the exchange can alter the default risk faced by an individual market participant. If you buy a futures contract from a specific individual, the default risk you face is determined by the default rate of that specific counterparty. If instead you buy the same futures contract through an exchange, your default risk depends on the default rate not just of your counterparty but on the rate of the entire market. Moreover, to the extent that the exchange is capitalized by equity from its members, the default risk you face is reduced further because you have a claim not against some specific counterparty but rather against the exchange. Therefore, when you trade through the exchange, you are in a sense purchasing an insurance policy from the exchange.

The primary economic function of the exchange is to reduce the costs of transacting in futures contracts. The anonymous trades made possible through the exchange, together with the homogeneous nature of the futures contracts — standardized assets, exercise dates (four per year), and contract sizes — enable the futures markets to become relatively liquid. However, as was made clear by recent experience of the London Metal Exchange, the exchange structure, marking-to-market, and margin accounts do not eliminate default risk. In November 1985, the "tin cartel" defaulted on contracts for tin delivery on the London Metal Exchange, thereby making the exchange liable for the loss.[6]

In sum, a futures contract is much like a portfolio of forward contracts. At the close of business each day, in effect, the existing forwardlike contract is settled and a new one is written.[7] This daily settlement feature combined with the margin requirement allows futures contracts to reduce substantially the credit risk inherent in forwards.

SWAP CONTRACTS[8]

Because they were publicly introduced only in 1981, swaps are commonly portrayed as one of the latest financing innovations. But as we hope to be able to convince you, a swap contract is in essence nothing more complicated than a portfolio of forward contracts. We will also demonstrate that the credit risk attending swaps is somewhat less than that of a forward contract with the same maturity but greater than that of a comparable futures contract.

As implied by its name, a *swap contract* obligates two parties to exchange, or swap, some specified cash flows at specified intervals. The most common form is the *interest rate swap,* in which the cash flows are determined by two different interest rates.

---

6. A description of this situation is contained in "Tin Crisis in London Roils Metal Exchange," *The Wall Street Journal,* November 13, 1985.
7. A futures contract is *similar* to a portfolio of forward contracts; however, a futures contract and a portfolio of forward contracts become identical only if interest rates are *deterministic*—that is, known with certainty in advance. See Robert A. Jarrow and George S. Oldfield, "Forward Contracts and Futures Contracts," *Journal of Financial Economics 9,* (1981) and John A. Cox, Jonathan E. Ingersoll, and Stephan A. Ross, "The Relationship between Forward Prices and Futures Prices," *Journal of Financial Economics 16,* (June 1986).
8. This section is based on Clifford W. Smith, Jr., Charles W. Smithson, and Lee M. Wakeman, "The Evolving Market for Swaps," *Midland Corporate Finance Journal,* (Winter 1986).

FIGURE 2-3

(a) An Interest Rate Swap   *(b)* An Interest Rate Swap as a
Portfolio of Forward Contracts

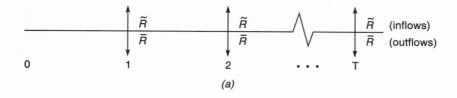

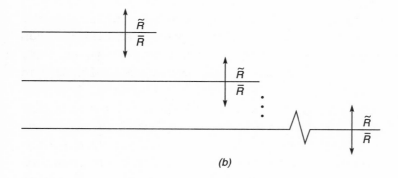

(b)

Panel (a) of Figure 2–3 illustrates an interest rate swap from the perspective of a party who is paying out a series of cash flows determined by a fixed interest $(\bar{R}_T)$ and receiving a series of cash flows determined by a floating interest rate $(\tilde{R})$.[9]

---

9. Specifically, the interest rate swap cash flows are determined as follows: The two parties agree to some notional principal, P. (The principal is notional in the sense that it is only used to determine the magnitude of cash flows; it is not paid or received by either party.) At each settlement date, 1, 2, . . ., T, the party illustrated makes a payment $\bar{R}_T = \bar{r}_T P$, where $\bar{r}_T$ is the T-period fixed rate that existed at origination. At each settlement, the party illustrated receives $\tilde{R} = \tilde{r}P$, where $\tilde{r}$ is the floating rate for that period—that is, at settlement date 2, the interest rate used is the one-period rate in effect at period 1.

Panel (b) of Figure 2–3 demonstrates that this swap contract can be decomposed into a portfolio of forward contracts. At each settlement date, the party to this swap has an implicit forward contract on interest rates: The party illustrated is obligated to sell a fixed-rate cash flow for an amount specified at the origination of the contract. Also in this sense, a swap contract is like a portfolio of forward contracts.

In terms of our earlier discussion, this means that the solid line in Figure 2–2 also represents the payoff from a swap contract. Specifically, the solid line in Figure 2–2 illustrates a swap contract in which the party receives cash flows determined by P (say, the U.S. Treasury bond rate) and makes payments determined by another price—say, the London InterBank Offer Rate (LIBOR). Thus, in terms of their ability to manage risk, forwards, futures, and swaps all function in the same way.

But similar payoff profiles notwithstanding, the instruments differ with respect to their default risk. As we know, the performance period of a forward is equal to its maturity; because no performance bond is required, a forward contract is a pure credit instrument. Futures reduce the performance period (to one day) as well as requiring a bond, thus virtually eliminating credit risk. Swap contracts typically use only one of these mechanisms to reduce credit risk; they reduce the performance period.[10] This point becomes evident in Figure 2–3. Although the maturity of the contract is T periods, the performance period is generally not T periods long but is instead a single period. Thus, given a swap and a forward contract of roughly the same maturity, the swap is likely to impose far less credit risk on the counterparties to the contract than the forward. This credit risk difference between swaps and forwards is analogous to that between an amortized loan and a zero coupon bond.

---

10. There are instances in which a bond has been posted in the form of collateral. As should be evident, in this case the swap becomes more like a futures contract.

At each settlement date throughout a swap contract, the changes in value are transferred between the counterparties. To illustrate this in terms of Figure 2–3, suppose that interest rates rise on the day after origination. The value of the swap contract illustrated has risen. This value change will be conveyed to the contract owner not at maturity (as would be the case with a forward contract) nor at the end of that day (as would be the case with a futures contract). Instead, at the first settlement date, part of the value change is conveyed in the form of the "difference check" paid by one party to the other. To repeat, then, the performance period is reduced from that of a forward, albeit not to so short a period as that of a futures contract.[11] (Keep in mind that we are comparing instruments with the same maturities.)

At this point let us stop to summarize the two major points made thus far. First, a swap contract, like a futures contract, is like a portfolio of forward contracts. Therefore, the basic payoff profiles for each of these three instruments are similar. Second, the primary differences among forwards, futures, and swaps are the settlement features of the contracts and amount of default risk these instruments impose on counterparties to the contracts. Forwards and futures represent the extremes, with a swap being the intermediate case.

It is important to note that swaps do impose some credit risk. For this reason it is not surprising that commercial banks have become increasingly active in a market that was initiated, for the most part, by investment banks. The sharp difference of opinion that has arisen between commercial and investment banks over the "most advisable" evolutionary path for the swap market to follow is also understandable. Because investment banks are not in the business of extending credit,

---

11. Unlike futures for which all of any change in contract value is paid or received at the daily settlements, swap contracts convey only part of the total value change at the periodic settlements.

they would much prefer swaps to become more like futures—
that is, exchange-traded instruments with bonded contract
performance. Commercial banks, by contrast, have a comparative advantage in credit extension and thus stand to
benefit if swaps remain credit instruments. Accordingly, they
would prefer the credit risk to be managed by imposing capital
requirements on the financial institutions arranging the swaps.

OPTION CONTRACTS

As we have seen, the owner of a forward, futures, or swap
contract has an *obligation* to perform. In contrast, an *option*
gives its owner a *right*, not an obligation. An option giving its
owner the right to buy an asset—a *call option*—is provided
in Figure 2–4. (Here, once again, the financial price P could
be an interest rate, a foreign exchange rate, the price of a
commodity, or the price of some other financial asset.) The

F I G U R E   2 – 4

The Payoff Profile of a Call Option

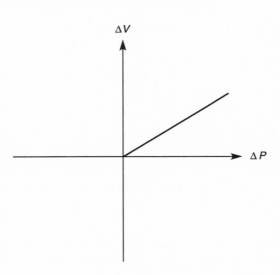

owner of the contract illustrated has the right to purchase the asset at a specified future date at a price agreed upon today. Consequently, if P rises, the value of the option also goes up. But the value of the option remains unchanged (at zero) if P declines because the option contract owner is not obligated to purchase the asset if P moves to an unfavorable price.[12]

The payoff profile for the owner of the call option is repeated in panel (a) of Figure 2–5. In this case, the contract owner has bought the right to buy the asset at a specified price—the exercise (strike) price. (In Figures 2–4 and 2–5, the exercise price is implicitly equal to the expected price.)

FIGURE 2–5

Payoff Profiles of Puts and Calls

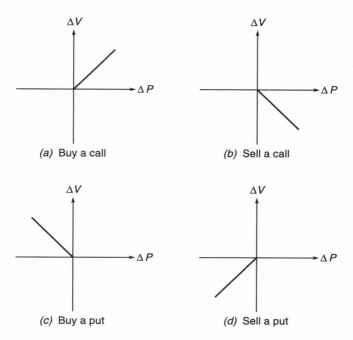

(a) Buy a call

(b) Sell a call

(c) Buy a put

(d) Sell a put

---

12. For continuity, we continue to use the ΔV, ΔP convention in figures. To compare these figures with those found in most texts, treat ΔV as deviations from zero ($\Delta V = V - 0$) and remember that ΔP measures deviations from expected price ($\Delta P = P - {}^-P$).

The payoff profile for the party who sold the call option (also known as the *call writer*) is shown in panel (b). Note that in contrast to the buyer of the option, the seller of the call option has the *obligation* to perform. For example, if the owner of the option elects to exercise his or her option to buy the asset, the seller of the option is obligated to sell the asset.

Aside from the option to buy an asset, there is also the option to sell an asset at a specified price, known as a *put option*. The payoff to the buyer of a put is illustrated in panel (c) of Figure 2–5, and the payoff for the seller of the put is shown in panel (d).

In many instances, jargon does more to confuse than to make clear, and this is particularly true in the buy/sell, call/put jargon of options. Suppose you were exposed to rising interest rates—that is, an increase in interest rates reduced your wealth. As illustrated by the left side of Figure 2–6, you could eliminate the down-side exposure by buying a call on the interest rate (that is, you could buy an interest rate cap). Expressed in terms of bond prices, however, the proper strategy for hedging the same exposure would be to buy a put on bonds. As Figure 2–6 illustrates, a call on interest rates is equivalent to a put on bonds. The same thing occurs, moreover, in the foreign exchange market; a put on DM/$ is equivalent to a call on $/DM. (There have been times when two persons arguing about whether something was a put or a call were, in fact, both right.)

To this point, we have considered only the payoffs for the option contracts. Figures 2–4 through 2–6 assume in effect that option premiums are neither paid by the buyer nor received by the seller. By making this assumption, we have sidestepped the thorniest issue, the valuation of option contracts. We now turn to option valuation.

The breakthrough in option pricing theory came with the work of Fischer Black and Myron Scholes in 1973. Conveniently for our purposes, Black and Scholes took what might be described as a building-block approach to the valuation of

FIGURE 2 – 6

Hedging Exposures with Options

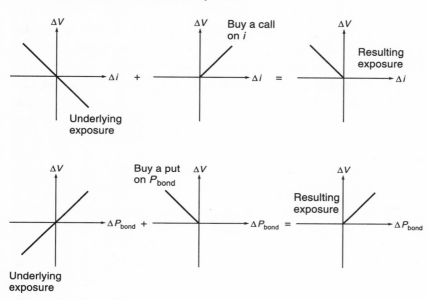

options. Look again at the call option illustrated in Figure 2–4. For increases in the financial price, the payoff profile for the option is that of a forward contract. For decreases in the price, the value of the option is constant, like that of a riskless security such as a Treasury bill.

The work of Black and Scholes demonstrates that a call option could be replicated by a continuously adjusting (dynamic) portfolio of two securities: (1) forward contracts on the underlying asset and (2) riskless securities. As the financial price rises, the call-option-equivalent portfolio contains an increasing proportion of forward contracts on the asset. Conversely, the replicating portfolio contains a decreasing proportion of the asset as the price of the asset falls. Because this replicating portfolio is effectively a synthetic call option, arbitrage activity should ensure that its value closely approximates the market price of exchange-traded call options. In this sense, the value of a call option—and thus the premium that would be charged its buyer—is determined by the value of its option-equivalent portfolio.

Panel (a) of Figure 2–7 illustrates the payoff profile for a call option that includes the premium. This figure (and all of the option figures thus far) illustrates an *at-the-money option,* an option for which the exercise price is the prevailing expected price. As panels (a) and (b) of Figure 2–7 illustrate,

FIGURE 2–7

(a), (b) "At-the-Money" Option
(c), (d) "Out-of-the-Money" Option

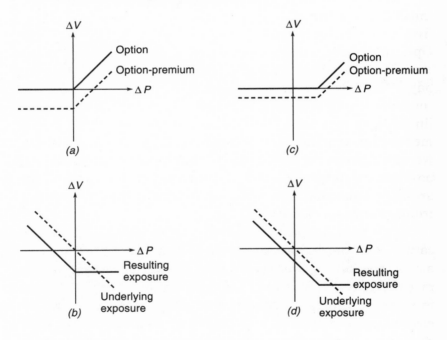

(a) The payoff profit for buying an at-the-money call option
The dashed line reflects the premium.
(b) The resulting exposure from buying the at-the-money option.
(c) The payoff profit for buying an out-of-the-money call option.
(d) The resulting exposure from buying the out-of-the-money option.

an at-the-money option is paid for by sacrificing a significant amount of the firm's potential gains. However, the price of a call option falls as the exercise price increases relative to the prevailing price of the asset. This means that an option buyer who is willing to accept larger potential losses in return for paying a lower option premium should consider using an out-of-the-money option.

An *out-of-the-money call option,* illustrated in panel (c) of Figure 2–7, provides less downside protection than other instruments, but the option premium is significantly less. The lesson here is that option buyers can alter their payoff profiles simply by changing the exercise price.

For the purposes of this discussion, however, the most important feature of options is that they are not as different from other financial instruments as they might first seem. Options do have a payoff profile that differs significantly from that of forward contracts (or futures or swaps). But option payoff profiles can be duplicated by a dynamically adjusted combination of forwards and risk-free securities. Thus, we find that options have more in common with the other instruments than is immediately apparent. Futures and swaps, as we saw earlier, are in essence nothing more than particular portfolios of forward contracts; options, as we have just seen, are very much akin to portfolios of forward contracts and risk-free securities.

This point is reinforced if we consider ways that options can be combined. Consider a portfolio constructed by buying a call and selling a put with the same exercise price and maturity. As the top row of Figure 2–8 illustrates, the resulting portfolio (long a call, short a put) has a payoff profile equivalent to that of buying a forward contract on the asset. Similarly, the bottom row of Figure 2–8 illustrates that a portfolio constructed by selling a call and buying a put (short a call, long a put) is equivalent to selling a forward contract. The relation illustrated in Figure 2–8 is known more formally as *put–call parity*. The special import of this relation, at least

FIGURE 2-8

Put–Call Parity

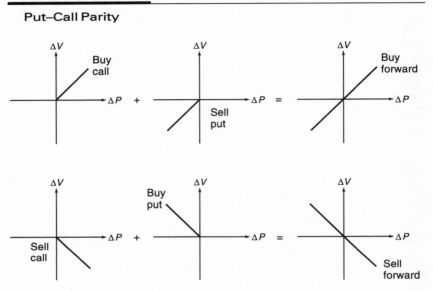

Same strike price and maturity is equivalent to the payoffs to buying a forward.
Selling a call and buying a put are equivalent to selling a forward.

in this context, is the building-block construction it makes possible: Two options can be "snapped together" to yield the payoff profile for a forward contract.

At the beginning of this section, then, it seemed that options would be very different from forwards, futures, and swaps; in many ways they are. But we discovered two building-block relations between options and the other three instruments:

1. Options can be replicated by snapping together a forward, futures, or swap contract with a position in risk-free securities.

2. Calls and puts can be snapped together to become forwards.

THE BOX OF FINANCIAL BUILDING BLOCKS

Forwards, futures, swaps, and options—to the novice, they all look so different. And if you read the trade publications or talk to the participants in the four markets, the apparent differences among the instruments are likely to seem even more pronounced. It looks as if the only way to deal with the financial instruments is to pick one and then become a specialist in that market, to the exclusion of the others.

However, it turns out that forwards, futures, swaps, and options are more like building blocks—to be linked together into complex creations—and less like stand-alone, individual constructions. To understand the off-balance-sheet instruments, you don't need a lot of market-specific knowledge; you just need to know how the instruments can be linked to one another. As we have seen, (1) futures are built by snapping together a package of forwards; (2) swaps are similarly built by snapping together a package of forwards; (3) options can be built by snapping together a forward with a riskless security; and (4) options can be snapped together to yield forward contracts, or forwards can be snapped apart to yield a package of options.

Figure 2–9 characterizes each of the four instruments we have been discussing according to the shapes of their payoff profiles. It also reminds us of the put–call parity relation between options and forwards, futures, or swaps. In so doing, Figure 2–9 in effect provides the instruction manual for our box of financial building blocks. A quick look shows that though there can be many pieces in the box, there are only six basic shapes with which to concern yourself. The straight pieces come in three colors: We know we can obtain a forward payoff profile either with forwards (the red ones), futures (the yellow ones), or swaps (the blue ones). The kinked pieces are all the same color (white) because options can be combined to replicate a forward, a future, or a swap.

FIGURE 2-9

The Financial Building Blocks

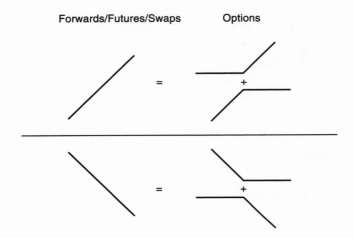

Accounting for "Free Standing" Interest Rate, Commodity, and Currency Derivatives— Futures, Forwards, Swaps, and Options*

Raymond J. Beier
Robert H. Herz

Financial innovations have challenged the financial community's use of existing authoritative guidance for new financial instruments. Accounting standard-setters have not kept up with the innovations of the financial community; that is, the creation of new financial products has outpaced the establishment of relevant accounting standards. Although existing literature by the Financial Accounting Standards Board (FASB) has addressed the accounting for certain types of derivative financial instruments (derivatives) in connection with hedging transactions, the prescribed guidance is narrowly focused as it only applies to a limited number of financial instruments and their uses. To compound the confusion, the existing accounting guidance was developed on a piecemeal basis, resulting in inconsistent and conflicting accounting standards. Thus industry practices, while not authoritative, have evolved within the marketplace.

---

* The authors would like to acknowledge Jeff Kotowity of Coopers & Lybrand, LLP, for his valuable assistance in preparing this chapter.

The climate of confusion caused the FASB to commence a major project on financial instruments[1] and off-balance-sheet financings in order to develop a more complete and consistent framework for all financial instruments including derivatives. Because of the project's complexity, the FASB's progress has been slow. In the meantime, the savings and loan crisis and well-publicized losses incurred by several companies through derivatives activities have prompted the financial community and regulators to urge the project's swift completion. As an interim step, the FASB has issued several standards to improve disclosure about derivatives, of which the most recent was SFAS No. 119, *Disclosure about Derivative Financial Instruments and Fair Value of Financial Instruments*. A detailed discussion of the disclosure requirements of SFAS No. 119 and the other disclosure-related standards is presented in Chapter 6.

As a result of the perceived riskiness of certain derivative activities, the accounting for derivatives and financial instruments has been heading in the direction of fair value accounting, which effectively oversteps historical cost, the underlying foundation of generally accepted accounting principles (GAAP). Although opponents of this trend have vigorously argued that fair value accounting (mark-to-market) creates unnecessary earnings volatility and "user unfriendly" financial statements, all of the FASB's recent standards on disclosure of derivatives and the accounting for financial instruments have contained

---

1. The FASB defines "financial instruments" in Statement of Financial Accounting Standard No. 107, *Disclosure about Fair Value of Financial Instruments,* as "cash, evidence of ownership interest in an entity, or a contract that both:
   a. Imposes on one entity a contractual obligation (1) to deliver cash or another financial instrument to a second entity or (2) to exchange other financial instruments on potentially favorable terms with the first entity.
   b. Conveys rights to that second entity a contractual right [footnote omitted] (1) to receive cash or (2) exchange other financial instruments on potentially favorable terms with the first entity."

significant elements of fair value accounting. Most significantly, in May 1993 the FASB issued SFAS No. 115, *Accounting for Debt and Equity Securities,* which requires companies to carry significant portions of their debt and equity securities portfolio at fair value. So it appears that the wave of fair value accounting will encompass derivatives as well. (Further discussion of the FASB's progress on its derivatives project is included at the end of this chapter.)

This chapter covers (1) the existing accounting rules and practices applicable to investors in and users of free-standing derivatives, (2) the FASB's ongoing efforts in this area, and (3) the Securities and Exchange Commission's current views on derivatives. Chapter 4 will cover derivatives that are embedded in other financial instruments.

CURRENT AUTHORITATIVE GUIDELINES

The existing authoritative guidance for derivatives, which is neither complete nor entirely consistent, is based on several sources. The Securities and Exchange Commission (SEC) has the power to set financial reporting guidelines for publicly traded companies. Although the SEC generally defers to the FASB and the FASB's Emerging Issues Task Force (EITF) regarding the accounting treatment of new products, the SEC's staff has been increasingly proactive in expressing its views on certain hedging and disclosure issues related to derivatives. The FASB and EITF pronouncements on financial instruments and derivatives are presented in Table 3–1.

The American Institute of Certified Public Accountants (AICPA) offers practical guidance—although not authoritative pronouncements—to the profession on accounting and financial reporting. The AICPA issues Statements of Position (SOPs) and industry accounting guides to assist in the planning of audit engagements, the application of FASB pronouncements, and the dissemination of industry GAAP. The AICPA also publishes issues papers on accounting topics such as

T A B L E   3 – 1

Published Guidelines for Accounting for Derivatives

Document	Title	Application
Statement of Financial Accounting Standards (SFAS)		
SFAS No. 52	Foreign Currency Translation	Hedge accounting for foreign currency contracts and currency swaps.
SFAS No. 80	Accounting for Futures Contracts	Hedge accounting for futures contracts.
FASB Interpretation Number (FIN)		
FIN 39	Offsetting of Amounts Related to Certain Contracts	Offsetting receivables and payables arising from derivatives transactions.
EITF Issues		
EITF No. 84–36	Interest Rate Swap Transactions	General guidance on interest rate swaps.
EITF No. 86–25	Offsetting Foreign Currency Swaps	As described in title.
EITF No. 87–31	Sale of Put Options on Issuer's Stock	As described in title.
EITF No. 88–9	Put Warrants	Warrants that contain the features of a put option and a stock warrant.
EITF No. 90–17	Hedging Foreign Currency Risks with Purchased Options	Hedging anticipated foreign currency transactions with purchased options.
EITF No. 91–1	Hedging Intercompany Foreign Currency Risks	As described in title.
		(Continued)

Document	Title	Application
EITF No. 91–4	Hedging Foreign Currency Risks with Complex Options and Similar Transactions	Hedging anticipated foreign currency risk.
EITF No. 94–7	Accounting for Financial Instruments Indexed to, and Potentially Settled in, a Company's Own Stock	Derivatives linked to a company's own stock.
EITF No. 95–2	Determination of What Constitutes a Firm Commitment to Foreign Currency Transactions Not Involving Third Parties	Clarification of EITF No. 91–1.
EITF No. 95–11	Accounting for Derivative Instruments Containing an Option-Based and a Forward-Based Component	Accounting for compound derivatives such as amortizing swaps and cancelable swaps. No consensus was reached.
EITF No. 96–1	Sale of Put Options on Issuer's Stock That Require or Permit Cash Settlement	As described in title.
SEC Related		
Accounting Series Release No. 268	Presentation in Financial Statements of Redeemable Preferred Stock	Applied by analogy to certain derivatives that settle in a company's own stock.
American Institute of CPAs		
Issues Paper 86–2	Accounting for Options	
EITF 96–13	Accounting for Sales of Call Options or Warrants on Issuers Stock with Various Forms of Settlement	As described in title.

Issues Paper 86–2, *Accounting for Options,* which many rely on when accounting for options and option strategies though it is not recognized as authoritative.

Finally, the consensus views reached by the FASB's Emerging Issues Task Force are a very important source of guidance. In June 1984 the FASB established the EITF as part of its plan to provide timely guidance on implementation questions and emerging accounting issues. The 13-member EITF includes representatives of major public accounting firms, smaller public accounting firms, the Financial Executive's Institute, the Institute of Management Accountants, and the Business Roundtable. The chief accountant of the SEC attends EITF meetings as an observer, and the FASB's director of research and technical activities is the EITF's chairman. As three dissenting votes preclude a consensus on any given issue, an EITF consensus view indicates that significant diversity in practice is not expected. Moreover, an EITF consensus is regarded by auditors and by the staff of the SEC as authoritative and as part of GAAP. It is noteworthy that over half of the issues dealt with by the EITF since its inception have related to financial instruments and new financial products, including many issues dealing specifically with derivatives. Table 3–1 presents the most significant EITF issues in this regard.

GENERAL ACCOUNTING APPROACH FOR DERIVATIVES

The primary goal of accounting is to produce relevant information that is reliable, neutral, and capable of being compared among different entities. Also, embedded in accounting theory is the belief that the costs of obtaining information should not exceed the benefits (broadly defined) of such information.[2] The "matching principle," under which gains and

---

2. For example, see the discussion of SFAS No. 107. Under that pronouncement, disclosures are to be made to the extent that the costs of computing "fair market value" are practicable (that is, the costs do not exceed the benefits).

losses on related items should be recognized in the same period, is the foundation for a special accounting treatment commonly referred to as *hedge accounting*.

When transactions are commenced to hedge the risks associated with other transactions and meet specific requirements, hedge accounting may be applied. Hedge accounting generally means that gains or losses from the hedge position are recognized in the same period as the losses or gains on the hedged item. Because derivatives are commonly used as hedging tools, the accounting for such derivatives is premised on hedge accounting.

The FASB defines derivative financial instruments as futures, forwards, swaps, option contracts, or other financial instruments with similar characteristics such as interest rate caps and floors, and fixed-rate loan commitments which settle in cash or another financial instrument.[3] That definition, excludes those contracts that settle in a nonfinancial commodity (such as wheat or oil); however, a contract indexed to the price of wheat but settled in cash would be considered a derivative financial instrument.

The FASB's definition of a derivative is specifically directed toward *free-standing derivatives*—those derivatives that are not embedded in another instrument. Accordingly, the FASB's definition excludes all on-balance-sheet receivables and payables, including those that "derive" their values or contractually required cash flows from the price of some other security or index, such as mortgage-backed securities, interest-only and principal-only obligations, and indexed debt instruments. Accounting for many of those types of financial instruments is covered in Chapter 5.

Generally, a free-standing derivative is carried at fair value and unrealized gains and losses are recorded currently in earnings (that is, marked-to-market) unless the derivative qualifies for hedge accounting in which both realized and unrealized gains and losses on the derivative are recognized

---

3. SFAS No. 119, paragraph 5.

concurrently with the hedged position (consistent with the matching principle). Thus, if the hedged position is carried at historical cost (debt, for example), the unrealized gains and losses on the hedge (such as a futures contract) are deferred and included in the cost basis of the hedged position. Conversely, if the hedged position is carried at fair value with unrealized gains or losses recognized currently in income, the unrealized gains and losses on the hedge will also be recognized currently in income.

However, because the accounting for derivatives is not comprehensive and was developed on a piecemeal basis, some of the hedge accounting guidelines differ by derivative type. For that reason, the determination as to whether a transaction may be accounted for as a hedge should be assessed on a case-by-case basis. Consequently, the accounting for derivatives is presented below by derivative type. When the next edition of this book is issued, the FASB will have developed a comprehensive accounting standard for derivatives.

FUTURES CONTRACTS

A futures contract is a legal agreement between a buyer or seller and a clearinghouse of a futures exchange, such as the Chicago Board of Exchange. The accounting for futures contracts is set forth in SFAS No. 80, *Accounting for Futures Contracts*. Under SFAS No. 80, gains and losses resulting from changes in the fair value of a futures contract may be deferred under hedge accounting if all of the following criteria are met:

- The item to be hedged exposes the enterprise to price or interest rate risk.

- The hedged position reduces the exposure (as when there is high correlation between changes in the market value of the hedged position and the inverse changes in market value of the hedged item).

▪ The hedge position is designated as a hedge.

Exposure to Risk

As specified in the first criterion, risk must be present to account for a futures contract under hedge accounting; otherwise, hedging is superfluous. Also the entire enterprise, not just a specific transaction, must be exposed to risk. When determining whether an enterprise is subject to risk, natural hedges must be considered. *Natural hedges* are other assets, liabilities, firm commitments, or anticipated transactions that already offset or reduce the exposure to risk posed by the item to be hedged. For example, a wholesale firm is exposed to risk when an increase in the price of corn could reduce its profits after it has committed to sell the corn at a fixed price yet purchase it at prevailing market prices. In that situation the wholesaler is exposed to enterprise risk. However, if the wholesaler has committed to buy the corn at the prevailing market prices, the wholesaler's exposure to price risk will be offset by the corresponding fluctuations in the future sales price. The wholesaler is therefore naturally hedged. Furthermore, realizing that many large companies manage risk on a decentralized basis by business unit rather than on an entire enterprise basis, SFAS No. 80 also permits risk assessment at the business unit level.

Reduction of Risk

The hedge position must also reduce the exposure created from the risk. This means that changes in the market value of the hedging instrument and the hedge position are correlated or inversely related; that is, gains or losses on the hedging instrument and hedge position will offset. SFAS No. 80, however, requires that a high degree of correlation exist at inception and throughout the transaction's term based on such factors as historical correlation and future expected variations in correlation in order for the hedge to qualify for hedge accounting.

The probability of high correlation is to be evaluated both at the inception of the hedge and throughout the hedge period. This means that changes in the market value of the hedging instrument must track the changes in the market value of the hedged item. Demonstrating the effectiveness of a hedge is essential because it is the basis for entering into the hedge transaction in the first place (meaning that the gain or loss on the hedged item will be offset by the loss or gain on the hedging instrument). When determining whether high correlation is likely, an enterprise must consider such factors as actual correlation during relevant past periods and variations in correlation that could be expected.

Companies may use a variety of approaches to evaluate expected future correlation, but *regression analysis* is the statistical method most commonly used to measure this relationship. Regression analysis techniques examine historical data relevant to each variable and calculate the expected value of one variable based on the value of the other. The result is a measure of the expected sensitivity of the movement in one variable to movement in another variable—a measurement known as the *correlation coefficient*. Once the correlation coefficient has been calculated, statistical analysis must verify its *strength;* knowing the strength of this coefficient is critical to a successful hedging program.

The strength of the correlation coefficient is indicated by the *R-square statistic*. An R-square statistic of 1 (its maximum value) means that 100 percent of a change in one variable can be explained by a change in the other variable. For example, if a 1 percent change in the value of item A triggers a 0.5 percent change in the value of item B and there is an R-square statistic of 0.90, then there is a 90 percent assurance that if the value of item A moves 1 percent, the value of item B will move 0.5 percent. The price movements would then be said to be *highly correlated.* In this situation, selling futures contracts on item B equal to two times the value of hedged item A will be highly effective in offsetting the effects of price changes on item A.

The assessment of correlation requires that judgments must be made on a case-by-case basis. Although measurement and analysis of correlation is an evolving process and it is difficult to establish precise guidelines, a hedging instrument that is 80 percent or more correlated with the hedged item (an R-square statistic of 0.80) is generally considered to meet the test of high correlation.

In addition to the requirement of assessing high correlation at the inception of the hedge, SFAS No. 80 requires an ongoing assessment of high correlation during the hedge period. Although statistical techniques such as regression analysis may be used to assess probable future correlation at hedge inception, the test of actual correlation—the ongoing correlation during the hedge period—generally should be measured based on the actual results of the hedge since inception. A common way of measuring the degree of ongoing correlation is to divide the cumulative price change for the hedging instrument (the futures contract) by the cumulative price change of the hedged item. Again, precise guidelines are not prescribed, but to qualify for ongoing high correlation the cumulative changes in the value of the futures contracts generally should be between 80 and 125 percent of the cumulative changes in the value of the hedged item. In addition to these percentage guidelines, the materiality of the absolute dollar amounts of net gains or losses to be deferred should also be considered to determine whether continuation of hedge accounting would be appropriate.

The assessment of ongoing high correlation should be made at least as often as financial results are reported externally. SFAS No. 80 requires termination of hedge accounting if high correlation ceases to exist. However, an isolated incidence of inadequate correlation—as when the cumulative hedge ratio falls beyond the range of 80 and 125 percent—

may not require the termination of hedge accounting if there is sufficient basis for concluding that the incident was isolated, with an identifiable, nonrecurring cause.

If a futures contract that has been accounted for as a hedge is terminated even though the hedged item still exists, the correlation test is no longer relevant. Once the futures contract is terminated, the deferred hedge results are treated as part of the hedged item's carrying amount.

Designation as Hedge

The third criterion for a futures contract to qualify for hedge accounting under SFAS No. 80 is that the futures contract must be designated as a hedge. This means that an entity cannot designate a position as a hedge after it incurs a loss in order to defer that loss; it must designate the instrument as a hedge first and then begin to apply hedge accounting.

SFAS No. 80 permits hedge accounting contracts that hedge firm commitments and anticipated transactions in addition to existing assets and liabilities. A *firm commitment* is a legally enforceable obligation under which performance is probable because of significant large disincentives for nonperformance. An *anticipated transaction* is a transaction that an entity expects to occur but is not obligated to carry out in the normal course of business. An example of a hedge of a firm commitment is the sale of Treasury futures contracts to lock in the interest rate on a borrowing that the company has committed to incur in three months. The entity may be able to designate the futures contracts as a hedge and defer the gains and losses until the borrowing is incurred, at which point the deferred gain or loss will become part of the borrowing's cost basis and be amortized as part of the interest cost or yield.

The same transaction would be considered an anticipated transaction if the company is not legally bound to enter into the borrowing but expects to. Because of the inherent uncertainty of recording an asset or liability (especially an asset) related to an anticipated event (that would occur when the gains or losses on a hedging instrument are deferred) SFAS No. 80 requires that, in addition to meeting the above hedge accounting criteria, the significant characteristics and expected terms of the future transaction must be identified and the likelihood of the anticipated transaction to occur must be probable.

See Illustration 3–1 in the appendix to this chapter for an extended illustration of hedge accounting involving futures contracts.

FORWARD CONTRACTS

Forward Contracts Not Involving Foreign Currencies

Forward contracts do not use a central exchange, but otherwise the economic characteristics of forward contracts are quite similar to future contracts. SFAS No. 80 specifically excluded forward contracts from its scope, but paragraph 34 states:

> The exclusion of forward contracts from the statement should not be construed as either acceptance or rejection by the Board of current practice for such contracts, nor should the exclusion be interpreted as an indication that the general principles of this statement might not be appropriate in some circumstances for certain forward contracts, and it may address the conceptual aspects of accounting of executory contracts generally.

Accordingly, practice to date has accepted the requirements of SFAS No. 80 for forward contracts not involving foreign currencies (which are specifically addressed in SFAS No. 52). Yet without specific authoritative guidance certain industries have formulated their own accepted accounting practice for forward contracts. For example, in the mining and other extractive industries, commodity forwards are used to fix the price of future sales and production. Common practice has been to account for these forward contracts as if they were fixed price sales (referred to as "synthetic" fixed price contracts) at the time the sales are recorded without any interim mark-to-market and hedge accounting for the forward contract. It is noteworthy that substantial markets exist for the commodities in which other accounting is accepted.

FOREIGN CURRENCY CONTRACTS

SFAS No. 52, *Foreign Currency Translation,* provides guidance on the accounting for foreign currency transactions including forwards, futures, and currency swaps. As previously discussed, hedge accounting requirements differ among certain types of derivative products and the differences are clearly exemplified by comparing SFAS No. 52 and SFAS No. 80.

As with SFAS No. 80, SFAS No. 52 permits hedge accounting if the item to be hedged creates risk, the hedging instrument used to minimize that risk is designated as a hedge, and the hedging instrument is effective in minimizing risk. However, the mechanisms to satisfy those criteria highlight the conceptual differences between the two statements.

Rather than using the SFAS No. 80 enterprise approach, SFAS No. 52 requires risk assessment to be performed at the transaction level. For example, a U.S. entity with a firm commitment to buy a machine for 100 million yen in three months and an unrelated firm commitment to sell 100 million yen worth of goods is naturally hedged from movements in yen (thus, if the yen appreciates, the increased cost of acquiring the machine will be naturally offset by the increased revenue on the sale of goods). SFAS No. 52 permits hedge accounting for instruments used to hedge one or both of those transactions even though the entity is naturally hedged on a enterprise basis.

SFAS Nos. 80 and 52 also differ with respect to cross-hedging. SFAS No. 80 allows cross-hedging provided the high correlation provision is met. SFAS No. 52 generally prohibits cross-hedging even if there is high correlation and a clear economic relationship between the hedged position and hedging item. SFAS No. 52 permits cross-hedging only if it is not "practical or feasible" to hedge in identical currencies. For example, even if a company could demonstrate that it was economically hedged by entering into a forward exchange contract for Australian dollars to hedge its British pound debt, SFAS No. 52 does not permit hedge accounting for the forward exchange contract because British pound forward exchange contracts are available. The phrase "practical or feasible" refers to the availability of a hedging instrument in the exposed currency, not whether it is less expensive to hedge in a tandem currency.

Hedge Accounting as Defined by SFAS No. 52

Under SFAS No. 52, all foreign-denominated monetary assets and liabilities[4] are remeasured into the entity's reporting currency at each balance sheet date. Any changes in value attributable to foreign currency movements are currently included in earnings. Thus, hedges of existing foreign-denominated monetary assets and liabilities should also be measured currently in income rather than deferred. This approach matches the foreign exchange gains or losses on the hedged item with those of the hedging instrument.

For example, on April 1, a U.S. company borrows 5 million Deutsche marks (DM) due in one year when the current

---

4. Monetary assets and liabilities are assets and liabilities whose amounts are fixed in terms of units of currency or by contract (such as accounts receivable, debt, and so on).

exchange rate (DM/\$) is 1.25. To hedge its DM exposure, the company simultaneously enters into a forward contract to buy DM 5 million in one year at the current rate. On June 30, the next reporting date, the company remeasures the borrowing and forward at a current exchange rate of 2.00.

	4/01 Balance Sheet	6/30 Balance Sheet	6/30 Income Statement
FX Rates	1.25	2.00	gain/(loss)
Borrowing	\$4,000,000	\$2,500,000	\$1,500,000
Forward	\$0	\$1,500,000	(\$1,500,000)
FX Gain (Loss)			\$0

Note that hedge accounting for foreign currency transactions (other than firm commitments and net investments in foreign entities[5]) generally does not consider deferring gains and losses on the hedging instrument, unlike what occurs under SFAS No. 80.[6]

SFAS No. 80 permits hedge accounting for firm commitments and anticipated transactions, but SFAS No. 52 only permits hedge accounting for firm commitments, not anticipated transactions. At the time SFAS No. 52 was issued, the FASB had concluded that there was too much uncertainty with respect to whether an anticipated transaction would occur, which of course increased the likelihood that a loss on a hedge could be deferred unjustifiably.

For example, if a U.S. manufacturer of heavy machinery enters into a firm commitment (that is, it has entered into a legally enforceable contract under which performance is probable because of sufficiently large disincentives for non-performance) to sell machinery to a German customer for DM

---

5. The accounting for investments in foreign entities and related hedging transactions is beyond the scope and is therefore not addressed in this chapter.

6. As an additional note, SFAS No. 52 does not allow companies to offset receivables or payables relating to hedging instruments against the assets or liabilities being hedged, unless a legal right or setoff exists (discussed in section on Netting of Positions).

2 million, it could hedge against future DM movements by entering into a forward contract to sell DM 2 million on the date of the sale. The manufacturer may be able to designate the forward contract as a hedge of the fixed price contract and defer gains and losses on the forward contract until the sales date (at which point the deferred gains and losses are included in the manufacturer's cost price). Conversely, if the manufacturer expects or anticipates to sell the machinery to the German customer but does not have a firm commitment (in this case, it does not have a signed sales contract), the manufacturer would not be able to defer gains and losses on the forward contract because the transaction is not firm—it is only anticipated.

However, to make matters more confusing, companies using purchased foreign currency options to hedge anticipated transactions may use hedge accounting for those options. This accounting relies on the rules for accounting for options, which are further explained in the next section of this chapter.

See Illustration 2 in the appendix to this chapter for an extended illustration of hedge accounting involving forward exchange contracts.

OPTIONS (OTHER THAN FOREIGN CURRENCY OPTIONS)

As explained in more detail in Chapter 2, an option contract gives its owner the right, but not the obligation, to buy (call) or sell (put) a specified item at a certain price (exercise or strike price) during a specified period.[7] To obtain this right, the buyer pays a nonrefundable fee (the premium) to the seller (the writer).

The EITF has addressed the accounting for options that are intended to hedge foreign currency risk (discussed later in this chapter), but otherwise no authoritative guidance exists

---

7. *American-type options* can be exercised at any time during the exercise period; *European-type options* can be exercised only on the expiration date.

for the accounting for options. The American Institute of Certified Public Accountants (AICPA) released the March 6, 1986, Issues Paper 86–2, *Accounting for Options*. Although it is not authoritative, the issues paper recommends certain approaches that have helped shape current practice.

Issues Paper 86–2 recommends an accounting treatment similar to that of futures contracts based on SFAS No. 80. Accordingly, under this approach options may qualify for hedge accounting provided they meet certain criteria. In addition, the issues paper contains other general guidelines:

- Options should generally be marked-to-market unless they qualify for hedge accounting.

- For speculative options (that is, those that don't qualify for hedge accounting) the mark-to-market adjustment should be reflected immediately in income.

- For options that qualify for hedge accounting, the mark-to-market adjustment should be deferred and recorded as an adjustment of the carrying value of the item being hedged. Hedge accounting is generally available for purchased options and *certain* combination or complex options (as explained later in this section), but not for written options.

- As with SFAS No. 80, the dollar amount of the item underlying the option (into which the option is exercisable) is not included in the company's balance sheet.

- The requirements for an option to qualify as a hedge are the same as SFAS No. 80 (that is, risk reduction, high correlation, and designation), except that risk assessments are made only on a transaction-by-transaction basis. This differs from both foreign currency options and futures contracts used as hedges where the risk assessment test is on an enterprise level.

- When determining the probability for high correlation (which is necessary to qualify for hedge accounting), the company should consider the correlation during relevant past periods and also the correlation that could be expected at higher or lower price levels. Cross-hedging is permitted if there is a clear economic relationship between prices and high correlation is probable.

- Written options may qualify as a hedge only to the extent of the premium received (as explained later in this section).

- Options can be used to hedge existing assets or liabilities, firm commitments, and anticipated transactions.

Although Issues Paper 86–2 analogizes to the accounting for futures, options are quite different than futures and, therefore, the accounting is adjusted to reflect those differences. An option is a unilateral contract where the holder has a right, but no obligation, to call or put a delivery of the item underlying the options contract, whereas a futures contract is two-sided. Because a futures contract is a legally binding bilateral agreement, the holder of a contract position will benefit or suffer 100 percent of the consequences of a change in price of the underlying commodity. With a purchased option, the holder pays a price or premium to cover risk of adverse price changes but, at the same time, retains the benefits of favorable price changes. The premium is composed of time value and, in certain situations, intrinsic value.

Time value represents the market's estimation of the probability that the option will become valuable or in-the-money before it expires.

Intrinsic value is the amount that is in-the-money; thus, only in-the-money options have intrinsic value.

An option with a three-month expiration date has greater time value than the same option with a one-month expiration date; that is, time value deteriorates over time or as the expiration date approaches. The option with a three-month term has a greater probability of becoming in-the-money. Also, if the option is deeply out-of-the-money, the probability of that option becoming valuable or in-the-money is not likely to occur; therefore, its time value will be lessened. Time value is, in effect, an insurance premium that runs out at expiration.

Issues Paper 86–2 recommends that if an option qualifies for hedge accounting, the option's time value and intrinsic value should generally be bifurcated and accounted for separately because of their inherent differences. Time value is amortized as an expense over the life of the option while the intrinsic value is marked-to-market with gains and losses deferred under hedge accounting. For example, an entity buys a call option on XYZ common stock for $12 that expires in three months and has a strike price of $50. The current price of XYZ common is $40; thus, the option is out-of-the-money and the premium is purely time value. Accordingly, the entity will record the $12 premium as an asset and amortize over its remaining life (three months). If the stock price at the date of the purchase had been $52, the option purchased for $12 would have an intrinsic value of $2 ($52 – $50) and a time value of $10 ($12 – $10). The intrinsic value would be marked-to-market and the time value would be amortized.

When an option is purchased to hedge a position that is carried on a mark-to-market basis (such as equity securities classified in the trading category under SFAS No. 115), the option is not split. Rather, the entire option contract is carried on a mark-to-market basis. For example, an entity purchases puts on Company XYZ stock for $1,000 to hedge against a price decline of its position in Company XYZ, which is classified as trading and marked-to-market. The entity would record that option in its trading inventory and carry it at market value.

If a purchased option is used to hedge equity securities classified as available-for-sale, the option also is accounted for on a mark-to-market basis by recording the mark in stockholders' equity associated with the mark on the securities being hedged. If an equity option position is closed out prior to the sale of the hedged equity securities, the realized gain or loss would be included as part of the securities' carrying amount. Likewise, if a treasury option designated as a hedge of a debt security classified as available-for-sale is closed out, the realized gain or loss on the option would be amortized into income as a yield adjustment on the debt security.

Issues Paper 86–2 based many of its views on the standards prescribed by SFAS No. 80 including the ability of an option strategy to hedge an anticipated transaction to qualify for hedge accounting. The portion of time value of the option used to hedge a forecasted transaction (that is, an anticipated or firmly committed transaction) that relates to the period prior to the expected transaction date may be included in the measurement of the transaction or, alternatively, amortized to expense over that period.

When a purchased option is closed out, the difference between the initial time value and the time value received on closing out the option should be treated in the same manner as was the time value prior to being closed out. If the time value was being amortized into income, the difference should be included in income. If the time value was being deferred (as when hedging an anticipated transaction or firm commitment), the difference should be deferred as well.

Written Options

Issues Paper 86–2 recognizes that written options can only provide an economic hedge to the extent of the premium received by the writer; therefore, any losses to the writer beyond the amount of the premium received must be charged to income. Conversely, the SEC has consistently held the position that the deferral of losses on written options is generally not appropriate because written options do not reduce but rather increase risk.[8]

Complex and Combination Options (Other Than Foreign Currency)

The usefulness and flexibility options as hedging instruments can be enhanced when two or more options are combined. Some examples of common types of complex and combination options include:

Call Bull Spreads   A purchased and written call on the same underlying item and with the same expiration date, but the exercise price of the purchased call is less than the written call's exercise price—a "bullish" outlook. Call bull spreads are used to hedge against price increases on short positions, but only provide hedge protection up to the written call's strike price. For example, a company with a short position in stock XYZ with a market price of $50 wants to hedge against price increases, but does not believe that it needs to hedge against increases above $60. By purchasing a call with an exercise price of $50 and writing a call with a strike price of $60, the company is hedged against increases up to $60 but not above that price.

Put Bear Spreads   A purchased and written put on the same underlying item and with the same expiration date, but the exercise price of the purchased put is greater than the

---

8. The SEC staff originally expressed its views on written foreign currency options in EITF 91–4, *Hedging Foreign Currency Risk with Complex Options and Similar Transactions,* and has subsequently reaffirmed the same view for all other written options including written caps, floors, and swaptions.

written put's exercise price—a "bearish" outlook. Put bear spreads are used to hedge against price decreases on long positions, but do not provide hedge protection at prices below the written put's exercise price.

Synthetic Futures Contract A purchased put and written call on the same underlying item at the same strike price with the same expiration date; the hedger effectively locks in the selling price like a futures contract, minimizing price increases and decreases. For example, if a company wants to hedge against price risk on a long position in stock XYZ and lock in its current price of $50, the company can buy a put on XYZ stock with an exercise price of $50 and sell a call on the security with the same exercise price and expiration date. If the price of the security increases to $55, the put would be worthless (because the exercise price is $50), and the call would be exercised whereby the company would sell the stock for $50. If the stock price dropped to $45, the call would be worthless because the call holder could buy the XYZ stock in the market at the current price, and the company would exercise the put and sell the stock for $50.

Interest Rate Collars A purchased call and written put on interest rates "collars" interest rate movements within a specified range. For example, an issuer of variable rate debt may not want interest movements to exceed 300 basis points. To minimize interest rate movements, the issuer can purchase a series of long calls and write a series of short puts expiring on the dates of the interest rate reset dates (European-type expiration). In addition, each call and put option would have a strike price of 150 basis points above and below the initial interest rate, respectively.

Participating Forward Purchased put and written call at the same strike price but the call is written for a smaller quantity than the put. The purchased put provides a hedge against future price declines and the written call reduces the cost of the put in exchange for sacrificing some of the benefit of price increases. Thus, if a company wants to hedge its investment in 200 shares of stock XYZ from price decreases below $50, it could purchase two puts and write one call with strike prices of $50. Therefore, if the price of XYZ decreases, the company will exercise the puts and sell its shares at $50, and the call will expire unexercised. Conversely, if the price increases to $60, then the written call will be exercised at $50, the puts will expire unexercised, and the company will be able to sell (or hold) its remaining 100 shares at $60.

As with "simple" purchased and written options, no authoritative guidance exists for complex and combination options; nevertheless, the financial community has generally accepted the guidance of Issues Paper 86–2 for these options transactions as well. The accounting for complex and combination options (other than foreign currency options) has typically been as follows:

1. A call bull spread or a put bear spread should be accounted for as one unit. The premium on the purchased option will typically exceed the premium received on the written option;[9] accordingly, the accounting for these spreads follows the accounting for purchased options. A call bull or put bear spread can qualify for hedge accounting if the purchased option alone qualifies for hedge accounting. If so, the spread should be accounted for in accordance with the guidance for purchased options.

2. Call bear spreads and put bull spreads are treated as written options because a net premium is typically received on these spreads; thus, the combination may only qualify for hedge accounting to the extent of the premium received.

---

9. As previously discussed, the exercise price of the purchased call on a call bull spread is lower than the exercise price of the written call. As a result, the purchased call will be deeper or closer to being in-the-money than the written option and will command a higher premium. Likewise, the exercise price of the purchased put on a put bear spread will be greater than the exercise price of the written put.

3. Synthetic futures should be accounted for as a unit and follow futures accounting under SFAS No. 80.

4. Other combination options should be accounted for as a unit as follows:

- If the combination provides unlimited protection after a deductible,[10] the criteria for a purchased option should be used to determine whether the combination qualifies for hedge accounting.

- If the combination provides only limited protection, the criteria for a written option should be used to determine whether the combination qualifies for hedge accounting.

- If the combination qualifies for hedge accounting and the time value paid exceeds the time value received, the net time value should be accounted for in accordance with the guidance for purchased options.

- If the combination qualifies for hedge accounting and the time value received exceeds the time value paid, the net time value should be accounted for in accordance with the guidance for written options.

Foreign Currency Options

Although SFAS No. 52 does not permit hedge accounting for anticipated foreign currency transactions, EITF 90–17 reached a consensus that hedge accounting is permissible for anticipated transactions when a purchased foreign currency option (with little or no intrinsic value at the date of purchase) is used to hedge a foreign currency transaction provided that the hedge accounting conditions of SFAS No. 80 are satisfied (see page 32 of this chapter). Recall that SFAS No. 80 hedge

---

10. For example, an entity buys an out-of-the-money put with an exercise price of $90 to hedge against a price decrease in a security with a current fair value of $100. The entity is willing to accept a deductible or loss of $10 before the put is effective as a hedge.

accounting criteria require that risk be evaluated on an over-all enterprise basis rather than on the individual transaction basis prescribed by SFAS No. 52. In addition, the nature of the foreign currency risk to be evaluated should be based on the provisions set forth in SFAS No. 52 which defines it as risk associated with transactions and commitments in curren-cies other than the transacting entity's functional currency.

The EITF also discussed the propriety of hedge account-ing in a number of specific situations using purchased foreign currency options with little or no intrinsic value.

▪ One situation addresses an enterprise that estimated its minimum probable foreign sales for the next several years and wished to reduce its exposure to the related foreign exchange risk. In this case, the propriety of hedge accounting depended on whether the transactions met the SFAS No. 80 anticipated transaction criteria. The EITF observed that the likelihood of meeting the criteria diminishes the farther into the future the anticipated transaction is expected to occur.

▪ Another situation addressed whether a U.S. parent could qualify for hedge accounting when it hedged the fore-casted net income of its foreign subsidiary. The foreign sub-sidiary generated revenues and incurred costs denominated in its functional currency. In this case, the EITF concluded that hedge accounting would not be appropriate because

1. The parent would not have foreign currency risk, as defined in SFAS No. 52, because its subsidiary's transactions are denominated in the subsidiary's functional currency.

2. Future net income does not qualify as a hedgable transaction because it is the net result of many transactions and accounting allocations rather than a single identified transaction.

▪ Hedge accounting would also not be appropriate when foreign currency options are purchased as a "strategic" or "competitive" hedge, when the gains on the options are intended to offset lost operating profits from increased competitive pressure associated with exchange rate changes that benefit competitors. To qualify for hedge accounting, EITF 90–17 requires that the options be designated as a hedge of an existing asset (including a net investment in a foreign entity), an existing liability, a firm foreign currency commitment, or an anticipated foreign currency transaction.

Foreign Currency Complex and Combination Options

EITF 91–4 addresses the use of hedge accounting for those option transactions that were specifically excluded from EITF 90–17, such as deep-in-the-money purchased options, written options, options purchased and written as a unit (combination options), and similar transactions, including synthetic forwards, range forwards, and participating forwards. EITF 90–17 addressed only foreign currency options with little or no intrinsic value. EITF 91–4 is limited to combinations that are established as contemplated integral transactions in which the components are entered into at or about the same time, are designated as a unit, and have the same expiration date.

At the March 19, 1992, EITF meeting, the chief accountant of the SEC indicated that the SEC staff will object to the deferral of gains and losses arising from complex options and other similar transactions used to hedge anticipated transactions. In addition, the chief accountant noted that the SEC's staff will object to deferral of losses with respect to written options because of their belief that written options increase rather than decrease risk.

Intercompany Foreign Currency Risk

Economically, intercompany transactions denominated in foreign currencies do not expose an enterprise to currency risk because the related cash flows remain within the enterprise.

For instance, assume a U.S. enterprise has two subsidiaries:
A and B. A's functional currency is the U.S. dollar and B's
functional currency is a foreign currency ("FC"). Subsidiary
A purchases goods from B for FC100 when the exchange rate
is FC1.00 = $1.00. If, at settlement date, the exchange rate
is FC1.00 = $2.00, A needs to disburse $200 to buy FC100 in
the spot market. Thus, A incurs a loss of $100. On the other
hand, the value of the U.S. parent's net investment in B
increases by $100 because B received cash of $200. Therefore,
on an enterprise basis, there is no economic gain or loss.

Notwithstanding, EITF 91–1 provides that transactions
or commitments among members of a consolidated group with
different functional currencies can present foreign currency
risk that may be hedged for accounting purposes. This is
consistent with the functional currency approach in SFAS No.
52 which treats each identified group (such as a subsidiary
or division) as a separate entity.

When hedging foreign currency commitments, SFAS No.
52 requires that the foreign currency commitment must be
firm. The EITF also concluded in EITF 91–1 that an intercompany foreign currency commitment may be considered
firm if there is a firm commitment to a third party obligating
the affiliates to comply with the terms of the intercompany
agreement. In the event that a third-party commitment is not
present, a firm commitment exists only if the agreement is
legally enforceable and performance is probable because of
sufficiently large disincentives for nonperformance. Examples of disincentives for nonperformance include satisfying
fiduciary responsibilities to lenders or minority interests,
complying with existing laws or regulations, a significant
economic penalty to the consolidated entity for nonperformance. In EITF 95–2, the task force attempted to clarify this
provision by concluding that a significant economic penalty
exists when a penalty imposed by an unrelated party provides
a sufficiently large disincentive for nonperformance such that

performance under the intercompany foreign currency commitment is probable, even if corresponding anticipated transactions with a third party do not occur.

INTEREST RATE SWAPS

An interest rate swap is a contractual agreement between two parties to exchange interest payments on a specified principal or notional amount for a specified period. Interest rate swaps typically involve the exchange of variable interest rate payments for fixed interest rate payments and vice-versa. These *fixed for floating interest rate swaps* are commonly referred to as "plain vanilla." While interest rate swaps are used for many purposes, they generally provide a user with greater flexibility in achieving a desired interest rate risk profile.

Currently, there is no authoritative literature that deals with the accounting for interest rate swaps. Although interest rate swaps can be viewed as equivalent to a series of forward contracts as discussed in Chapter 2, in general the accounting treatment for interest rate swaps has not been analogized to accounting for forwards because accountants have considered swaps to have unique characteristics. A general accounting framework has evolved from current practice, influenced by the SEC staff comments and EITF consensus.

The accounting for interest rate swaps, like other derivatives, is affected by whether an interest rate swap is used for hedging or speculative purposes; and its risk composition may further impact the accounting treatment. Plain vanilla interest rate swaps that are related to underlying debt instruments have generally been accounted for on an accrual basis (that is, they are *not* marked-to-market), but speculative plain vanilla interest rate swaps are marked-to-market. The SEC staff requires that interest rate swaps that contain embedded features such as written options or leverage must be marked-to-market even if used for hedging purposes. These swaps are commonly referred to as "leveraged swaps." Still, another type of swap is an index-amortizing swap, in which the notional amount decreases over time. Index-amortizing swaps contain provisions of both plain vanilla and leveraged swaps.[11] The accounting for interest rate swaps will be discussed further in Chapter 4, Accounting for Embedded Derivatives.

Plain Vanilla Interest Rate Swaps

The accounting for plain vanilla interest rate swaps has generally been as follows:

▪ Because most swaps are entered into either as an integral part of a borrowing arrangement or to hedge interest rate exposure, recognizing a gain or loss related to changes in value of the swap contract is generally inappropriate except in instances in which the associated assets and liabilities are also being adjusted for changes in value (marked-to-market). Accordingly, interest expense should be adjusted for the net amount receivable or payable under the swap arrangement. This treatment is commonly referred to as "accrual" or "settlement" accounting.

▪ The typical interest rate swap transaction provides a legal right of offset for amounts due under the arrangement. Accordingly, any receivable or payable related to such a transaction should be presented net in the balance sheet (that is, the swap should not be presented broad by recording a gross receivable and payable).

---

11. In EITF 95–11, *Accounting for Derivative Instruments Containing Both Written Option-Based Component and a Forward-Based Component,* the task force attempted to provide guidance on the accounting for free-standing derivatives with embedded written options. The goal was to marry the SEC staff's views (that the deferral of losses on written options is not appropriate) with current practice, which has not always followed mark-to-market accounting especially with index-amortizing swaps. Several alternatives were considered, but after lengthy discussions, the task force decided to discontinue its discussions as further progress seemed unlikely.

- With the exception of certain specialized industry practices, fees received or paid for entering into the swap should be amortized over the life of the swap as yield adjustments. However, fees received by an intermediary for arranging a swap when there is no continuing involvement may be recognized in income.

- Unrealized gains and losses for changes in market value of speculative swaps (that is, swaps that do not qualify for accrual accounting) generally should be recognized currently in income.

- Gains and losses on early termination of swaps originally accounted for as integral to a borrowing arrangement or as a hedge should be associated with the related debt and spread over the remaining original life of the swap.

See Illustration 3 in the appendix to this chapter for an illustration of accounting for interest rate swaps.

SYNTHETIC INSTRUMENT ACCOUNTING

The accounting method previously described for interest rate swaps that are linked to borrowings or to interest-bearing assets is an example of what has become known as *synthetic instrument accounting.* Although the topic of synthetic instrument accounting cannot be found in the current authoritative accounting literature, a number of articles on the subject and recent FASB discussion documents[12] have acknowledged its existence.

As applied in practice, synthetic instrument accounting involves treating two or more distinct financial instruments as having synthetically created a single recognizable instrument and, accordingly, accounting for those multiple instruments as that single instrument. Thus, floating-rate

---

12. For example, see Chapter 8 of the 1992 FASB Discussion Memorandum, *Recognition and Measurement of Financial Instruments;* also see the discussion in this chapter of the FASB staff's June 1993 document on hedging and risk-adjusting activities.

debt together with a swap of the floating interest payments into fixed payments is treated as fixed-rate debt. The same holds true for the reverse where fixed-rate debt is swapped into floating, or basis swaps modify the interest rate characteristics of debt, or interest rate swaps combine with interest-bearing assets. In all cases, the swap is not accounted for separately in the income statement; only the net payments under the swap and the related interest on the debt or asset are combined as an adjustment to periodic interest expense or income. Generally, any receivable or payable for the swap is presented separately from the debt or the asset in the balance sheet unless it meets the offsetting criteria specified in FIN 39 (discussed in the section "Netting of Positions").

Although this treatment seems logical and appropriate, the absence of authoritative standards or guidelines on the subject means that questions about when to apply synthetic instruments accounting frequently arise in practice, even in the case of simple interest rate swaps. Must the swap be entered into at the inception of the borrowing or lending transaction to be afforded synthetic instrument accounting? Under current practice as it has evolved the answer is generally no. The interest rate swap can be entered into after the related borrowing or lending transaction and need not even be held through the maturity of the linked debt or asset.

Should a Deutsche mark borrowing whose principal has been effectively converted into U.S. dollars via a currency swap be accounted for as synthetic U.S. dollar debt? Here the answer under current accounting rules is no. Under SFAS No. 52 on foreign currency translation, current exchange rates are used to translate the foreign currency debt, the foreign currency element of the currency swap is marked-to-market and the resulting gains and losses are included in the current period's earnings. Thus, to the extent the loss or gain on the swap offsets the gain or loss on the debt, reported earnings are unaffected. For balance sheet purposes the debt and the swap must be shown "broad"; that is, in accordance with the consensus in EITF 86–25 the current foreign currency receivable or payable on the swap must be shown separately and cannot be offset against the debt.[13] Accountants argue that this treatment properly reflects the fact that the debt and the currency swap are with different counterparties.

Synthetics involving options and swaptions raise additional accounting issues due to the one-sided nature of these instruments. Take the example of synthetic noncallable fixed-rate debt that arises from the combination of issuing callable fixed-rate debt and selling a swaption against the embedded call. Assume the entity issues five-year callable (after three years) fixed-rate debt while simultaneously writing a swaption exercisable concurrently with the call date of debt. The swaption would be structured such that, if exercised, the issuer receives LIBOR and pays fixed rate during years four and five.

In this example, if interest rates have fallen at the call date in three years, the company will likely call the debt and may refinance it short term with commercial paper. Similarly, the holder of the swaption will likely exercise it and enter into the two-year swap, paying the company LIBOR and receiving the now above market fixed interest payment. But if interest rates have risen, presumably the company would not call the debt and the swaption would not be exercised. In either case, some accountants argue that the company has effectively created noncallable five-year fixed-rate debt with the up-front premium received on the swaption providing a reduction of the effective financing cost. Therefore, they might treat this transaction as a single instrument, synthetic five-year fixed-rate debt and amortize the premium received on the swaption

---

13. This assumes the debt and the swap are with different parties. Where the debt and the swap are with the same party, balance sheet netting would be permitted provided there is a legal right of offset (as previously discussed).

as a reduction of interest expense over the five years. The difficulty encountered in reaching this view relates to the presumption that the company's decision whether or not to call the debt in three years and the swaption holder's decision whether or not to exercise the swaption at that date is symmetrical.

Such symmetry might not always exist as when, for example, a call premium is involved; or when, as in the above example, different floating rates are involved (such as refinancing by the company at commercial paper rates versus receipt of LIBOR on the swap); or when in three years, for whatever reason, the company would be unable to refinance the called debt. Most accountants would therefore carefully assess the facts and circumstances surrounding a particular transaction of this kind before concluding on the propriety of using synthetic instrument accounting. Such facts and circumstances would include the company's financial condition and likely ability to refinance at the call date as well as the range of interest rates under which, given any call premium and/or differences in the floating rate bases of the refinancing and the swap under the swaption, there might be asymmetry between the actions of the company and the swaption holder at the call date. Moreover, the longer the term of the debt and the farther out the call date—for example, in the case of 20-year debt with a call at year 10—the more difficult it is to convince auditors of the propriety of applying synthetic instrument accounting to this type of transaction.

In summary, at present there are no authoritative rules or guidelines governing the accounting for synthetics. Generally, in the absence of such guidance, accountants have only permitted synthetic instrument accounting in those cases where there is clear evidence that the multiple instruments create another recognizable financial instrument and that there is a high probability of the company achieving and maintaining the intended synthesis.

ACCOUNTING FOR DERIVATIVES INDEXED TO AND POTENTIALLY SETTLED IN A COMPANY'S OWN STOCK

Numerous forms of free-standing derivative transactions exist whose value is linked to a company's own common stock that are settled in company shares and/or cash. These transactions introduce significant accounting issues as they possess characteristics of a derivative instrument that could be marked-to-market and an equity transaction that historically in GAAP does not give rise to any earnings impact.[14]

These derivatives are structured in various formats for numerous purposes. Some examples include:

- A company may issue debt with detachable stock purchase warrants to lower the cost of financing.

- A company may sell put options to lock-in or reduce the cost of a future stock repurchase program.[15]

- A company may use purchased call options to hedge the earnings impact from stock appreciation rights.[16]

- A company may use short forward contracts or purchased put options to hedge the proceeds of future issuances of stock.

---

14. APB 9, *Reporting the Results of Operations,* paragraph 28.
15. If the market price of the stock is greater than the strike price, the put holders will not exercise their options and the company will absorb the full premium which will offset the increased cost of repurchasing shares at a higher market price. Conversely, if the market price of the stock is below the strike price, the put holders will exercise their options and the company would have to pay an above market price (less the premium received) to repurchase its stock. Nevertheless, the company locks in its "target" price.
16. SFAS No. 123, *Accounting for Stock-Based Compensation,* requires cash settled stock appreciation rights to be marked-to-market as a component of compensation expense.

The accounting for these derivatives or related transactions has been addressed, to some degree, in the authoritative literature. APB 14 addresses the accounting for convertible debt and debt issued with detachable stock purchase warrants (see Chapter 4), and APB 25, as amended by SFAS No. 123 addresses the accounting for stock options and stock appreciation rights granted to employees. Generally, the accounting follows an approach that treats noncompensatory-related transactions as equity transactions which do not affect reported earnings.

On a few occasions, the EITF has addressed the accounting for these types of derivatives. In Issue No. 87–31, the EITF addressed the accounting for the sale of put options on a company's own stock and concluded that the sale is an equity transaction and the premium received should be recorded as equity. For SEC registrants, in accordance with SEC Accounting Series Release (ASR) No. 268, an amount equal to the strike price of the option should be transferred from permanent equity to temporary or "mezzanine" equity.

In Issue No. 88–9, the EITF addressed the accounting for a financial instrument that contains the elements of both stock purchase warrants and put options, referred to as a "put warrant." This instrument enables the holder to (1) purchase the issuer's common stock at a strike price, (2) put the warrant back to the issuer for cash, or (3) in some cases, to purchase the stock and sell it back to the issuer for cash.

The EITF concluded that put warrants should be accounted for similarly to mandatorily redeemable preferred stock in accordance with ASR No. 268 (applicable to SEC registrants only). Thus, issuers must record the warrant proceeds as mezzanine capital (presented in the balance sheet in a separate category between debt and permanent equity). Further, the task force noted that put warrants are more akin to a debt instrument than equity if the put price is significantly higher than the issuance price. In that situation, the issuer would record the proceeds received as a liability.[17] Going forward, the liability should be accreted from the value assigned at the date of issuance to the redemption price.

As with other forms of derivatives, the complexity of these instruments has elevated over time. For instance, the transactions discussed above historically were settled with common stock. Now, transactions are settled not only in common stock, in cash or the option of either common stock or cash.

In response to the creation of these derivatives indexed to a company's own stock that possess alternative settlement mechanisms, EITF 94–7 created a "quasi standard." The EITF's consensus included the following:

- Free-standing contracts that require net cash settlement should be accounted for as assets and liabilities and should be measured at fair value. Any gains or losses on those contracts should be included in earnings.
- Free-standing contracts that require physical settlement or settlement in net shares are equity instruments and should be initially measured at fair value. Subsequent changes in fair value should not be recognized.
- Free-standing contracts that give the company a choice of net cash settlement or settlement in its own shares should be classified as equity instruments. If such contracts are ultimately settled in cash, the amount of the cash paid or received should be included in contributed capital.
- Free-standing contracts that give the counterparty (such as an investor) a choice of net cash settlement or settlement in shares should be accounted for as assets or liabilities and initially and subsequently be

---

17. The accounting for this form of warrant was originally addressed in EITF 86–35.

measured at fair value. Any gains or losses on those contracts including any arising from ultimate settlement in shares should be included in earnings.

It is important to note that the SEC observer to the EITF stated that the SEC staff has consistently held the position that hedge accounting is not permitted for contracts indexed to or potentially settled in a company's own shares because existing assets, liabilities, firm commitments, and anticipated transactions are not being hedged which is one of the requirements needed in order to achieve hedge accounting under SFAS No. 80. Accordingly, if a company is interested in the economics of such contracts, it should consider how different settlement approaches affect the desired accounting treatment.

In EITF 96–1, the task force readdressed EITF 87–31 as the means of settlement had not been discussed and applied. Based on earlier conclusions in EITF 94–7, EITF 96–1 reached the following consensus:

- Written put options on an issuer's stock that are either net cash settled or that give the counterparty a choice of a net cash settlement or share settlement should be classified as a liability and marked to market. Any gains or losses on those contracts should be included in earnings and disclosed in the financial statements.

- Written put options on an issuer's stock that give the issuer a choice of a net cash settlement or share settlement should be classified as an equity instrument and should be measured initially at market value. Subsequent changes in market value should not be recognized. If the put options are ultimately settled in cash, the amount of cash should be included in stockholders' equity. For SEC registrants, written put options to be settled in cash should be classified in mezzanine equity.

The task force currently attempts to resolve additional balance sheet classification and accounting issues in EITF 96-13 involving calls or puts on an issuer's stock. As of the close of the September 1996 meeting, this is unresolved.

NETTING OF POSITIONS

The lack of comprehensive accounting guidance has also affected how companies report their derivatives activities in their financial statements. In the past, the reporting and disclosing of receivables and payables in connection with derivatives was inconsistently applied. For instance, amounts were only being reported net if a legal right of offset[18] existed as set forth in FASB Technical Bulletin (FTB) No. 88–2, *Definition of a Right of Setoff*. However, many broker/dealers, banks, and other entities active in the derivative markets believed that the provisions of FTB 88–2 did not apply to their industries. Derivative dealers regularly have many open derivative positions with varying durations and a number of counterparties over various product lines (such as forwards, options, swaps, and so on). Nevertheless, they reported and disclosed the fair value amounts of all their positions as one net receivable or payable. They believed that the receivables and payables arising from derivative activities are valuation adjustments, not separate assets and liabilities.

To standardize the reporting for offsetting, the FASB issued FASB Interpretation No. 39, *Offsetting of Amounts Related to Certain Contracts*. That ruling incorporates the principles of FTB No. 88–2 in relation to the legal right of offset with the existence of certain industry practices. Under FIN 39 and consistent with FTB No. 88–2, a legal right of offset must exist in order to net positions, and that right exists only if the following conditions are satisfied:

1. Each of the two parties owes the other determinable amounts.

---

18. The legal right of offset is defined as a debtor's legal right, by contract or otherwise, to discharge all or a portion of the debt owed to another party by applying against the debt an amount that the other party owes the debtor.

2. The reporting party has the right to set off the amount owed with the amount owed with the other party.

3. The reporting party intends to set off.

4. The right of set off is enforceable at law.

Recognizing the differences inherent in the derivatives business, FIN 39 permits offsetting of positions with the same counterparty if (a) the positions are covered by a valid master netting agreement, and (b) the reporting entity carries the positions at fair value. Thus, derivative dealers, who typically carry their derivative positions at fair value, can satisfy the requirements of FIN 39 by establishing a master netting agreement with each counterparty with whom it conducts business.

FASB PROJECT ON ACCOUNTING FOR DERIVATIVES

As discussed earlier in this chapter, the current set of accounting rules provides inconsistent guidance and fails to explicitly cover a number of today's hedging instruments and techniques. To rectify the above problems, the FASB has been working on the financial instruments project that began in 1986 and which has increasingly gained momentum as derivative instruments and their utilization as risk management tools have become more sophisticated and widely accepted. Over the ten year life of this project, the Board formulated, discussed, and rejected numerous approaches, but in June 1996, the Board's views finally evolved into a draft accounting statement as described in detail below.

Over the ten year period, many publications have been written about the financial instrument project which identified numerous issues and discussed various alternatives. In June 1993, the Board issued a *Report on Deliberations, Including Tentative Conclusions on Certain Issues Related to Accounting for Hedging and Other Risk-Adjusting Activities,* representing a preliminary set of thoughts by the Board. The thought process included carrying all derivatives at fair value, and permitting hedge accounting for existing assets, liabilities, and firm commitments. Hedge accounting was to be prohibited for anticipated transactions as several FASB members, sharing the views of the chief accountant of the SEC, had difficulty accepting the deferral of gains or losses on hedges related to transactions which may never materialize.

Another hedge accounting model was introduced in the 1993 report described as the "partial effectiveness method," whereby a hedge would be considered effective to the extent that changes in the fair value of the hedging instrument did not exceed the inverse change in the fair value of the item being hedged. The partial effectiveness method would have simplified and broadened the current rules. However, the heightened focus on derivatives, in particular, by Congress, the GAO, and the SEC, together with the wave of several highly publicized reported losses involving derivatives undoubtedly impacted the Board's thinking.

The Board continued its deliberations in 1994 and started to examine possible alternative mark-to-market approaches but found them to be either too complex and/or yielding results that were conceptually difficult to justify. Accordingly, in November 1994, the Board tentatively agreed on an approach conceptually similar to SFAS No. 115. That approach would classify all free-standing derivative instruments in one or two categories—trading or other than trading. Derivatives classified as "trading" would be measured at fair value with changes in values recognized in earnings in the period in which they occur. Derivatives not classified as "trading" would be measured at fair value with changes in value excluded from earnings and reported in a separate component of equity until realized. Realized gains or losses would be recognized in earnings (i.e., realized gains and losses cannot be deferred).

While this approach met the FASB's general belief that all derivatives should be carried at fair value and would have been relatively simple to apply by financial statement preparers, it was roundly criticized. Critics believed that it would create greater volatility in stockholders' equity—the mark-to-market on derivatives used for risk management purposes would flow through stockholders' equity while the related assets and liabilities would be carried at cost. Also, by disallowing the deferral of realized gains and losses, futures contracts—in which realized gains and losses are generated daily since daily cash settlement is required—would become less popular and would have forced derivatives users to enter into potentially more risky over-the-counter derivatives.

As a result of the criticism, the FASB began researching other potential approaches. In October 1995, the FASB presented another "fair value approach" but by January 1996, it agreed to abandon the new approach and pursue one similar to the current hedge accounting rules. In this approach hedge results would be reported as adjustments to the carrying amounts of existing assets, liabilities, and firm commitments, and permit the deferral of the earnings impact of certain transactions designated as hedges of forecasted transactions. Based on those parameters, the FASB finally issued an exposure draft in June 1996 entitled, *Accounting for Derivative and Similar Financial Instruments and for Hedging Activities (the "ED")*. While certain concepts of current GAAP are carried forward within the ED, the accounting for derivatives would substantially change.

The ED would standardize the accounting for derivatives and certain other financial instruments[19] that have similar characteristics by requiring that an entity measure those instruments at fair value and recognize them as assets or liabilities on the balance sheet. If certain conditions are met,

---

19. Although plain-vanilla cash instruments are excluded, the scope of the ED is intended to include financial instruments that have both cash instrument and derivative characteristics when the embedded derivative contains implicit or explicit leverage, such as structured notes (for example, a debt instrument with a stated coupon that multiplies changes in LIBOR times an amount greater than the face value of the contract).

an entity may elect to designate a derivative or other similar financial instrument as:

1. A hedge of the fair value exposure of an existing asset or liability, including a firm commitment, ("fair value hedge");

2. A hedge of the cash flow exposure of a forecasted transaction ("cash flow hedge"); or

3. A hedge of the foreign currency exposure of a net investment in a foreign operation

In accordance with the ED, changes in fair value of the derivative financial instruments would be recognized in earnings in the period of change unless a derivative is designated as a hedge of:

- A forecasted transaction (changes in fair value would be recorded in comprehensive income outside of earnings), or

- A net investment in a foreign entity (the foreign currency transaction gain or loss component of the change in fair value would be recorded in comprehensive income[20] outside of earnings as part of the cumulative translation adjustment).

Balance sheet recognition and mark-to-market basis of accounting for derivatives would be a change from current practice for many types of derivatives. As a result, the balance

---

20. In a separate ED, *Reporting Comprehensive Income,* issued in June 1996, the Board has proposed a new financial statement that would include net income, as currently defined, and other comprehensive income with the sum of the two categories designated as "comprehensive income." Gains and losses currently presented in the stockholders' equity section (such as gains and losses on available-for-sale securities and translation adjustments) would be included instead in other comprehensive income. Because of the interrelationship between the two projects, the Board intends to have a new statement on comprehensive income effective prior to or simultaneously with a new statement on accounting for derivatives.

sheet size of many entities may increase. Also, the treatment of gains and losses on hedges of forecasted transactions may result in fluctuations of comprehensive income that would directly impact a company's net worth and earnings per share.

Fair Value Hedges (Hedges of Existing Assets, Liabilities, and Firm Commitments)

An entity must specifically identify the asset, liability, or firm commitment being hedged or the proportion[21] being hedged. The change in the fair value of the hedged item would be recognized in earnings in the period of change (with a corresponding adjustment of the carrying amount or "basis" of the hedged item) only to the extent that cumulative changes in the fair value of the hedging instrument from the inception of the hedge offset the cumulative changes in the fair value of the hedged item from the inception of the hedge. The effect of that accounting is an adjustment to the basis of the hedged item by the amount of the gain or loss on the hedging derivative. The basis is adjusted to the extent that those gains or losses offset losses or gains experienced on the hedged item.

The following example illustrates the basis adjustment of hedged inventory.

Hedged item: Inventory
Hedging instrument: Purchased put option contract

	Situation A	Situation B	Situation C	Situation D
Change in fair value of:				
Inventory	$10 gain	$20 loss	$30 gain	$50 loss
Option	$8 loss	$25 gain	$40 loss	$35 gain
"Basis" adjustment to inventory	Add $8	Reduce $20	Add $30	Reduce $35
Net Income statement effect	$0	$5 gain	$10 loss	$0

---

21. The proportion of the hedged item refers to its percentage, not the period of time (for example, 40 percent of a five-year loan, not 100 percent of the loan to be hedged for the first two years).

The basis adjustment to inventory is limited to the change in fair value of the inventory unless the change is greater than the change in fair value of the option.

For a derivative to qualify as a hedge of an existing asset, liability, or a firm commitment, *all* of the following criteria must be met:

1. At the inception of the hedge, there is formal documentation of the hedging instrument and the hedged item, including the nature of the risk being hedged. Unlike SFAS No. 80, ED does not require enterprise risk reduction.

2. The use of the derivative financial instrument is consistent with the entity's established policy for risk management.

3. The hedged item is specifically identified as either all or a proportion (expressed as a percentage) of an entire asset or liability.

4. The hedged item is a single asset, liability, or firm commitment or is a portfolio of similar assets and liabilities.[22] If hedged items are aggregated and hedged as a portfolio, the hedged items must share common characteristics so that they are expected to respond to changes in market variables in an equivalent way.[23]

5. The hedged item has a reliably measurable fair value, and changes in the fair value of the derivative are expected (both at inception and on an ongoing basis) to offset substantially all changes

---

22. Under current GAAP, companies must designate individual items to be hedged which can result in burdensome record keeping, but the ED permits hedging on a portfolio basis (the portfolio must be of similar assets), a welcomed provision among the financial community.

23. For example, when aggregating loans for portfolio hedging, the following characteristics should be considered: loan type, loan size, nature and location of collateral, coupon interest rate, maturity, period of origination, prepayment history, interest rate type, and so forth.

in the fair value of the hedged item attributable to the risk being hedged. However, if a derivative (such as a purchased option contract) provides only one-sided protection against the hedged risk, the increases in the fair value of the derivative are expected (both at inception and on an ongoing basis) to offset substantially all of the decreases in fair value of the hedged item attributable to the hedged risk.[24]

6. The hedged item individually, or combined with other items, presents an exposure that could affect reported earnings if prices change. The purpose of this criterion is to prohibit hedge accounting for hedges of items that would never affect earnings, such as treasury stock purchases and intercompany transactions.

7. The derivative designated as the hedging instrument is not a written option. For purposes of the ED, a combination of options, whether free-standing or embedded in a derivative, would be considered a net written option if, either at inception or over the life of the contract, a net premium is received in cash or has a favorable rate or other term. This criterion is consistent with the SEC's view that written options to do not reduce risk and therefore should not be eligible for hedge

---

24. This criterion is similar to the "high correlation" requirement in SFAS No. 80. In order to determine whether a hedging instrument is effective, an entity may have to bifurcate the risks (for example, interest rate and foreign currency) in a hedged asset, liability, or a firm commitment. However, subsequent to inception of the hedge, the change in fair value of the hedged item would be the total change caused by all risk factors— hedged or unhedged. As such, the change in fair value of a hedged item may be greater or smaller than that of the hedging instrument even when the hedging instrument is 100 percent effective for the type of risk hedged. In such cases, the proposal limits the recognition of change in fair value of the hedged item to the change in fair value of the hedging instrument.

accounting. It appears this criterion would eliminate deferral accounting for certain synthetics, such as a written swaption strategy used to monetize the embedded call in callable debt. With respect to combination options, it appears hedge accounting would be permitted if a net premium is paid and the transaction meets all the other hedging criteria.

8. The entity is able to allocate to the hedged item (a single item or a portfolio) any "general reserves" (valuation accounts), deferred fees and costs, or purchase premiums and discounts established for a group of items of which the hedged item is a part. The purpose of this criterion is to ensure that the portfolio of items hedged are similar. Otherwise the allocation of such costs would be quite difficult.

9. The hedged item is not:

   - A debt security classified as held-to-maturity[25] in accordance with SFAS No. 115;

   - Oil or gas in the ground, unmined mineral ore, an agricultural product in process, or similar item; or

   - An intangible asset, a lease, or a liability for written insurance contracts.

10. At the inception of the hedge, the variable cash flows related to the hedged item are not being hedged as a forecasted transaction. For example, variable rate debt is a hedgable item, provided the anticipated interest payments are not hedged as a forecasted transaction.

---

25. A held-to-maturity security would not qualify as a hedgable item under the proposal because it does not satisfy the "earnings exposure" criterion in (6) above; however, the foreign currency risk of a held-to-maturity security can qualify the hedge accounting.

Cash Flow Hedges (Hedges of Forecasted Transactions)

In accordance with the ED, changes in the fair value of the derivative designated as a hedge of a forecasted transaction would be reported as a component of comprehensive income when the forecasted transaction was expected to occur. At that point, the cumulative gains or losses are recognized in earnings. For example, if the forecasted transaction is sales, then the gains and losses on the hedging instrument would be recognized in earnings when the sales (on an accrual basis) are forecasted to occur. If the forecasted transaction is the receipt of cash from the sale, the hedging gains and losses would be recognized in earnings when the cash was expected to be received.

If an entity hedges forecasted purchases of raw materials, the hedging instrument (such as a futures contract) would be marked-to-market and the change in fair value would be initially recorded in comprehensive income. However, the change in fair value would be transferred to income on the initially-specified date expected, presumably when the raw materials are received. This treatment would be a change from current practice under which the deferred gain or loss is not recognized in income until the inventory is sold since the gain or loss is included in the inventory's basis.

In order to qualify as a hedge of a forecasted transaction, the following criteria must be met:

1. At the inception of the hedge, there is formal documentation of the hedging instrument and the specifically identified hedged forecasted transaction, including the nature of the risk being hedged.

2. The use of the derivative is consistent with the entity's established policy for risk management.

3. The derivative designated as the hedging instrument is not a written option.

4. Both at inception and on an ongoing basis, the derivative is expected to have cumulative cash flows that will offset substantially all of the changes in cash flows of the hedged forecasted transaction that are attributable to the risk being hedged. If a derivative designated as a hedge (such as a purchased option contract) provides only one-sided protection against risk, the cumulative cash inflows from the derivative are expected to offset substantially the corresponding increased cash outflows (or reduced cash inflows) of the hedged transaction that are attributable to the risk being hedged. In addition, the contractual maturity or repricing date of the derivative is expected to occur on or about the same date as the projected date of each forecasted transaction.

5. The forecasted transaction is probable (such as, it is likely to occur), is part of an established business activity, and presents an exposure to price changes that would produce variations in cash flows and would affect reported earnings.

6. The forecasted exposure is a transaction—an external event involving an exchange with a third party. Accordingly, forecasted transactions between members of the consolidated group would not qualify as a hedgable exposure.

7. The forecasted transaction is not the acquisition of an asset or incurrence of a liability that will be measured at fair value subsequent to the recognition of the asset or liability (the purchase of equity securities classified as trading under SFAS No. 115).

8. At the inception of the hedge, the variable cash flows of the forecasted transaction do not relate to an asset or liability that is being hedged by a fair value hedge.

The qualifying criteria described above are generally consistent with the concepts in SFAS No. 80, but some differences include: (i) enterprise risk reduction is not required; (ii) maturity date of the derivative must match with the projected date of the forecasted transaction;[26] and (iii) intercompany transactions do not qualify as hedges.

FOREIGN CURRENCY RELATED ISSUES

In connection with the above provisions of the ED, the following should be noted with respect to foreign currency related transactions:

An entity may have a firm commitment to purchase a nonfinancial asset, such as inventory or equipment, from a foreign manufacturer. Such a firm commitment involves two components: (i) a nonfinancial component (the right to receive a nonfinancial asset) and (ii) a financial component (the obligation to pay foreign currency). Consistent with current practice, the ED permits the designation of a derivative such as a forward exchange contract as a hedge of the financial component of the firm commitment without affecting the accounting for the nonfinancial component. Therefore, only the change in the fair value of the financial component would be reported in earnings to the extent of offsetting changes in fair value of the hedging instrument.

SFAS No. 52 provisions that allow entities to hedge their net investment in foreign enterprises would not be changed. Under SFAS No. 52, foreign currency transaction gain or loss on the instrument that hedges a net investment is reported in the same manner as translation adjustments (such as, deferred in stockholders' equity until the net investment is liquidated).

---

26. This means that the use of a series of short-term derivatives (e.g., "rolling or stacking" futures contracts) to hedge a forecasted transaction is prohibited; this limitation has been strongly opposed by many constituents.

EFFECTIVE DATE AND TRANSITIONAL REQUIREMENTS

The ED proposes that its provisions be mandatory for fiscal years beginning after December 15, 1997, and may not be applied retroactively to financial statements of prior periods except that earlier application would be permitted for fiscal years beginning after the issuance of the new statement. Initial application would occur at the beginning of the entity's fiscal year. At the date of initial application of the ED, companies would be required to recognize "transition adjustments" as follows.

1. At the effective date, all derivatives would be recorded at fair value. The difference between a derivative's fair value and its previous carrying value would be recorded as a transition adjustment.

2. Any recorded deferred debit or credit existing at the effective date relating to deferred gains and losses on derivatives would be eliminated. Resulting gains and losses would be recorded as transition adjustments.

3. To the extent that gains or losses recognized in 1 and 2 above relate to hedges of existing assets, liabilities, or firm commitments, offsetting adjustments would be made to the hedged items. That is, the carrying amount of the hedged items would be adjusted to the extent of offsetting and opposite changes in fair value.

4. Existing hedges would be designated as fair value hedges if they relate to changes in value of existing assets, liabilities, or firm commitments, or cash flow hedges if they relate to variable cash flows of forecasted transactions. Transition adjustments relating to fair value hedges would be recorded as of the effective date as a single-line item in net income outside of operations in the manner required for the cumulative effect of changes in accounting principles. Transition adjustments relating to cash flow hedges would be similarly reported at transition as part of other comprehensive income and would eventually be recognized in net income on the forecasted date of the projected cash flows.

5. Adjustments not encompassed by the above would be recognized as cumulative-effect adjustments in net income.

While complicated and quite lengthy, the ED does represent a comprehensive accounting standard for all derivatives. In addition, it promotes the matching principle, to a certain degree, as gains and losses on a hedging instrument may be recognized concurrently with the gains and losses of the hedged item. Nevertheless, derivatives are a controversial, widely publicized topic, and the ED represents a significant change to current practice. Accordingly, the ED will undergo extensive scrutiny from the public during the ED's comment period (expressed in written responses and public hearings), and the final form of a derivatives accounting standard may be significantly different from the proposed guidance presented above.

Illustrations of Accounting for Free-Standing Derivatives

ILLUSTRATION 3–1: FUTURES CONTRACTS

As discussed earlier, SFAS No. 80 describes the accounting for a futures contract. It requires all futures contracts to be marked-to-market and, if serving as a hedge, to defer the gain or loss until the loss or gain on the hedged item is recognized. Accounting for a futures contract that is hedging an anticipated borrowing is illustrated by the following hypothetical transaction.

Situation

On May 2, 19X1, a manufacturer expects to borrow $10 million on May 20, 19X1, for 90 days, with an interest rate tied to LIBOR (London Interbank Offered Rate), to finance the acquisition of inventory. The manufacturer expects to renew the loan for an additional 90 days, repay half the loan in November, and roll over the $5 million balance for another 90 days. Ninety days later, the manufacturer will roll this $5 million over again. The manufacturer is exposed to risk of increasing interest rates. Assume that the transactions meet the probability and other criteria specified in SFAS No. 80 for hedge accounting for anticipated transactions.

Hedge Strategy

To lock in the 9 percent interest rate in effect on May 2, 19X1 for a period of one year, the manufacturer sells a strip of Eurodollar futures contracts that coincide with the dates when it expects to borrow and roll over the debt:

- Ten[1] June 19X1[2] Eurodollar contracts are sold to lock in the interest rate on the $10 million to be borrowed on May 20, 19X1.

- Ten September 19X1 Eurodollar contracts are sold to lock in the interest rate on the $10 million loan when it is rolled over on August 18, 19X1.

- Five December 19X1 Eurodollar contracts are sold to lock in the interest rate on the $5 million when it is rolled over on November 16, 19X1.

- Five March 19X2 Eurodollar contracts are sold to lock in the interest rate on the $5 million when it is rolled over on February 14, 19X2.

Contracts are closed as the debt is actually borrowed or rolled over. Eurodollar futures contracts are expected to reduce the manufacturer's risk of loss because the price of these contracts and the interest expense associated with the loan are highly correlated.

---

1. Eurodollars futures contracts are sold in units of $1 million, each of which represents a certificate of deposit with a major London bank maturing in 90 days. Therefore, 10 contracts are needed to cover each 90-day $10 million.
2. These months represent the nearest relevant settlement months for which Eurodollar futures contracts are available.

Calculating Hedge Effectiveness

The basis gain or loss on a particular contract determines the overall effectiveness of that contract. The futures contract results are compared with the additional interest incurred because of rate changes. For example, the effectiveness of hedging the first rollover period is calculated as follows:

Additional interest cost:	
Principal	$10,000,000
Change in rate (9% to 10.18%)	× 1.18%
Cost for 360 days	$ 118,000
Cost for 90 days	$ 29,500
Gains on September futures contracts:	
Gain through May 20	$ 11,750
Gain for May 20 through August 18	20,000
	$ 31,750
Net basis gain	$2,250

This calculation shows that high correlation was achieved; the gain on the futures contracts offset 108 percent of the increased borrowing costs. The effective interest rate for this period as a result of the hedge can be calculated as follows:

Principal	$10,000,000
Target interest for 90 days (9%)	$ 225,000
Less basis gain	(2,250)
	$ 222,750

$$\text{Effective rate for quarter: } \frac{\$222,750}{10,000,000 \times 90 / 360} = 8.91\%$$

Summary

The net futures gains realized by the manufacturer reduced its overall borrowing cost from what would have resulted had the company not hedged. The impact of the hedge results can be summarized as follows:

	May 20– August 18	August 19– Nov. 16	Nov. 17– Feb. 14	Feb.15– May 16	Cumulative
Target interest (9%)	$225,000	$225,000	$112,500	$112,500	$675,000
Additional interest cost because of rate increases paid	6,250	9,500	10,875	12,500	59,125
Total interest paid	231,250	254,500	123,375	125,000	734,125
Gain on futures contracts	(9,000)	(31,750)	(8,500)	(7,250)	(56,500)
Net final interest cost	$222,250	$222,750	$114,875	$117,750	$677,625
Target rate on May 2	9.00%	9.00%	9.00%	9.00%	9.00%
Hedged rate	8.89%	8.91%	9.19%	9.42%	9.04%

Accounting Entries

	Debit	**Credit**
May 2, 19X1		
Amount due from broker ....$	30,000	
Cash ....$		30,000
(To record initial margin deposit.)		
May 20, 19X1		
Cash..$	10,000,000	
Loan payable ....$		10,000,000
(To record 90-day borrowing.)		
May 2–May 20, 19X1		
Amount due from broker ....$	32,250	
Deferred gain on futures contracts ....$		32,250
(To record deferral of cumulative gain		
on futures contracts.)		
May 21–August 18, 19X1		
Interest expense..$	231,250	
Deferred gain on futures contracts	9,000	
Cash ....$		231,250
Interest expense		9,000
(To amortize cumulative deferred gain		
on June contracts over the hedge period,		
and to record interest expense on the		
$10,000,000 borrowing.)		

(Continued)

	Debit	Credit
Amount due from broker ....$	45,250	
Deferred gain on futures contracts ....$		45,250
(To record deferral of gain on futures		
contracts since May 20, 19X1.)		
August 19–November 16, 19X1		
Interest expense..$	254,500	
Deferred gain on futures contracts	31,750	
($11,750 + $20,000)		
Cash ....$		254,500
Interest expense		31,750
(To amortize cumulative deferred gain		
on September contracts over the hedge		
period, and to record interest expense		
on the $10,000,000 borrowing that was		
rolled over on August 18, 19X1.)		

Hedge Results

The manufacturer's position in the futures contract can be illustrated as follows:

(Hedge Results, Continued)

Date	Cash Position	Futures Position	Initial Margin	Variations Margin‡
May 2, 19X1		Sell 10 June 19X1 Eurodollar contracts @ 91.00* Sell 10 Sept. 19X1 Eurodollar contracts @ 90.86 Sell 5 Dec. 19X1 Eurodollar contracts @ 90.62 Sell 5 Mar. 19X2 Eurodollar contracts @ 90.42	$30,000†	
May 20, 19X1	Borrow $10,000,000 @ 9.25%	Buy 10 June 19X1 Eurodollar contracts @ 90.64 Market values: 10 Sept. contracts—90.39 5 Dec. contracts—90.18 5 Mar. contracts—89.94		($9,000) (11,750) (5,500) (6,000) ($32,250)
Aug. 18, 19X1	Roll $10,000,000 @ 10.18%	Buy 10 Sept. 19X1 Eurodollar contracts @ 89.59 Market values: 5 Dec. contracts—89.18 5 Mar. contracts—88.92		($20,000) (12,500) (12,750) ($45,250)
Nov. 16, 19X1	Roll $5,000,000 @ 9.87%	Buy 5 Dec. 19X1 Eurodollar contracts @ 89.94 Market values: 5 Mar. contracts—89.54		$9,500 7,750 $17,250
Feb. 14, 19X2	Roll $5,000,000 @ 10.00%	Buy 5 Mar. 19X2 Eurodollar contracts @ 89.84		$3,750

* Eurodollar contracts are quoted using an index of 100 minus the annualized LIBOR for 90-day deposits. A quotation of 91.00 means the annualized LIBOR is 9.00 percent. A price change of one basis point (.01 percent) equals $25.00 ($1,000,000 x .0001 x 90/360).

† A margin deposit of $1,000 per contract was deposited with the broker, as required by the futures exchange.

‡ Changes in market value of futures contracts will result in the requirement for increased (decreased) margin to be posted. See calculations below.

Calculating Gains and Losses on Futures Contracts

Because interest rates changed during the period covered by the futures contracts, the company incurs gains and losses equal to the increases and decreases in variation margin shown in the hedge results. The gains and losses on the futures contracts are the decreases or increases in their market value. For example, the gain of $32,250 as of May 20 is calculated as follows:

	June Contracts	September Contracts	December Contracts	March Contracts
Market value on May 2	91.00	90.86	90.62	90.42
Market value on May 20	90.64	90.39	90.18	89.94
Market value change (in basis points)	36	47	44	48
Value per basis point	× $25	× $25	× $25	× $25
Market value decrease per contract	$900	$1,175	$1,100	$1,200
Number of contracts sold	× 10	× 10	× 5	× 5
Total gain on contracts as of May 20	$9,000	$11,750	$5,500	$6,000

	Debit	Credit
Deferred gain on futures contracts ....$	17,250	
Amount due from broker...$		17,250

(To record loss on futures contracts
since August 18, 19X1 as a reduction
of the deferred gain account.)

November 16, 19X1

| Loan payable ....$ | 5,000,000 | |
| Cash ....$ | | 5,000,000 |

(To record repayment of half the loan.)

November 17, 19X1–February 14, 19X2

Interest expense ....$	123,375	
Deferred gain on futures contracts		
($5,500 + $12,500 − $9,500)	8,500	
Cash ....$		123,375
Interest expense		8,500

(To amortize cumulative deferred gain
on December contracts over the hedge
period, and to record interest expense
on the $5,000,000 borrowing when it was
rolled over on November 16, 19X1.)

| Deferred gain on futures contracts ....$ | 3,750 | |
| Amount due from broker...$ | | 3,750 |

(To record loss on futures contracts
since November 16, 19X1, as a reduction
of the deferred gain account.)

| Cash ....$ | 86,500 | |
| Amount due from broker...$ | | 86,500 |

(To record receipt of margin deposit when
hedge is terminated on February 14, 19X2.)

February 15–May 16, 19X2

Interest expense ....$	125,000	
Deferred gain on futures contracts		
($6,000 + $12,750 − $7,750 − $3,750)	7,250	
Cash ....$		125,000
Interest expense		7,250

(To amortize cumulative deferred gain
on March contracts over the hedge period,
and to record interest expense on the
$5,000,000 borrowing when it was rolled over
on February 14, 19X2.)

(Continued)

	Debit	Credit

May 16, 19X2
Loan payable ....$ 5,000,000
Cash ....$ 5,000,000
(To record final principal payment due
on the $10,000,000 loan.)

ILLUSTRATION 3–2: FORWARD EXCHANGE CONTRACTS

On July 1, 19X1, a U.S. company (the "Company") borrows Foreign Currency ("FC") 10 million at a fixed interest rate of 10 percent per annum, with a maturity date of one year. Interest is payable on December 31 and June 30. The Company immediately converts the FC10 million to U.S. dollars at the spot (the current) rate. Simultaneously, the Company enters into two forward exchange contracts:

Contract 1. To hedge the first interest payment, the Company enters into Contract 1, to purchase FC500,000 (semiannual interest of FC.5 million) for delivery on December 19X1 at a fixed contract price of FC1.00 = U.S.$0.665 (U.S.$332,500).

Contract 2. To hedge the second (and final) interest payment as well as the repayment of the borrowing, the Company enters into Contract 2, to purchase FC10.5 million (principal of FC10 million plus semiannual interest of FC0.5 million) for delivery on June 30, 19X2 at a fixed contract price of FC1.00 = U.S.$0.685 (U.S.$7,192,500).

FC/U.S.$ Exchange Rates
July 1, 19X1:   FC1.00 = U.S.$0.65
December 31, 19X1: FC1.00 = U.S.$0.68
June 30, 19X2:   FC1.00 = U.S.$0.70

Accounting Entries

	Debit	Credit

July 1, 19X1

1. Cash (FC10,000,000 x U.S. $0.65) .... $ 6,500,000
   Debit .... $ 6,500,000
   (To record the FC borrowing.)

2. No entry is required with respect
   to the forward contract.

December 31, 19X1

3. Interest Expense (FC500,000 x U.S.$0.68) .... 340,000 *
   Cash 340,000
   (To record the first interest payment.)

4. Amortization of Premium on Contract 1
   (FC500,000 x U.S. $0.015)† .... 7,500 *
   Forward Premium Payable 7,500
   (To record the amortization of the premium
   on the forward contract.)

5. Forward Receivable .... 15,000 *
   Gain on Contract 1
   [FC500,000 x U.S.$(0.68 − 0.65)] 15,000
   (To record the change in FC
   exchange rates.)

6. Forward Premium Payable 7,500
   Cash 7,500
   Forward Receivable 15,000
   (To record the settlement of Contract 1.)

7. Amortization of Premium on Contract 2 183,750
   (FC10,500,000 x U.S.$0.035 x 6/12
   months.)‡
   Forward Premium Payable 183,750
   (To record the amortization of the premium
   on the forward contract.)

8. Forward Receivable
   (FC10,000,000 x U.S.$ (0.68 − 0.65)) .... 300,000 *
   Transaction Gain (July to December) 300,000
   (To record the change in FC
   exchange rates.)

9. Transaction Loss (July to December) .... 300,000 *
   Debt 300,000
   (To remeasure the borrowing based
   on the FC spot rate.)

(Continued)

	Debit	**Credit**

June 30, 19X2

10. Interest Expense (FC500,000 x U.S.$0.70) .... $ 350,000
    Cash ....$ 350,000
    (To record the final interest payment
    on the borrowing.)

11. Amortization of Premium on Contract 2
    (Refer to entry 7)   183,750
    Forward Premium Payable   183,750
    (To record the amortization
    of the premium on the
    forward contract.)

12. Forward Receivable   25,000
    Gain on Contract 2
    (FC500,000 x U.S. $0.70 − 0.65)   25,000
    (To record the change in FC
    exchange rates.)

13. Forward Receivable
    [FC 10,000,000 x U.S. $(0.70 − 0.68)]   200,000
    Transaction Gain (January to June)   200,000
    (To record the change in FC
    exchange rates.)

14. Transaction Loss§   200,000
    Debt   200,000
    (To remeasure the borrowing
    based on the FC spot rate.)

15. Forward Premium Payable (entries 7 and 11)   367,500
    Cash   157,500
    Forward Receivable (entries 8, 12, and 13)   525,000
    (To record the settlement of Contract 2.)

16. Debt (FC10,000,000 x U.S.$ 0.70)   7,000,000
    Cash   7,000,000
    (To record the settlement of the borrowing
    at maturity date.)

* Typically, companies would accrue these charges on a monthly basis.

† Calculated as the difference between the spot rate at July 1 of 0.65 and the December 31 forward rate of 0.665.

‡ Calculated as the difference between the spot rate at July 1 of 0.65 and the June 30, 19X2, forward rate of 0.685.

§ Calculated as the difference between the July 1, 19X1, spot rate of 0.65 and the June 30, 19X2, spot rate of 0.70, or 0.05 times the FC10,000,000 debt ($500,000). $300,000 of the loss was recorded at December 31, 19X1, leaving $200,000 to be recorded at June 30, 19X2.

Income Statement

Interest Expense, December 31, 19X1

Interest July to December (entry 3)	$ 340,000
Amortization of Forward Premium (entry 4)	7,500
Amortization of Forward Premium (entry 7)	183,750
Gain on Closed Contract (entry 5)	(15,000)
	516,250

Interest Expense, June 30, 19X2

Interest January to June (entry 10)	$ 350,000
Amortization of Forward Premium (entry 11)	183,750
Gain on Closed Contract (entry 12)	(25,000)
	508,750

Total Expense	$ 1,025,000**

** This agrees with the negative cash balance as of June 30, 19X2:

Debt proceeds:	U.S.$6,500,000
Interest paid: (U.S.$340,000 + 350,000)	(690,000)
Proceeds from settlement of forward contracts: (U.S.$7,500 + 157,500)	165,000
Debt payment:	(7,000,000)
	U.S.$(1,025,000)

At each reporting date, the effect on net income is a net interest cost equal to the FC interest cost multiplied by the forward contract rate, adjusted for the amortization of the premiums on the forward contracts. The net interest cost can also be described as the sum total of the U.S. dollar cash paid plus the premium/loss on forward contract minus the discount/gain on forward contract.

Balance Sheet

December 31, 19X1

Cash
($6,500,000 + 7,5000 − 340,000) ...... U.S.$ 6,167,500
Forward Receivable ....   300,000 †

Debt	U.S.$ 6,800,000
Forward Premium Payable	183,750 †
....U.S.$ 6,467,500	U.S.$ 6,983,750

June 30, 19X2

Cash .... U.S.$ (1,025,000) *

---

* This agrees with the negative cash balance as of June 30, 19X2:

Debt proceeds .... U.S.$ 6,500,000
Interest paid (U.S.$340,000 + 350,000) .... (690,000)
Proceeds from the settlement of forward contracts
  (U.S.$7,500 + 157,500) 165,000
Debt payment .... (7,000,000)
                                                                U.S.$(1,025,000)

† Although the receivable and payable are shown here separately, they can be presented net on the balance sheet if both amounts relate to a single counterparty with a legal right of offset.

Conclusion

By entering into the forward exchange contract, the Company locked in its debt cost at:

Interest:	FC500,000 x U.S.$0.665	U.S.$ 332,500
	FC500,000 x U.S.$0.685	342,500
Premium:	FC10,000,000 x U.S.$(0.685 − 0.65)	350,000
		U.S.$ 1,025,000

The cost to the Company for this protection is the premiums on the forward contracts based on the difference between the spot rate and the "locked-in" forward rate.

ILLUSTRATION 3–3: CURRENCY SWAPS

Company A issues a £1,000,000 bullet note that matures in five years and bears interest at a rate of 10 percent a year. Company A hedges this transaction by entering into a currency swap. The currency swap consists of three elements: (1) an initial exchange, (2) the intervening payments, and (3) the maturity exchange. The payment dates of the swap are matched to those of the foreign currency debt.

Exchange rates and LIBOR rates for the next two years are as follows:

Year	Rate	LIBOR
0	1.6	
1	1.65	11.0%
2	1.58	11.5%

The pertinent cash flow information is shown on page 91.

(Currency Swaps, Continued)

Year	Debt		Currency Swap			Total Cash Flow per Period
	Principal	Interest	Initial Exchange	Intervening Payments	Maturity Exchange	
0	£1,000,000		£(1,000,000) $1,600,000			$1,600,000
1		£(100,000)		($LIBOR) £100,000		($LIBOR)
2		£(100,000)		($LIBOR) £100,000		($LIBOR)
3		£(100,000)		($LIBOR) £100,000		($LIBOR)
4		£(100,000)		($LIBOR) £100,000		($LIBOR)
5	£(1,000,000)	£(100,000)		($LIBOR) £100,000	£1,000,000 $(1,600,000)	($LIBOR) $(1,600,000)

The journal entries for the first two years to record the transaction are shown below.

Year	Description	Debit	Credit
0	Cash ....$ 1,600,000 F/X debt ....$ 1,600,000 (To record the issuance of the £-denominated debt. Note: no entry is made to initially record the currency swap.)	1,600,000	1,600,000
1	Interest expense .... Accrued liability... (To record the net swap payment and the interest due on the debt [$1,600,000 × 11%].)	176,000	176,000
1	Transaction loss .... F/X debt... (To record the unrealized F/X loss on the debt [$1.65 − $1.60 × £ 1,000,000].)	50,000	50,000
1	F/X contract receivable .... Transaction gain .... (To record the unrealized transaction gain on the currency swap.)	50,000	50,000
2	Interest expense .... Accrued liability... (To record the net swap payment and the interest due on the debt [$1,600,000 × 11.5%].)	184,000	184,000
2	F/X debt .... Transaction gain .... (To record the unrealized F/X gain on the F/X debt [£ 1,000,000 × 1.58 − $1,650,000].)	70,000	70,000
2	Transaction loss .... F/X contract receivable .... F/X contract payable .... (To record the unrealized transaction loss on the currency swap.)	70,000	50,000 20,000

CHAPTER 4

Accounting for Embedded Derivatives

James A. Johnson

This chapter covers derivatives embedded in other financial instruments. Sometimes the derivative is embedded in an asset; for example, an investor might own preferred stock in another enterprise that is convertible into the other enterprise's common stock. The preferred stock's conversion option is an embedded derivative. Sometimes the derivative is embedded in a liability; for example, a borrower might issue a long-term note that is callable by the borrower well before maturity. The call option is embedded in the terms of the debt.

But sometimes derivatives embed other derivatives. For example, one counterparty to a three-year interest rate swap might have the option to extend the interest rate swap for two years. The counterparty holding the embedded extension option can be viewed as owning a call option on a two-year interest rate swap beginning in three years. Alternatively, the same counterparty could be viewed as owning a put option on a five-year swap, exercisable once at the end of three years.

Chapter 3 demonstrated that accounting for free-standing derivative financial instruments is often complex. The task is further complicated when the derivative is embedded in a *cash instrument*. Accounting for the cash instrument itself may be complex, especially if the cash instrument is a debt or equity security accounted for under the provisions of SFAS No. 115, *Accounting for Certain Investments in Debt and Equity Securities,* or is denominated in a foreign currency. But further complexity exists when the derivative is embedded in another *derivative,* because the accounting for most derivatives is in large part unsettled. Only a few derivatives are addressed by authoritative accounting pronouncements. As discussed in Chapter 3, established standards contain significant inconsistencies, making it difficult to apply these rules to other derivatives by analogy.

Over the past 15 years the growth in derivatives as risk management, investment, and speculative tools has been astounding, notwithstanding the dearth of generally accepted accounting principles in the area. As a result, since 1984 the FASB's Emerging Issues Task Force has had to deal with many narrow financial instrument issues, often concerning embedded derivatives. A significant portion of this chapter will be devoted to highlighting relevant EITF consensus decisions. But until standard-setters develop comprehensive guidance for derivatives, it is likely that derivative accounting, especially when the derivative is embedded in another instrument, will be established ad hoc, requiring diligent monitoring by financial statement preparers and auditors.

APB 14 AND THE SINGLE INSTRUMENT APPROACH

The fundamental question when a financial instrument embeds a derivative is whether each component should be separately accounted for or whether the entire instrument should be accounted for as an integrated whole. The accounting issue in APB Opinion No. 14, *Accounting for Convertible Debt and Debt Issued with Stock Purchase Warrants,* illustrates the significance of the question. Further, APB 14's resolution of the issue—that an embedded derivative should not be disaggregated from the balance of the overall financial instrument—continues to be applied by analogy in many other (but not all) situations. However, there now appears to be growing acceptance that disaggregation often is a superior resolution because it allows the accounting to capture the individual economic elements of an instrument. Nonetheless, the provisions of APB 14 constitute GAAP for instruments falling in its scope until the FASB amends or supersedes them.

APB 14 covers a company's accounting for the following situations:

- Debt and stock warrants (on company or affiliate stock) issued by the company to investors as a "package" (unit offerings).
- Convertible debt issued by the company to investors.

When a company issues conventional stock purchase warrants, it credits the fair value of the proceeds (usually cash) to shareholders' equity. When a company issues debt, it credits the fair value of the proceeds to a liability. But a unit offering and a convertible note allow an investor to acquire both an equity-type right and a debt investment. Has the issuer sold debt, equity, or some of each?

APB 14's conclusion is based on whether the terms of the securities give the investor the ability to separate the equity right (the warrant in a unit offering and the conversion privilege in convertible debt) and the debt right. If the rights are separable, the issuer should account for each feature independently. If the rights cannot be separated—that is, the equity right is embedded in the debt right—the issuer should account the investment as a single instrument.

Separable Rights

Generally, the debt and equity components in a unit offering are separable. That means the stock purchase warrant and the debt can be owned independently of one another. For example, an investor may exercise the warrant and still be entitled to future interest and principal payments on the debt. Alternatively, if a market exists for the debt, the warrant, or both, the investor could sell one instrument and retain the other.

Example

Assume that an issuer sells a unit consisting of a five-year, $1,000 note and 10 stock purchase warrants. Each stock purchase warrant enables the investor to acquire one share of common stock of the issuer company in exchange for the warrant and $100. The warrant is exercisable at any time but if it is unexercised, it expires without value at the end of five years. At the time the unit is offered, the market price for the issuer's stock is $90.

   According to APB 14, the issuer should allocate the $1,000 proceeds (debt issuance costs are ignored in this example) to the warrant and the note based on the relative fair values of each at the time of the unit offering. If the fair value of each warrant is $5 and the fair value of the debt without the warrants is $950, the issuer would make the following journal entry:

```
dr. Cash ............................................................................. 1,000
dr. Debt discount .................................................................. 50
      cr. Note payable ................................................................. 1,000
      cr. Stockholders' equity (Additional Paid-in Capital) ................................ 50
```

(to record proceeds of unit offering and to allocate proceeds to debt and equity warrants issued)

In subsequent periods, the issuer amortizes the debt discount as additional interest expense, using the interest method. Thus, interest expense consists of the contractual interest on the note plus the $50 allocated to debt discount and to the detachable stock purchase warrant.

Embedded Rights (Rights Not Separable)

Convertible securities covered by APB 14 have the following characteristics:

- An interest rate that is lower than the issuer could establish for nonconvertible debt,
- An initial conversion price that is greater than the market value of the common stock at time of issuance, and
- A conversion price that does not decrease except in accordance with antidilution provisions.

Example

An issuer sells a five-year, $1,000 note for $1,000. At any time before the note matures, the investor can exchange the note for 10 shares of the company's common stock (a $100 conversion price). At the time the note is offered, the market price for the issuer's stock is $90.

According to APB 14, no portion of the $1,000 proceeds should be allocated to the conversion feature. The issuer makes the following journal entry:

```
dr. Cash ........................................................................... 1,000
     cr. Convertible note payable ................................................. 1,000
```

(to record the proceeds of the issuance of a convertible note)

Although the APB was concerned about practical difficulties in valuing the conversion option, their decision was largely based on the fact that the conversion option and the debt are inseparable.[1] APB 14 also notes that some unit offerings of debt and stock warrants are the equivalent of convertible debt. This occurs when the note must be surrendered (usually

---

1. "The two choices [debt or the conversion option] are mutually exclusive; they cannot both be consummated. Thus, the security will either be converted into common stock or redeemed for cash. The holder cannot exercise the option to convert unless he forgoes the right to redemption, and vice versa" (APB 14, paragraph 7).

in lieu of a cash exercise price) when the warrants are exercised. Although there are two securities, one cannot exist without the other, making them inseparable.

Observations

Note that an investor in the unit offering and an investor in the convertible note have similar investment expectations. Both will benefit from appreciation in the issuer's stock if the price exceeds $100. If the stock fails to appreciate, both investors hold a $1,000 obligation of the issuer. Further, in both cases, the coupon interest rate will be less than the coupon rate on issuer debt, which is otherwise identical but sold without the equity rights (warrants or the conversion feature). This lower coupon interest rate represents the option premium "paid" by the option holder (the investor) and "received" by the option writer (the issuer). Note that no actual premium is exchanged. The investor pays the premium by agreeing to accept lower coupon interest income; conversely, the issuer receives the premium by incurring less coupon interest expense.

In spite of the similarities, the accounting treatment required by APB 14 yields very different results as summarized in the following table:

	Debt with Separable Stock Purchase Warrants	Convertible Debt
Debt	Initially lower, due to discount	Higher
Equity	Initially higher, due to proceeds allocated to warrants	Lower
Interest expense	Higher, due to amortization of debt discount	Lower
Earnings per share treatment (see APB 15)	Generally treasury stock method	Generally if-converted method

This table points out why the question of whether to disaggregate an embedded derivative is important. The APB's decision not to require disaggregation of the stock purchase option embedded in convertible debt affects reported liabilities, equity, expense—even earnings per share—when compared to the accounting for a similar instrument whose rights are separable rather than embedded.

Implications of the Single Instrument Approach

Because of the conclusions reached in APB 14, to date accountants have usually decided that derivatives should not be separately accounted for from the balance of the financial instrument in which they are embedded. However, this does not mean that the effect of the derivative is automatically ignored. Sometimes the embedded derivative alters the accounting for the entire instrument. In other words, the accounting for the entire instrument differs from that which would be applied to a similar instrument that does not embed the derivative. In other cases, the effect of the derivative does not change the accounting for the balance of the instrument. Unfortunately, no guiding principal has yet been established by standard-setters nor has one evolved in practice.

As a result, the balance of this chapter deals with individual financial instrument situations, many of which have been addressed by the EITF. First, derivatives embedded in cash instruments are discussed; then the chapter concludes with a discussion of derivatives embedded in other derivatives.

DERIVATIVES EMBEDDED IN CASH INSTRUMENTS

Conventional Issuer Call Options Embedded in Debt Instruments

A typical call option gives the borrower the right to retire debt before its contractual maturity, often in exchange for the payment of a premium (for example, 3 to 5 percent) above the principal amount of the obligation. The borrower holds a purchased call option, written by the lender. The call option gives borrowers the ability to retire fixed-rate debt before maturity, which is often desirable if prevailing interest rates have declined in periods after the debt was issued.

Until a call of the type discussed in this section is exercised, it usually does not affect the accounting for the debt instrument by either the borrower or the lender.[2] The FASB staff has concluded that a call feature does not preclude an investor from classifying callable debt securities as held-to-maturity.[3]

Prepayment (Borrower Put) Options in Mortgage-Backed Securities and Similar Assets

Paralleling the growth of the derivatives market has been the growth of asset securitizations. Securitizations enable investors to acquire a creditworthy security whose cash flow depends on (1) the specific terms of the security and (2) the performance of a pool of large numbers of receivables, often mortgages on single-family homes. Despite their creditworthiness, investments in mortgage-backed securities have the potential of significant market risk because of an embedded option.

A mortgage typically permits the borrower to prepay the obligation at any time, without penalty. This privilege represents an embedded put option, purchased by the borrower and

---

2. In some cases, the call price establishes a ceiling on the amount of interest income that an investor can accrue using the interest method if the loan's stated interest rate increases during the term of the loan. See SFAS No. 91, *Accounting for Nonrefundable Fees and Costs Associated with Originating or Acquiring Loans and Initial Direct Costs of Leases,* paragraph 18a.
3. See Question 19 in L. F. Seidman and R. C. Wilkins, *Special Report — A Guide to Implementation of Statement 115 on Accounting for Certain Investments in Debt and Equity Securities* (Norwalk, CT: Financial Accounting Standards Board, 1995).

written by the lender (and transferred to investors in a mortgage securitization). In periods of declining interest rates, the put option is valuable to the borrower and represents a significant risk to the investor. A fixed-rate borrower can prepay the mortgage and refinance at the lower prevailing rate. A variable-rate borrower is also motivated to prepay the mortgage in periods of lower interest rates. Although the floating-rate borrowers may not be able to reduce their financing costs, they can "lock-in" lower rates by switching to a fixed-rate mortgage.

A variety of securitization techniques can be used to reduce the prepayment risk of certain classes of mortgage-backed securities. However, these techniques shift the prepayment risk to remaining security classes, compounding the latter classes' exposure.

Example

This example greatly simplifies the potential complexities of mortgage-backed securities but is also a useful illustration of fundamental issues arising from the embedded option. Two classes of securities, backed by a pool of single-family home mortgages, are offered to investors: an *interest-only* class and a *principal-only* class. Each month, holders of the interest-only class are entitled to all of the pool's mortgage payments representing interest and holders of the principal-only class are entitled to the remainder, representing principal.

Investors in each class are buying the right to a series of future cash inflows. Thus, the purchase price that each pays is today's value for the future cash flows considering interest rates and prepayment expectations (possible credit losses are ignored in this example). But an important difference exists: Because the principal-only class is entitled to all of the principal of the pool (regardless of whether borrowers pay on schedule or prepay), the principal-only investor is certain of the amount of total cash inflows he or she will receive—the uncertainty is limited to the *timing* of the receipt.

An investor in the interest-only class is uncertain as to both the *timing* and *amount* of future cash receipts. As mortgages in the pool prepay, pool mortgages decrease and the remaining assets generate less interest income available to the interest-only investor. Thus, if prepayments exceed the investor's original expectations, his or her return will diminish accordingly. At the extreme, the interest-only investor could receive a negative yield (this occurs if prepayments are so dramatic that the total cash the investor receives is less than the original investment).

Observations

The following observations apply to mortgage-backed securities investments:

- The embedded option increases the volatility of the fair value of the asset.

- The embedded option makes a precise determination of the all-in-yield to the investor impossible unless the investor's cost exactly equals his or her share of the underlying mortgages' principal (in this case the yield will exactly equal the interest—less servicing— on the pool). The greater the premium or discount from the underlying principal, the more unexpected prepayments will affect the ultimate yield.

- Investors who pay a premium for their investments risk losing the unamortized premium if the underlying mortgages prepay. Investors who acquire securities at a discount face quicker-than-expected recovery of their investment if prepayments exceed their expectations.

Although a comprehensive review of accounting for mortgage-backed securities is beyond the scope of this chapter, the following summarizes key guidance:

- SFAS No. 91 guides investors on the application of the interest method of recognizing interest income.

- SFAS No. 115 prescribes the accounting for investments in debt securities, including mortgage-backed securities. An investor must have the positive intent and ability to hold a debt security to maturity in order for the investor to account for the investment at amortized cost.[4] Otherwise, the investor classifies the investment as available for sale or trading. EITF Appendix Topic D-39 discusses the application of GAAP to a mortgage security that potentially could be designated (that is, meet criteria established by depository institution regulators) as *high risk.*

- EITF 94–4 dealt with whether mortgage-backed interest-only certificates may be classified as held-to-maturity (due to the uncertainty over realization of the asset) under SFAS No. 115. The EITF did not reach a consensus; however, a majority of the members observed that held-to-maturity classification would be rare because the risk and volatility of the asset make active management more likely.

Some assets have many or all of the characteristics of interest-only classes. Normally, when a mortgage lender pools individual loans and sells them in a securitization, it retains the obligation to service the loans. As compensation, the seller

---

4. After its December 31, 1996, effective date, SFAS No. 125, *Accounting for Transfers and Servicing of Financial Assets and Extinguishments of Liabilities,* will require that interest-only strips, loans, or other receivables that can be prepaid or otherwise settled in such a way that the holder would not recover substantially all of its investment must be accounted for like investments in debt securities classified as available-for-sale or trading under SFAS No. 115.

receives a servicing fee, usually payable monthly and calculated as a percentage of the outstanding principal. The servicing fee has the same economic characteristics of an interest-only strip.

Complicating the accounting analysis is a distinction between *normal* and *excess* servicing fees. Normal servicing fees represent a portion of total mortgage servicing fees as defined in FASB Technical Bulletin 87–3; excess servicing fees are any remainder. In addition to retaining the right to service mortgages via a securitization, a mortgage servicer can acquire the service rights via purchase.[5]

The following accounting guidance applies to mortgage servicing rights:

▪ SFAS No. 65 and SFAS No. 122 discuss how a mortgage banking enterprise initially records and subsequently amortizes these assets. A mortgage banker amortizes them in proportion to, and over the period of, net servicing income. Normal servicing rights are stratified according to one or more predominant risk characteristics. Each stratum is carried at lower of cost or fair value via a valuation allowance.

▪ EITF 86–38 discusses impairment of excess mortgage service fee assets. Generally, the asset is written down if the carrying amount exceeds the present value of estimated remaining future excess service fee revenue (the discount factor used in the original calculation of the asset should be used for this present value calculation).[6]

Convertible Bond with Issuer Option to Settle for Cash upon Conversion

An EITF Issue deals with various ways in which an issuer settles embedded equity appreciation right in a bond convertible into a fixed number of the issuer's shares. APB 14 covers

---

5. See SFAS No. 65, *Accounting for Certain Mortgage Banking Activities,* and SFAS No. 122, *Accounting for Mortgage Servicing Rights,* for guidance related to the servicer's initial recognition of mortgage service fee assets.
6. See note 4. SFAS No. 125 eliminates the distinction between excess and normal servicing fees.

physical settlement: The investor receives the shares. Three instruments are compared and in all cases, at maturity, the issuer must repay the accreted value of the debt in cash if the investor does not exercise the conversion option:

> *Instrument A*   Upon conversion, the issuer pays cash to settle the obligation equal to the fixed number of shares multiplied by the stock price on the date of conversion (the conversion value).

> *Instrument B*   Upon conversion, the issuer has the option to satisfy the entire obligation in stock or in cash equal to the conversion value.

> *Instrument C*   Upon conversion, the issuer must pay cash to satisfy the accreted value of the obligation (the note may be a "zero coupon" obligation and thus sold, and originally carried, at a discount to face). The issuer has the option for settling the conversion spread (the excess of the conversion value above the accreted value) in either cash or stock.

Although the EITF considered separate accounting for the embedded equity appreciation right and the debt obligation, it reached a consensus in EITF 90–19 that single instrument accounting for the two features is appropriate. This treatment is consistent with APB 14's conclusions regarding convertible debt securities.

The EITF considered two further issues: how the issuer should account for the excess of the conversion value over the accreted value, and how an issuer would treat each instrument in computing earnings per share.

The EITF concluded that instrument B should be accounted for as conventional convertible debt. That is, the interest expense consists of coupon interest on the debt (none if the note is a zero coupon obligation) and accretion of debt discount. If the issuer satisfies an exercise of the conversion option in cash, the debt is extinguished, giving rise to a current period gain or loss accounted for in accordance with APB 26 and SFAS No. 4. The issuer would use the if-converted method for determining the effect of instrument B on earnings per share.

The EITF concluded that neither instrument A nor C were conventional convertible instruments under APB 14. The consensus illustrates how an embedded option can affect the accounting for an otherwise conventional cash instrument, even when the embedded option is not separated for accounting purposes. In both cases, the issuer would adjust the carrying amount of the instrument in each reporting period to reflect the higher of the current period stock price or the accreted value of the instrument. Period to period adjustments are included in current income (not spread over future periods).

Because conversion of instrument A will not result in the issuance of stock, it has no effect on earning per share computations (however, the adjustment of the carrying value of the debt affects the determination of current income). Instrument C is handled in this fashion for calculating primary earnings per share. However, conversion of instrument C may result in the issuance of additional stock. Thus, in calculating fully diluted earnings per share, the issuer should use the if-converted method applicable to fully diluted calculations.

Indexed Debt Instruments

Many debt instruments are referenced to an index—prevailing market interest rates at the date the debt is issued and, in the case of variable-rate debt, on-going interest rates such as LIBOR or a bank lender's prevailing prime interest rate. However, the consensus in EITF 86–28 is broadly applicable to a wide variety of debt instruments that are tied to nontraditional indexes. Even the retail customers of many commercial banks can invest in an indexed debt instrument. These certificates of deposit mature at the higher of a stipulated face amount or an amount based on the S&P 500 common stock index prevailing at maturity. In addition to stock indexes, EITF 86–28 contemplates other unusual indexes, such as the price of a commodity (such as oil) or even the fair value of a piece of real estate property,[7] perhaps owned by the borrower.

The EITF considered an example of a 5 percent bond (interest payable in cash periodically). At maturity, the investor receives cash equal to the higher of the initial proceeds or an amount based on the S&P 500 index. In this case, the investor has economically purchased a cash-settled call option, written by the borrower and embedded in the bond.[8] EITF 86–28 also covers separable contingent payment rights; in this case the cash-settled call option is detachable rather than embedded.

The EITF reached a consensus that if the contingent payment right is separable, the issuer should allocate the proceeds between the debt instrument and the investor's contingent payment right. The resulting premium or discount is amortized as a yield adjustment using the interest method. This approach is similar to the APB 14 accounting for a unit

---

7. The Accounting Standards Executive Committee of the American Institute of Certified Public Accountants has issued a proposed statement of position, *Accounting by Participating Mortgage Loan Borrowers*. In certain participating mortgages, the principal amount of the mortgage note is linked to the fair value of the mortgaged property. If adopted, the SOP—rather than the EITF consensus—would apply to transactions within its scope.

8. Throughout this chapter, many embedded options are settled in cash (as opposed to physical delivery of an asset) and do not require explicit "exercise" by the holder. However, these embedded options have the economic characteristics of traditional options. In the case of indexed bonds, the holder normally "pays" a premium by accepting a lower coupon on the debt instrument (say 5 percent instead of 5.5 percent on a similar bond without the index feature). If, at maturity, the indexed bond is in-the-money, the option holder enjoys any upside benefit (which could greatly exceed the value of the premium paid). Conversely, borrowers are option writers. Their maximum benefit is the amount of the premium received (the lower relative coupon); however, the downside risk could substantially exceed this amount. The fact that many embedded options do not require explicit exercise is usually not relevant. Only irrational investors permit an in-the-money option to expire unexercised, absent unusual circumstances.

offering except that the contingent payment right is credited to a liability account rather than additional paid-in capital.

The EITF did not reach a consensus on separate accounting for a contingent payment feature that is not separable from the debt obligation. Such a requirement would have been at odds with APB 14's approach to convertible debt.

The EITF also reached a consensus that as the applicable index value increases and goes "into-the-money," the issuer should recognize a liability for the amount that the contingent payment feature exceeds the amount originally attributed to the contingent payment (the latter is zero if the contingent payment feature is not separable and the issuer decides not to ascribe a value at the date the note is issued). If no proceeds are originally allocated to the contingent payment feature, the liability is accounted for as an adjustment of the carrying amount of the debt. The liability should be based on the applicable index value at the balance sheet date and should not anticipate any future changes in the index value.

Is the offset to the liability adjustment an expense? Yes, although the EITF discussed two exceptions without reaching a consensus. The first exception dealt with the appropriateness of the issuer using hedge accounting (the discussion was conducted in the context of an indexed bond with a separable cash-settled contingent payment feature). Presumably, if the issuer applied hedge accounting, the offset to the liability adjustment would adjust a designated asset, liability, or future transaction. A majority of the task force did not support hedge accounting, and the EITF's chairman expressed serious reservations. See Chapter 3 for a discussion of hedge accounting issues related to written options.

The second exception the task force discussed involved a bond with a separable contingent payment feature, indexed to a commodity. Although the minutes do not use the term, this possible exception deals with the accounting effects of a physically settled covered call option. If the contingent payment feature can be settled by physical delivery of the commodity and if the issuer owns the commodity (or has the ability to acquire it at a favorable price), the FASB staff would view the possibility that the issuer would settle the contingent payment feature via physical delivery as "fixing" the issuer's cost of settlement. Thus, subsequent increases in the value of the commodity and the resulting value of the contingent payment feature would not be recognized. Despite this view, certain EITF members would call for expense recognition even if the issuer has a "cover" for the call option it wrote.

Written Call Options That Enable the Holder to Acquire Stock of Another Entity

Certain call options enable the holder to acquire the stock of a company, owned as an investment by the issuer of the option. In some cases the call option takes the form of a detachable warrant issued in conjunction with debt. In other cases, the holder's call right is embedded in, rather than separable from, the debt—in these cases, the exchangeable debt must be exchanged for the common stock.

EITF 85–9 concluded that a liability should be recognized for the value of detachable warrants (presumably using a method similar to a unit offering under APB 14). The liability is not eliminated by a credit to income until the option expires unexercised or is exercised.

The EITF was unable to reach a consensus on whether, for accounting purposes, the issuer should disaggregate an embedded call option from the balance of exchangeable debt or whether single-instrument accounting should be applied. Initially, the SEC observer indicated that he did not believe that APB 14 applied, suggesting that he supported disaggregation. Some task force members disagreed and research indicated that most issuers of exchangeable debt did not disaggregate the embedded call option.[9] The FASB's staff did not believe that the transaction warranted a reconsideration

---

9. Relatively few exchangeable debt issuances were noted in 1985 when the EITF considered the topic.

of APB 14 (at least apart from the overall financial instruments project). The SEC observer commented that he may request more timely consideration of the issue if the number of exchangeable transactions increases or becomes more material.

Investor Put Options Embedded in Debt

Put options are less common than call options embedded in debt instruments. Generally, the debt instrument embeds an option, written by the issuer, that enables the investor to redeem the instrument prior to its stated maturity. Redemption terms can vary significantly. Put options enable investors to avoid the risk of unfavorable market developments, assuming that the issuer has the financial wherewithal to honor the put.

If the debt instrument is a security, investors should consider whether, or under what circumstances, they would ever exercise the put. According to the FASB staff, the exercise of a put option on a security classified as held-to-maturity will call into question an investor's stated intent to hold other debt securities to maturity in the future.[10] The issuer should consider the effect of the put on classification of the debt as current or noncurrent.

Convertible Bonds with a Premium Put

Convertible bonds with a "premium put" are instruments issued at par. The premium put allows investors to redeem the bonds for cash, at a multiple of the bond's par value at a date or dates prior to maturity. For example, a bond issued at par of $1,000 may be put to the issuer for 1.5 times par, or $1,500. The $500 represents the "put premium." When the bonds are issued, their carrying amount is in excess of the

---

10. See Question 20, Seidman and Wilkins, *Special Report.*

market value of the common stock that would be issued under the conversion terms. The put expires if the investor fails to exercise it. Thus, unless the stock appreciates to at least equal the put price—a multiple of par—it is likely that the investor will put the bonds rather than convert them or hold them to maturity.

EITF 85–39 reached a consensus that the issuer should accrue a liability for the put premium over the period from the date of debt issuance to the initial put date. Accretion would continue regardless of any changes in the market value of the debt or the underlying common stock. Accounting for the expiration of the put feature depends on market conditions:

- If the market value of the common stock under conversion exceeds the put price at the time the put expires, the issuer should credit the put premium to additional paid-in capital.
- If the put price exceeds the market value of the common stock under conversion at the time the put expires, the put premium should be amortized as a yield adjustment (reducing interest expense) over the remaining term of the debt.

The EITF did not cover the investor's accounting. On the surface, it would appear reasonable for the investor to include the put premium in income as it is earned. However, the onerous terms of the instrument may suggest that the issuer has limited financial flexibility and realization of the put premium may not be reasonably assured.

Increasing Rate Debt

In the case of increasing rate debt, the borrower has the option to extend three-month debt for three months at each maturity date until final maturity five years from original issuance. Each time the note is renewed, the interest rate on the note increases by a specified amount.

EITF 86–15 was a consensus that the borrower's periodic interest cost should be determined using the interest method based on the *estimated* outstanding term of the debt (considering plans, ability, and intent to service the debt).

The EITF did not cover investor accounting. However, from the investor's perspective, interest in subsequent renewal periods is contingent on the borrower exercising its option to extend the note.

Debentures with Detachable Stock Purchase Warrants

The instruments discussed in EITF 86–15 differ from a conventional APB 14 unit offering in the following ways (amounts shown in parenthesis are cited in the EITF minutes):

1. The holder of the detachable warrants, which expire several months after the maturity of the notes, can put the warrants back to the company for cash.

2. The warrant put price (at least $2,010 per share) substantially exceeds the warrant exercise price ($75 per share).

EITF 86–35 reached a consensus that is similar to the guidance of APB 14 in order for the issuer initially to record the transaction. Because the warrants are detachable, the proceeds of the unit offering should be allocated between the debt and the warrants. Thereafter, the issuer should accrue the carrying amount of the warrant to the put price, and charge the accrual as interest expense. Thus, issuer interest expense consists of coupon interest on the debt, accretion of the discount representing the original amount ascribed to the warrant, and the accrual of the difference between the original amount ascribed to the warrant and the put price. The EITF reached this conclusion because the put price is substantially higher than the value of the warrant exclusive of the put at the time of issuance. The EITF did not define "substantially higher," complicating the application of the consensus when the put is exercisable at a premium, but not an extraordinary premium, to the value of a similar warrant without the put.

The EITF did not address the investor's accounting. If the debt is a security, the investor would account for it under the provisions of SFAS No. 115. Because the puttable warrants are likely not marketable, as defined in SFAS No. 115, the investor should consider accounting for them in a manner similar to other nonmarketable investments in redeemable, nonmarketable equity securities. However, the onerous terms might suggest that the issuer has limited financial flexibility that could affect the investor's ability to realize the carrying amount of the warrant.

Dual Currency Bonds

In its basic form, the principal amount of a dual currency bond is payable in U.S. dollars. The periodic interest payments are denominated in a foreign currency. Further, the issuer cannot call the bond before maturity nor are the coupon payments detachable.

When the EITF discussed EITF 93–10, several members noted that issuers often treat dual currency bonds as though they were variable-interest rate debt obligations. The exchange rate acts like an interest rate index. Coupon payments, in U.S. dollar terms, will vary depending on the level of exchange rates between the U.S. dollar and the foreign currency in which the coupons are denominated. This treatment has the effect of postponing the effects of current exchange rate increases or decreases to future periods (as is the case in variable rate debt; if interest rates increase in a given period, the increase only affects the amount of interest expense attributable to the current period).

The SEC observer disagreed, saying that the staff had concluded that the portion of the liability representing the present value of future interest payments is a foreign currency transaction (SFAS No. 52 would thus require that the issuer translate and recognize the foreign currency amount of all remaining coupon payments based on the current spot rate of exchange at each financial reporting date). In effect, the SEC observer rejected single-instrument accounting—a different conclusion than that reached by APB 14—even though the separate rights are not detachable.

Because of the SEC observer's views, the task force was not asked to reach a consensus. The EITF also discussed ways to accomplish the disaggregation but did not select a particular method.

DERIVATIVES EMBEDDED IN OTHER DERIVATIVES

This section will discuss derivatives embedded in other derivatives. Many of these instruments combine a swap with an embedded written option. The option writer receives a premium in return for assuming risk, typically from potential changes in interest rates, foreign currency exchange rates, or commodity prices. The premium usually is received in the form of more favorable terms on the remaining instrument when compared to a similar instrument that does not embed the option. The question is whether the instrument's nonoption feature governs the accounting (for example, whether the instrument should be accounted for as a swap) or whether the written option feature governs. A third solution would be to independently account for each feature, even though they are not usually separable.

The EITF considered the topic in its deliberations of EITF 95–11, *Accounting for Derivative Instruments Containing Both a Written Option-Based Component and a Forward-Based Component.* Although the EITF appointed a working group to assist it and discussed the topic at five separate meetings, it was unable to reach a consensus. Apparently definitive guidance must await the FASB's completion of its project on derivatives and hedge accounting.

In the interim, the views of the SEC staff should be carefully considered by registrants. Before we describe these views, we must first discuss several instruments and risk management strategies.

Highly Leveraged Swaps

Typically, highly leveraged swaps are documented as interest rate swaps on standard ISDA forms. Periodically, one counterparty will pay an amount equal to the notional amount of the swap multiplied by a variable interest rate—say based on LIBOR—and receive an amount equal to the notional amount of the swap multiplied by a fixed interest rate (periodic cash exchanges are usually settled on a net basis). The variable rate formula embeds the option component. As interest rates increase, the variable interest rate (and hence the variable payment obligation) increases at a faster rate than the periodic increase in LIBOR. The multiplier or leverage effect can be significant. For example, the variable interest rate may equal LIBOR at the end of the period plus the cube of any increase in LIBOR from the beginning of the period to the end of the period. Table 4–1 shows the cash flow consequences of a sample swap embedding a similar formula.

If interest rates do not increase, the sample swap behaves like a conventional interest rate swap. But if this is the case, why does the variable rate payer agree to a formula that exposes him or her to added risk of increasing rates? Usually, the answer is found in the fixed rate. When compared to the terms available (at the outset of the sample swap) on a conventional swap, the fixed rate and hence the fixed payment amount are larger. If LIBOR does not increase over the term of the swap, the variable rate payer will benefit by the entire

TABLE 4–1

Sample Swap

Sample Swap

Notional Amount	150,000
Fixed Rate	6.75%

Variable Rate = LIBOR (begin) + Adjustment

Adjustment = the higher of (1) zero or (2) the cube of 100 times the change in LIBOR

Period	Variable Rate per Formula	Fixed Receipts	Sample Swap Variable Obligation	Net Exchange
1	5.00%	10,125	(7,500)	2,625
2	4.75%	10,125	(7,125)	3,000
3	4.50%	10,125	(6,750)	3,375
4	4.20%	10,125	(6,300)	3,825
5	5.76%	10,125	(8,644)	1,481
6	7.15%	10,125	(10,725)	(600)
7	9.04%	10,125	(13,556)	(3,431)

Interest Rate Assumptions

	LIBOR	
Period	Begin	End
1	5.00%	4.75%
2	4.75%	4.50%
3	4.50%	4.10%
4	4.10%	4.20%
5	4.20%	4.45%
6	4.45%	4.75%
7	4.75%	5.10%

amount of the excess fixed payments.[11] Only when LIBOR increases enough to eliminate this benefit will the variable rate payer be disadvantaged, assuming that the swap is held throughout its term.[12] However, because of the multiplier effect, the sample swap is sensitive to increases in LIBOR. Table 4–2 compares the cash flows on the sample swap to a vanilla swap. The latter bears a lower fixed rate, but the variable rate does not contain a leverage or multiplier feature.

TABLE 4–2

Sample Swap

Vanilla Swap					
Notional Amount	150,000				
Fixed Rate	6.50%				
Variable Rate = LIBOR (begin)					
Period	**Sample Swap Net Exchange (Table 4–1)**	**Fixed Receipts**	**Vanilla Swap Variable Obligation**	**Net Exchange**	**Difference**
1	2,625	9,750	(7,500)	2,250	375
2	3,000	9,750	(7,125)	2,625	375
3	3,375	9,750	(6,750)	3,000	375
4	3,825	9,750	(6,150)	3,600	225
5	1,481	9,750	(6,300)	3,450	(1,969)
6	(600)	9,750	(6,675)	3,075	(3,675)
7	(3,431)	9,750	(7,125)	2,625	(6,056)

11. The variable rate of a swap can also contain the written option premium. Assume the rates for a swap similar to a highly leveraged swap but without any embedded written option would require a fixed rate of 6 percent and a variable rate of LIBOR. Also assume the required written option premium is 1 percent per year. The option writer in a pay floating/ receive fixed swap embedding a written option could receive the premium by requiring an increase in the fixed rate to 7 percent or requiring a decrease in the component of the variable rate to LIBOR–1 percent.

12. Expectations of future interest rate increases will negatively affect the fair value of the swap from the variable rate payer's perspective.

FIGURE   4 – 1

Sample Swap versus Vanilla Swap

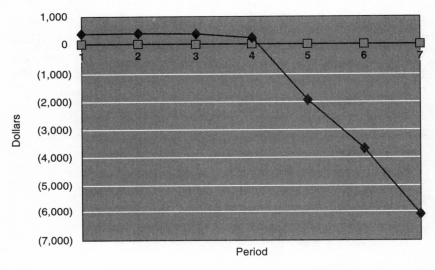

———— Represents the periodic payment difference between
the sample swap and the vanilla swap

A corporate treasurer might use a swap such as sample swap to convert fixed-rate debt to floating synthetically when the treasurer is confident that short-term interest rates will be stable or decline over the term of the swap. If the treasurer's interest rate view prevails, interest expense is lower than that which could be achieved by combining fixed-rate debt and a conventional pay floating-rate/receive fixed-rate swap because of the larger fixed receipts.

Note though that this risk management strategy entails the treasurer taking a view on interest rates. The benefit of the embedded written option will be subsumed and perhaps greatly overshadowed if interest rates increase. Figure 4–1 illustrates this possibility. It graphs the difference in cash flows between the sample swap (Table 4–1) and vanilla swap (Table 4–2) as LIBOR increases. Note that the graph replicates the payoff of a written option.

A number of large corporations incurred significant losses on leveraged/multiplier swaps due to unprecedented increases in short-term interest rates in the first half of 1994. In addition to raising questions about the accounting for such instruments, the attendant publicity has caused concern about the suitability of other derivatives for risk management purposes and about the adequacy of corporations' risk management control processes.

Extension or Cancellation Provisions

An otherwise conventional interest rate swap can enable one counterparty to cancel a swap, usually at a single date or periodically starting after a defined period. For example, a corporation that wants to create fixed rate debt synthetically can enter into a five-year swap under which it pays fixed and receives floating and links the swap for accounting purposes to existing commercial paper. The counterparty has the annual option to cancel the swap, beginning at the end of the third year. At the end of the third year, the counterparty will cancel the swap if short-term interest rates increase. Thus, the swap fails to "fix" the rate of commercial paper in years four and five, and the corporation will incur higher interest expense as the commercial paper reprices.

An opposite outcome results on a three-year swap that the counterparty can extend for two years at the swap's maturity. The counterparty will extend when short-term rates decrease. Thus, the corporation will lose the ability to enjoy the decline in interest rates in years four and five as the underlying commercial paper reprices.

A counterparty might engage in these swaps for reasons similar to those discussed in the preceding section. That is, the counterparty compensates the corporation for the option risk by offering it favorable rates on either leg of the swap. The treasurer seeks to reduce funding costs by the amount of this benefit.

Synthetic Callable Bond Asset

A corporation might enter into a five-year swap in which it pays floating rates and receives fixed rates. At year three, the counterparty has a cancellation option. The swap is linked to a five-year, noncallable floating interest rate asset owned by the corporation. The combination of the derivative and the underlying investment creates a synthetic asset, akin to an investment in a fixed-rate, five-year bond that is callable by the issuer at year three:

> *Interest rates remain stabile or increase*   The issuer of a callable bond would not call it (at least because of interest rate conditions). The callable swap replicates this outcome. The corporation has fixed net receipts throughout the five years of the asset and the matched swap.

> *Interest rates decline*   The issuer of a callable bond would call it. The investor would be exposed to reinvestment risk at the call date. The callable swap replicates this outcome. The swap is called and the corporation is "left" with the cash flows on the underlying floating rate asset.

Synthetic Noncallable Floating Rate Debt Obligations[13]

A corporation can seek intermediate-term variable-rate debt. To do so, it issues five-year, fixed-rate debt that is callable at

---

13. A debt issuer can also create a *synthetic noncallable fixed-rate debt* obligation. To do so, the corporation combines a written option and issues callable fixed-rate debt. The option permits the counterparty to compel the corporation to enter into a pay-fixed, receive-variable swap that commences on the date the underlying fixed-rate debt is callable and matures on the date the underlying debt originally matured. The counterparty usually pays the corporation cash as the written option premium. In this fashion, the corporation *monetizes* the value of the embedded call option it purchased from lenders. If the counterparty exercises the option, the corporation would refinance the underlying debt with variable rate debt.

    Technically, this structure does not utilize derivatives embedded in other derivatives—the option on the swap (a swaption) is a stand-alone derivative, potentially settleable in a derivative.

year three. Simultaneously, it enters into a five-year, receive-fixed, pay-floating interest rate swap. The swap embeds a cancellation option that permits the counterparty to terminate the swap at the end of year three.

If interest rates increase, the counterparty does not exercise its cancellation provision nor does the corporation call the underlying debt. Taken together, the fixed-rate debt and the swap combine to produce variable-rate interest expense. If interest rates decline, the swap counterparty exercises its option and the swap terminates. The corporation also exercises its call option on the underlying debt. It finances the call by issuing two-year, variable interest rate notes. Thus, it has achieved its original objective of obtaining variable cost debt for five years (via a combination of the swap and the notes in years 1–3 and on the variable rate notes in years 4–5).

This strategy is advantageous if the premium received by the corporation for the cancellation option (usually found in advantageous terms for the fixed or variable rate) has more economic value than the cost paid by the corporation for the call option it purchased and embedded in the debt (higher coupon payments than on otherwise similar noncallable debt and/or the call premium). A successful execution may indicate that the note lenders undercharged for the call risk they assumed.[14]

---

14. Embedded options can be difficult to value, and they are not priced in observable markets, presenting opportunities to corporate borrowers that engage in these strategies. However, the corporation faces similar difficulties in evaluating the premium it receives on embedded written options. Qualified personnel and valuation capabilities aid corporations in ensuring that they receive maximum value for the embedded written option. Also, competing bids from two or more dealers for the swap reduce the risk that the corporation will receive inadequate compensation for the embedded written option. Also see the discussion of embedded options in Chapter 8.

Highly Leveraged Swaps Compared to Extendible or Cancelable Swaps

The optionality of extendible or cancelable swaps is relatively less volatile than the optionality found in some highly leveraged or multiplier swaps, as explained in the following table.

Type of Swap	On-going Cash Flows at Option Exercise	Relationship of On-going Cash Flows to a Conventional Swap
Cancelable Swap	Terminate	Not applicable.
Extendible Swap	Continue	The relationship between the fixed rate and the variable rate approximate a conventional interest rate swap during the extension period.
Highly Leveraged/Multiplier	Continue	In sample swap, for example, the floating leg increases more than would the floating leg of a conventional swap during periods of increasing interest rates.

No standard criteria distinguishes highly leveraged swaps embedding a written option from non–highly leveraged swaps with less volatile optionality.

Indexed Amortizing Swaps

Indexed amortizing swaps have some similarity to cancelable swaps. A corporation (the floating-rate payer) and the counterparty agree to scheduled reductions in the notional amount of the swap in response to declines, if any, in an agreed upon interest rate index. The cash flows synthetically replicate the cash flows on an investment in fixed-rate mortgage-backed bonds (the fixed receipts) financed with short-term debt (the variable payments). As interest rates decline, the rate of prepayments on mortgage-backed bonds would tend to increase (replicated by the decline in the notional amount of the swap).

Thus, the corporation has written an embedded put option, purchased by the counterparty, that is similar to the home owner's put option in a mortgage. Some differences exist. For instance, the exercise of put options in a mortgage pool in response to interest rate declines is not perfectly predictable. Home owners prepay (or fail to prepay) for reasons other than interest rate declines—job changes, desire for a larger or smaller home, ability to qualify for a new mortgage, and so on. An index amortizing swap eliminates this element of unpredictability.

Index amortizing swaps have been popular with some financial institutions. In exchange for embedding the written option in the swap, these institutions enjoy a higher net interest spread because the fixed receipt (or the variable payment) contains the premium for the embedded put option. But, as is typical with embedded options, the payoff profile from the option writer's perspective is unequal. As interest rates increase, the instrument is "short" (as would be the case in fixed-rate, long-term cash instruments financed on a short-term basis). As interest rates decline, the instrument fails to deliver a corresponding upside; the beneficial spread is reduced by virtue of the declining notional amount. Thus, these instruments need to be carefully considered in an institution's overall asset/liability management process.

ACCOUNTING FOR WRITTEN OPTIONS EMBEDDED IN OTHER DERIVATIVES

General

In the absence of definitive FASB or EITF guidance, the views of the SEC staff on written options embedded in other derivatives are particularly important. *Leveraged* swaps that embed written options should be marked-to-market through income. The SEC staff has not offered a formal distinction between these and *nonleveraged* swaps that embed written options. It appears that the SEC is particularly concerned about swaps that have substantially more downside market risk than a plain vanilla swap of a similar term. (Downside risk being characteristic of a written option.) Modeling the cash flows and fair values of a swap under a number of different market scenarios (such as changing interest rates and yield curves) may help in assessing whether it is leveraged. Often, but not always, the formula for calculating the variable rate is complex in leveraged swaps.

And what are the SEC staff's views regarding nonleveraged swaps that embed written options? Conceptually, the SEC staff cannot distinguish them from leveraged swaps. In other words, the two categories differ in the degree—rather than in the nature—of the risk. Thus, it can be inferred that the SEC staff's preference is for mark-to-market accounting through income for all swaps that embed written options.

Before the EITF ended its deliberations on EITF 95–11, the SEC staff supported preliminary recommendations of a working group assisting the task force. The working group's recommendation would have required bifurcating the written option from the balance of the derivative and accounting for each component separately.[15] The written option component would be accounted for on a mark-to-market basis through income except under very narrow, specified conditions.

It now appears that resolution of the issue may await FASB's decisions on its derivatives and hedge accounting project (see the discussion in Chapter 3). Because of the SEC's

---

15. The bifurcation contemplated by this accounting can be complex. When it would not be practicable to bifurcate, the working group recommended accounting for the entire instrument on a mark-to-market basis through income.

views, counterparties in nonleveraged swaps that embed written options should monitor developments. Thorough disclosure of the terms and characteristics of these swaps is advisable. In fact, SFAS No. 119 notes that disclosure of the face or contract amount of financial instruments may be misleading when leverage features are not adequately disclosed. Thus, SFAS No. 119 requires a discussion of leverage features and their general effects on (1) the credit and market risk, (2) the cash requirements, and (3) the related accounting policy.

Mortgage Swaps

With the advent of indexed amortizing swaps, mortgage swaps (as contemplated by EITF 88–8) are rare. A mortgage swap is similar to an indexed amortizing swap except for the following:

1. The notional principal amount of the swap is indexed to an actual identified pool of mortgage-backed securities. As principal is collected on the pool, the notional amount of the swap declines.

2. At the termination of the swap, a net settlement payment or an exchange of mortgages for cash occurs between the counterparties.

From the perspective of the fixed-rate receiver, a mortgage swap contains embedded put options similar to those found by investors in mortgage-backed securities. In addition, the settlement alternatives at termination embed other options.
EITF reached the following consensus decisions:

- The notional amount of the mortgage-backed securities should not be recognized on the balance sheet at the inception of the transaction (this is conventional accounting for a derivative).

- If a mortgage swap did not qualify for hedge accounting, a market-adjusted method of accounting should be used (presumably, the subsequent issuance of SFAS No. 115 in 1993 would require mark-to-market—as opposed to lower-of-cost-or-market—accounting).

- Hedge accounting would be appropriate if the hedge criteria under GAAP are met. However, several task force members and the SEC observer expressed the view that it would be difficult to meet these criteria. Further, the SEC observer noted that hedges involving mortgage swaps and interest-only strips may require active management, leading to classification by financial institutions as trading account instruments recorded at market value.

CONCLUSION

Even a casual perusal of this chapter will convince the reader that accounting for embedded derivatives is a complex topic. At the outset, we noted that the unsettled nature of accounting for stand-alone derivatives, and the complex accounting for cash instruments in which derivatives can be embedded, ensure this outcome. There is an additional reason. The range of derivatives is vast—they can be linked to virtually any price or index and the linkage can occur in various ways, often employing unusual and conditional optionality.

To date, standard-setters have usually tackled the accounting for these instruments one by one. Given the flexibility of derivatives, this is a daunting task—users can employ them or combine them in virtually an unlimited number of ways. As a result, financial statement preparers, users, and auditors are looking to the FASB for resolution.

Yet the FASB's task is daunting as well. A broad-based solution to accounting for embedded derivatives could well challenge many of the tenets of the mixed-attribute, historical cost method presently in place. Thus, it is possible that final guidance will not be achieved soon. Readers should expect bodies such as the EITF, the AICPA, the SEC, and other regulators to provide interim guidance and must stay alert to ongoing developments.

CHAPTER 5

Accounting for Securitization Transactions

Benjamin S. Neuhausen

Securitization is the process of converting loans and other financial assets that are not readily marketable into securities that can be placed and traded in capital markets. The securities created, often called *asset-backed securities,* may be registered with the Securities and Exchange Commission and sold to retail investors. Other securities are not registered and are directed at institutional investors. The goal of securitization from the seller's point of view is to raise cash at a cost lower than the cost of general obligation borrowings or to achieve some other perceived advantage, such as off-balance-sheet treatment.

Securitization began with first mortgages on single-family homes, and those mortgage-backed securities remain the largest class of securities created from securitization transactions. In the past 10 years, securitization has blossomed, and structures and markets now exist to securitize virtually

---

This chapter is adapted with permission from *Accounting for Securitization Transactions by Sellers/Issuers,* (Chicago: Arthur Anderson & Company, 1989).

any kind of receivable: trade receivables, installment receivables, second mortgage loans, home equity loans, commercial loans (including commercial mortgages), lease receivables (auto, computer, airplane, and so on), credit card receivables, insurance premium loans, student loans, manufactured home loans, multifamily mortgage loans, receivables denominated in foreign currencies, and more. Securitization began in the United States and is far more prevalent in the United States than elsewhere. In recent years, however, securitization transactions have spread around the globe. Most major developed countries now have active markets to securitize, at a minimum, mortgages and trade or credit card receivables.

Syndications and participations of commercial loans by financial institutions are closely related to securitization. Like securitization, syndications and participations transfer interests in loans to outside investors (other financial institutions) and generate cash for the originating institution. Syndications and participations, however, typically do not create tradable securities. They create interests in loans, but those interests (1) are not securities, (2) may not be freely transferable, and (3) typically would be transferable only to another financial institution.

This chapter discusses the accounting issues that arise in securitization, syndication, and participation transactions and is organized as follows:

1. An overview of U.S. generally accepted accounting principles (GAAP) applicable to the sellers and issuers.

2. A detailed discussion of GAAP applicable to sellers and issuers for common transaction structures. This discussion includes relevant pronouncements of the Financial Accounting Standards Board (FASB), its Emerging Issues Task Force (EITF), and the Securities and Exchange Commission (SEC).

3. An overview of U.S. GAAP applicable to the investors.

4. A discussion of a new FASB statement and a recent
   FASB Exposure Draft that could significantly
   change the accounting by sellers and issuers.

This chapter does not cover regulatory accounting practices of, for example, banks, savings and loan associations, or
insurance companies. The chapter also does not cover the
income tax treatment of securitization transactions.

Securitization transactions take several forms. The key
differences involve who issues the securities, how many classes
of securities are issued, what is the nature of the securities,
and how many receivables are involved.

Who Issues the Securities?   Sometimes the securities
are issued directly by the originator of the receivables, and
any interests in the receivables not transferred to investors
continue to be owned directly by the originator. This structure
is common with syndications and participations of commercial
loans. More often, however, the originator transfers ownership of a pool of receivables to a special-purpose subsidiary,
trust, or partnership, which in turn issues the asset-backed
securities. The special-purpose subsidiary, trust, or partnership (generically, a special-purpose entity or SPE) is limited
by its organizational documents to buying receivables that
meet defined criteria and issuing asset-backed securities. The
primary purpose of creating an SPE is to isolate the receivables, and the investors' interests in them, from claims by the
originator's creditors if the originator becomes insolvent.
Usually originators transfer a 100 percent interest in the
receivables to an SPE, and receive cash and SPE asset-backed
securities (representing a partial retained interest in the
receivables) as consideration.

How Many Classes of Securities Are Issued?   In a
single-class securitization, one class of asset-backed securities
is issued. Each security represents a fractional undivided
interest in each receivable in the pool. Some of the securities

may be subordinated to others in the case of defaults or delinquencies by the obligors on the underlying receivables, but all of the securities represent equal undivided interests in all of the receivables. Single-class structures predominate for nonmortgage securitizations.

In a multiple-class securitization, several classes (or tranches) of asset-backed securities are issued. In one form of multiple-class securitization, each class represents a right to one fixed percentage of the principal collected on each receivable and a different fixed percentage of the interest collected on each receivable. A class that is entitled to a share of principal collected but no share of interest collected is a principal-only (PO) strip. A class that is entitled to a share of interest collected but no share of principal collected is an interest-only (IO) strip. In another form of multiple-class securitization, all principal collected (including prepayments) are paid to the class having the earliest stated maturity date until it is retired, then to the class with the next earliest maturity date until it is retired, and so on. It is also common to have one or more "zero coupon" classes that receive no payments of interest or principal until all or the other classes are retired. Until that time, the interest that accrues on the zero coupon class is added to its principal, and the cash interest collected on the underlying receivables is paid as additional principal on the prior classes. In this type of multiple-class securitization, the investor's interest is identifiable only at the level of the pool; the investor does not have an identifiable interest in any individual receivable.

What Is the Nature of the Securities Issued? The securities issued may be either debt securities (for example, notes, bonds, collateralized mortgage obligations, and so on) or securities representing a direct ownership interest in the underlying receivables (pass-through certificates, certificates of participation, and so on). The nature of the securities is important to identify the legal form of the securitization transaction, which in turn is important in determining the proper accounting by the originator.

How Many Receivables Are Involved? Most securitization transactions transfer interests in a large pool of relatively small receivables. Occasionally, an originator will securitize a small group of large receivables, or even a single large receivable. Participations and syndications of commercial loans typically involve just one loan.

OVERVIEW OF GENERALLY ACCEPTED ACCOUNTING PRINCIPLES

Securitization transactions span a wide spectrum. At one extreme are outright sales of assets or interests in assets with no continuing involvement by the seller. At the other extreme are borrowings collateralized by assets. In between are sales of assets with varying degrees of continuing involvement by the seller and nonrecourse borrowings collateralized by assets. The transactions at the ends of the spectrum usually are easy to account for because their substance follows their form; it is the transactions in the middle that create accounting issues. That is, transactions in the middle have characteristics of both sales and borrowings and raise questions of whether the seller/issuer should continue to include the receivables on its balance sheet by treating the transaction as a financing or record a sale of the receivables, with gain and loss recognition.

As a preface to discussing in detail the accounting considerations faced by sellers/issuers, it is worthwhile to provide an overview of the authoritative literature affecting securitization transactions. This overview helps set the stage for the complexities and potential controversies in accounting for these transactions.

The FASB has issued two accounting standards that are specifically relevant: FASB Statement (SFAS) No. 77, *Reporting by Transferors for Transfers of Receivables with Recourse* (December 1983), and FASB Technical Bulletin (FTB) No. 85–2, *Accounting for Collateralized Mortgage Obligations (CMOs)* (March 1985). In addition, SFAS No. 94, *Consolidation of All Majority-Owned Subsidiaries,* and EITF Issue 90–15, *Impact of Nonsubstantive Lessors, Residual Value Guarantees, and Other Provisions in Leasing Transactions,* provide guidance on consolidation of SPEs involved in securitization transactions.

Transfers (Sales) of Receivables with Recourse

In a sale of receivables with recourse, the seller is obligated to make payments to the buyer or to repurchase receivables sold under certain circumstances, typically for defaults up to a specified percentage that sometimes greatly exceeds likely credit losses. The amount of recourse can vary from a small percentage of the receivable balances to 100 percent. The form of the recourse also varies. In addition, the seller often guarantees to the buyer a specified return or yield during the term of the receivables.

SFAS No. 77 allows receivables to be removed from the balance sheet (with gain or loss recognition) if they are irrevocably transferred in a transaction that "purports to be a sale or a participation agreement." The seller can generally have no options or obligations to repurchase nondelinquent receivables (calls and puts). Off-balance-sheet treatment is allowed even though it is probable that the seller/transferor will make future payments to the buyer/transferee for credit losses, the effects of prepayments, or changes in interest rates—as long as the credit losses and the effects of prepayments can be reasonably estimated. SFAS No. 77 also allows off-balance-sheet treatment of transfers of partial interests in receivables. Any interests retained are recorded (or remain) as assets on the seller/transferor's balance sheet. In practice, it is not difficult to achieve sale accounting under SFAS No. 77, particularly for large pools of homogenous receivables.

Collateralized Mortgage Obligations

A collateralized mortgage obligation (CMO) is a debt security that is collateralized by a pool of mortgage loan receivables. The interest and principal payments of the mortgagors are accumulated, then used to pay interest and principal to the CMO holders. The CMOs are frequently nonrecourse to the general credit of the borrower/issuer; the holders may look only to the cash flow from the mortgage collateral for their interest and principal payments. Although the FASB had mortgage receivables in mind when it issued FTB No. 85–2, the FASB staff has indicated that it is appropriate to apply the technical bulletin by analogy to other types of receivables. The purpose of the technical bulletin was to give guidance as to when transactions that are in legal form debt instruments may be treated as sales for accounting purposes.

FTB No. 85–2 allows assets and debt to be removed from the balance sheet (with gain or loss recognition) in a CMO transaction if virtually all of the cash flows from the assets are irrevocably passed to the creditors and if the borrower/issuer cannot be required to make any future payments to the creditors other than from cash flows from the collateral. The borrower may not retain even secondary liability to pay the obligations. The technical bulletin does not allow off-balance-sheet treatment for passage of partial interests in the assets' future cash flows to creditors unless the interest retained by the borrower is "nominal," defined as "insignificantly small" or "trifling." Further, if a CMO transaction qualifies for off-balance-sheet treatment under the technical bulletin, the "nominal" interests retained by the borrower (if any) may not be recorded as assets; these interests are recorded as they accrue to the benefit of the borrower. Although the technical bulletin sets stringent criteria, it is unique in the accounting literature by permitting sale treatment even though the legal form is debt.

Conflicting Guidance

SFAS No. 77 and FTB No. 85–2 provide conflicting guidance. Receivables transferred in a transaction that purports to be a sale or a participation may be removed from the balance sheet under SFAS No. 77 even though the seller has substantial continuing involvement with those receivables. Conversely, receivables transferred in a transaction structured as a borrowing often are recorded on balance sheet even though the seller's continuing involvement is modest. The following paragraphs describe the effects of different forms of continuing involvement on the accounting for a transaction that purports to be a sale (SFAS No. 77) and a transaction that is structured as a borrowing (FTB No. 85–2).

Servicing   Servicing activities include: collecting payments from the obligors on the underlying receivables, pursuing delinquent obligors for payment, negotiating revised payment terms with or foreclosing on collateral of defaulted obligors, collecting escrow deposits for the payment of property taxes and insurance, investing funds collected until they are remitted to investors or others, forwarding payments and related accounting reports to investors, and paying taxes and insurance from escrow funds when due. The seller's retention of servicing rights does not affect the seller's accounting for a securitization transaction under either form.

Retention of a Partial Interest in the Receivables   If a transaction purports to be a sale, the seller's retention of partial interests in the receivables, even substantial interests, does not preclude sale accounting for the interests sold. By contrast, if a transaction is structured as a borrowing, the seller's retention of any more than a "trifling" interest in the receivables requires that the transaction be accounted for as a borrowing.

Recourse (Guarantees) for Credit Losses   If the seller agrees to absorb some or all credit losses (from delinquencies and defaults) on the underlying receivables in a transaction that purports to be a sale, off-balance-sheet (sale) accounting is not precluded if the seller can make a reasonable estimate of its exposure to loss. Under SFAS No. 77, sale accounting is not precluded even if the seller is obligated to reimburse the investors for 100 percent of credit losses. By contrast, if the investors have *any* recourse to the "seller" for credit losses in a transaction structured as a borrowing, the seller must account for the transaction as a borrowing.

Investor Put Option   If a transaction purports to be a sale, an investor's right to put receivables back to the seller for any reason other than delinquencies or defaults causes the transaction to be accounted for as a borrowing. If the investors put right is limited solely to putting delinquent or defaulted receivables, sale accounting is not precluded. If a transaction is structured as a borrowing, *any* investor's right to put receivables for *any* reason requires the transaction to be accounted for as a borrowing.

Seller/Originator Call Option   Under either structure, an option by the seller/originator to call the receivables requires the transaction to be accounted for as a borrowing. An exception is that a "clean-up call" to call the receivables when the remaining uncollected balance is below 5 percent to 10 percent of the original balance does not preclude sale accounting.

Guarantees of Prepayments   Under either structure, if the seller guarantees a certain level of prepayments to the investors (that is, agrees that the investors' principal will be repaid faster than indicated by the contractual payments on the underlying receivables), the transaction must be accounted for as a borrowing. This requirement applies even if the guaranteed level of prepayments is considered probable because it is consistent with the historic prepayment experience for the type of receivables sold. If the transaction purports to be a sale, however, the seller can reimburse the investors for losses caused by prepayments without precluding sale accounting. Thus, if the transaction purports to be a sale, the seller can't commit to prepay the investors' principal, but it can agree to reimburse the investors for lost interest income if the receivables prepay and the investor has to reinvest at rates lower than the yield on the securitization. If the transaction is structured as a borrowing, either type of agreement by the "seller" requires the transaction to be accounted for as a borrowing.

Retention of Interest Rate Risk If a transaction purports to be a sale, the seller's retention of interest rate risk does not preclude sale accounting for the interests sold. For example, the seller can sell fixed-rate receivables and promise to pay the investors a yield that fluctuates with LIBOR or Treasury note rates, or can sell floating-rate receivables and promise to pay the investors a fixed yield. By contrast, if a transaction is structured as a borrowing, the seller's retention of any interest rate risk in the receivables through a mismatch between the interest characteristics of the receivables and the securities requires that the transaction be accounted for as a borrowing.

SFAS No. 77 and FTB No. 85–2 are also inconsistent in that SFAS No. 77 permits the initial recording of a residual interest in a sales transaction (for example, due to a positive spread of the interest rates on the receivables over the investors' yields), while FTB No. 85–2 does not.

Ambiguous Transactions

The scope of SFAS No. 77, as noted, is limited to transactions that purport to be sales or participations, as opposed to collateralized borrowings, which may be an issue of legal form. Thus the FASB appears to place importance on legal form in an unsettled area of law.

The legal line between a sale of assets and a pledge of assets to secure a loan is not always clear. Some "buyers" have been unpleasantly surprised to learn that they may be classified as secured creditors in bankruptcy proceedings, in which case they could be forced to share their "collateral." For example, some attorneys believe that a sale of receivables with 100 percent recourse would be treated as a secured borrowing upon bankruptcy of the issuer, yet SFAS No. 77 clearly contemplates sale treatment for some transactions with 100 percent recourse.

These ambiguities, as well as other matters, have given rise to "scope" questions: How is one to determine whether SFAS No. 77, FTB No. 85–2, or some other pronouncement applies? These scope questions as well as other matters make accounting for transactions in the middle of the spectrum difficult.

Issuer Objectives

To summarize, the criteria included in the accounting literature for removing assets and liabilities from the balance sheet produce different accounting results for transactions in which the substance is similar or identical but the form is different. If the receivables transaction purports to be a sale or a participation, one standard applies; if the receivables transaction purports to be a borrowing, another—and radically different—standard applies, regardless of the seller/transferor/debtor's rights and obligations in the two transactions. Further, for some transactions the form is ambiguous.

Because the financial reporting treatment of a securitization transaction is, in large part, dependent on its form, the transaction form selected by an issuer may be influenced by its accounting objectives. Does it desire off-balance-sheet treatment and gain or loss recognition? Or does it desire to monetize "underwater" receivables (whose fair value is less than their carrying amount) by electing financing (on-balance-sheet) treatment and potentially avoid loss recognition?

Consolidation of Subsidiaries and Nonsubsidiaries

SFAS No. 94 requires that a parent company consolidate all subsidiary companies that it controls through ownership of a majority of the voting stock. In practice, that requirement extends to all entities controlled through ownership of a majority of the voting interests, including partnerships and trusts. Thus, parent companies and sponsors consolidate all majority-owned SPEs used for securitization transactions.

Sometimes sponsors transact securitization transactions through SPEs in which they do not hold a majority of the voting interests, or even no voting interest. These SPEs are sometimes referred to as "nonsubsidiary subsidiaries" or "orphan subsidiaries." In EITF 90–15 the task force issued guidance on lessees' consolidation of SPEs used in leasing transactions. The EITF concluded that a lessee should consolidate an SPE lessor if (1) the SPE's sole purpose was to lease assets to that lessee, (2) the terms of the leases resulted in the lessee having substantially all of the risks and rewards of the SPE's assets, *and* (3) the SPE does not have substantive equity at risk from an independent third party. That guidance has been extended by analogy to SPEs in other types of transactions, including securitizations.

DETAILED DISCUSSION OF GENERALLY ACCEPTED ACCOUNTING PRINCIPLES

This section discusses existing generally accepted accounting principles in more detail and is organized as follows:

- Recourse borrowings
- Sales of receivables with servicing retained

- Sales of partial interests in receivables
- Sales of receivables with recourse
- Sales of receivables with seller guarantee of prepayment experience
- Sales of receivables with seller retention of interest rate risk
- Sales of receivables with seller retention of foreign exchange risk
- Securitization of short-term receivables
- Collateralized mortgage obligation type structures
- Consolidation (transactions through subsidiaries or SPEs)

Recourse Borrowings

A recourse borrowing collateralized by a pool of receivables is a liability of the issuer for which the lender (noteholder) has recourse not only to the collateral but also to the general credit of the issuer. The instrument is an obligation of the issuing entity and not an ownership interest in the receivables. These transactions can take a variety of forms or possess various characteristics, including the following:

- Obligations for which scheduled payments on the receivables (collateral) are sufficient to meet the debt service on the obligations and any prepayments on the underlying assets are paid to the noteholders (so-called *pay-through bonds*).
- Multiclass obligations similar to CMOs, for which principal is paid by class, beginning with the class with the earliest stated maturity.
- Obligations that guarantee the noteholders a fixed maturity irrespective of the prepayment experience of the underlying assets (so-called *fixed-pay bonds*).

- Overcollateralized obligations, that is, the expected cash flows from the pledged assets exceed expected debt service or, stated differently, the fair market value of the pledged assets exceeds the amount of the obligations.

In any of these structures, the obligations may call for quarterly principal and interest payments—even though the payment schedule for the underlying assets is monthly, for example.

A recourse borrowing collateralized by assets is recorded as a liability like any other debt. The assets continue to be recorded as assets on the issuer's balance sheet and, assuming the intent and ability to hold until maturity, continue to be reported at their existing carrying amount (that is, no immediate gain or loss is recognized). Debt issuance costs should be deferred and amortized over the term of the borrowing. (This is also the case for nonrecourse borrowings and SFAS No. 77 transactions accounted for as financings.)

Sometimes these structures provide for the debt to be issued by a special purpose subsidiary. Typically, the operating parent company forms the subsidiary, which purchases the pool of receivables from its parent (or the receivables are otherwise transferred to the subsidiary) and issues the obligations secured by the receivables. This structure, which can also exist in nonrecourse debt arrangements as mentioned earlier, helps protect the investors by helping to isolate the receivables from bankruptcy concerns related to the parent. This structure also raises financial reporting issues concerning consolidation, which are discussed in the Consolidation section of this chapter (Page 5–65).

Sales of Receivables with Servicing Retained

If the *entire* principal balance of the receivables is sold at a price at or near par with servicing retained and the stated servicing fee rate differs from a "current (normal) servicing fee rate" or no servicing fee is specified, the sales price should be adjusted to provide for a normal servicing fee in each subsequent servicing period. This normal servicing fee should not be less than the estimated servicing costs. If the specified servicing fee is greater (or less) than the normal servicing fee rate, the sales price should be adjusted upward (or downward) by the present value of the difference over the estimated life of the receivables. In accordance with the EITF consensuses in EITF 84–21 and 88–11, estimates of excess (or deficient) servicing fees should be calculated using prepayment, default and interest rate assumptions that market participants would use for similar financial instruments subject to prepayment, and default and interest rate risks. They also should be discounted using an interest rate that a purchaser unrelated to the seller of such a financial instrument would demand. In essence, the objective is to adjust the actual sales price to an estimated sales price that would have been obtained had a normal servicing fee been specified. (Note that if the seller is not the servicer, it still will need to adjust the gain or loss for the present value of any difference between the stated rate on the receivables and the pass-through rate to the investors.)

If the excess of the stated interest rate on the receivables sold over the pass-through rate to the investors exceeds a normal servicing fee (excess servicing), but that excess over the receivables' lives cannot be reasonably estimated, the initial gain or loss on sale should not be adjusted. Rather, the excess should be recorded as income as received. A situation of this type might be the sale of receivables that can be prepaid at any time without penalty, where reasonable estimates of prepayments are not available.

SFAS No. 77 defines a current (normal) servicing fee rate as "a servicing fee rate that is representative of servicing fee rates most commonly used in comparable servicing agreements covering similar types of receivables." In practice, this definition was the subject of varied interpretation. In response thereto, the FASB issued FTB No. 87–3, *Accounting for Mortgage Servicing Fees and Rights* (December 1987), which provides guidance for residential mortgages. Specifically, the technical bulletin indicates that the normal servicing fee rate that should be used for mortgages is that set by the Government National Mortgage Association, the Federal Home Loan Mortgage Corporation, and the Federal National Mortgage Association (unless a higher rate is needed to cover the cost of servicing). That rate should generally be used whether the loans are sold to those organizations or to private sector investors.

In EITF 94–9, the task force discussed how to determine a normal servicing fee rate for a sale of Small Business Administration (SBA) loans in the absence of a major secondary market maker. The EITF reached a consensus that

> a seller-servicer should determine a normal servicing fee rate for SBA loans based on a representative survey of the direct and indirect costs of servicing of major servicers of SBA loans plus a reasonable profit margin. The Task Force observed that a recent survey of servicing costs conducted by the National Association of Guaranteed Government Lenders (NAGGL) at the request of the Federal Financial Institutions Examination Council concluded that 40 basis points is a normal servicing fee rate for SBA loans. The Task Force also agreed that if the seller-servicer's estimated servicing costs over the estimated life of the loan are expected to exceed normal servicing fees, the expected loss on servicing the loan should be accrued as of the date the loan is sold.

The FASB has not provided guidance for other types of receivables, but FTB No. 87–3 and EITF 94–9 should be looked to as analogies. Further, in discussing measurements of normal servicing fees for residential mortgages, EITF 85–26 reached a consensus that use of a normal fee developed as a function of the servicer's own cost is not appropriate. Determining normal service fee rates for nonmortgage receivables, such as automobile loans and credit card receivables, may be more difficult than mortgages. Some studies performed by investment banking and other firms exist and should be referred to.

Questions have also arisen with respect to accounting for the impact of changes in estimates due to prepayments on the net excess servicing fee receivable or net servicing fee deficiency payable that was initially established at the time of sale. Two approaches have been suggested:

1. If prepayment experience is unfavorable, the net excess servicing fee receivable (or deficiency payable) would be decreased (or increased) currently to the present value of the estimated remaining future excess (or deficient) service fee revenue, with the adjustment charged to income. The same discount rate used to calculate the original receivable or payable would be used to calculate the change. If prepayment experience is favorable, the receivable (or payable) would not be adjusted currently; however, amortization would be adjusted prospectively.

2. The seller would compute a new interest rate from the date of the initial sale based on the initial net receivable or payable balance recorded, but using the new estimate of the timing and amount of net cash flows for the excess (or deficient) servicing. The net receivable or payable would be adjusted to the amount at which it would have been stated had the current estimate of cash flows been used since inception. The catch-up adjustment (gain or loss) would be reflected in income currently.

In December 1986, the EITF addressed this issue for mortgages and reached a consensus that the first approach should be used (EITF 86–38). The second approach is based on SFAS No. 91, which was issued after the EITF consensus. The EITF has not changed its consensus, and both approaches have been used in practice. During a 1989 meeting of the EITF, the FASB staff announced that it is their understanding that the majority of enterprises use the first approach. Further, the staffs of the FASB, the Federal Home Loan Bank

Board, and the SEC believe that the first approach should be followed in all circumstances except when an enterprise previously changed to the second approach and financial statements reflecting the use of that method have been issued. In that instance the enterprise should continue to use that method.

Questions also arise with regard to income recognition for servicing activities. Assuming the fees can be reliably measured, they should be recognized on the accrual method as the servicing is performed, not on a cash basis. In transactions using an escrow account (see page 155), receipt of cash may be delayed until later in the term of the transaction.

Servicing Activities

Another issue arises when receivables pay monthly but payments to investors are made less frequently—for example—quarterly. When a seller acts as servicer on a pass-through, it administers payments and reinvests temporarily retained excess cash. In addition, it commits to pay the stated pass-through rate to investors and faces the risk that reinvestment income will fall short of that commitment. In return for taking this risk and performing the stipulated administrative functions, the seller enjoys the possible benefit of reinvestment rates in excess of the pass-through rate on funds temporarily held.

The fact that the seller in the pass-through retains funds temporarily generally does not preclude sale accounting because accumulating small payments on individual receivables and remitting larger periodic payments to investors is a normal function performed by sellers. Moreover, the compensation paid to the seller is in consideration of the services performed and the risk assumed. If the seller/servicer retains funds for extended periods before making payments to investors, however, the arrangement may take on many of the characteristics of a borrowing and the compensation to the seller may exceed the value of the services performed; therefore, sale accounting may not be appropriate. In practice, it has usually been concluded that quarterly periods are reasonable for monthly pay receivables and do not preclude sale accounting.

Sales of Partial Interests in Receivables

A sale of whole receivables is accounted for like any other outright sale. The receivables are removed from the balance sheet and gain or loss is recognized for the difference between the sales proceeds received and the carrying amount of the receivables sold (less transaction costs).

A sale of undivided interests in a receivable or pool of receivables (for example, a participation) is accounted for as a partial sale of the receivables. The percentage interest sold is removed from the balance sheet, and gain or loss is recognized for the difference between the sales proceeds received and the pro rata carrying amount of the interests sold. The percentage interest retained continues to be recorded as an asset. Stated differently, sale accounting is applied to the interests transferred, but not to the interests retained (allocation of carrying amounts in partial sales shall be discussed in the following paragraphs).

If the interests sold are not undivided interests or have different characteristics than the interests retained (for example, the interests retained are subordinated to the interests sold in the event of credit losses on the receivables), then the allocation of the carrying amount becomes harder. EITF 88–11 addressed, among other things, the SFAS No. 77 requirement for accrual of probable adjustments for senior/junior (subordinated) structures. The EITF reached a consensus that for purposes of determining gain or loss on sale, the seller should allocate its recorded investment (prior to considering any related amounts included in the allowance for credit losses) between the portion sold (the senior participation) and the portion retained (the subordinated participation and any excess servicing) based on their relative fair values. The seller should evaluate the adequacy of the allowance for credit losses considering the collectibility of the remaining recorded investment relating to the portion of the receivables retained and any recourse obligation relating to the portion of the receivables sold. Under this approach, market value estimates, in effect, would be the basis for the probable adjustments and may be more conservative than the seller's own estimates. If servicing fees are less than the estimated servicing costs, an additional loss accrual is needed.

A sale of interest or principal strips in a pool of receivables likewise is accounted for as a partial sale of the receivables. The seller should allocate the carrying amount of the receivable pool between the strips sold (for purposes of determining the gain or loss on the sale) and the strips retained (for purposes of determining the remaining recorded investment to be retained as an asset on the balance sheet). EITF 88–11 addressed the allocation methodology for partial sales. It reached a consensus that the seller should allocate the carrying amount of the receivable pool between the strips sold and the strips retained based on their relative fair values on the date that the receivable pool was acquired, adjusted for payments, and other activity from the date of acquisition to the date of sale. The EITF acknowledged that it may not be practicable to determine fair values as of the date of acquisition for the portions of receivables sold later. When this is the case, the allocation should be based on the relative fair values of the strips sold and the strips retained on the date of sale. The amount of any gain recognized when a strip is sold should not exceed the gain that would be recognized if the entire receivables pool were sold.

Unless the seller lacks the ability and intent to hold the remaining strips to maturity, the carrying amount allocated to the strips retained should generally continue to be accounted for as it was previously; that is, it continues to be recorded as an asset and should not result in a current gain or loss. An amount of premium or discount should be determined on the strips retained and amortized to income using the interest method.

Multiclass pass-through certificates representing interests in pools of mortgages became feasible under the REMIC provisions of the Tax Reform Act of 1986. Multiclass pass-throughs differ from interest and principal strips in that the investor's interest through a multiclass pass-through is identifiable only at the level of the pool; the investor does not have an identifiable interest in any individual receivable. The classes behave like the tranches in a CMO (that is, with different expected lives and cash-flow patterns). However, the structure is different—each class represents a specified ownership/participation interest in the cash flows of a pool of receivables rather than a class of a debt issue. Under the EITF 88–11 consensus, the seller should account for the sale of multiclass pass-throughs similarly to the sale of strips—allocate the carrying amount of the mortgage pool between the interests sold and the interests retained based on their relative fair values (as previously discussed) and recognize gain or loss on the interests sold. If *all* of the principal is sold via the multiclass pass-throughs at a price at or near par, the "excess servicing" method of computing gain or loss should be used (EITF 84–21 and 88–11). Under the excess servicing method, the entire pool of receivables is considered sold (versus a partial sale) for a price equal to the sum of (1) the proceeds received from investors and (2) the current fair or present value of the residual interest (excess servicing) retained by the seller (adjusted for a normal servicing fee when the issuer is the servicer). The present value of the residual asset (excess servicing) retained should be calculated using prepayment, default, and interest rate assumptions that market participants would use for similar financial instruments and should be discounted using an interest rate that a purchaser unrelated to the seller of such a financial instrument would demand (that is, a market-determined valuation). If the residual interest retained represents a small fraction of the receivables, the "excess servicing" method and the allocation of carrying amount based on relative values will generally result in similar gains or losses.

Sales of Receivables with Recourse

In a sale of receivables *with* recourse, the buyer has a right to receive payment from the seller for failure of debtors to pay when due and, in some cases, for the effects of debtor prepayments. As discussed below, the form of recourse can vary. Recourse is defined in SFAS No. 77 as "the right of a transferee of receivables to receive payment from the transferor of those receivables for (a) failure of the debtors to pay when due, (b) the effects of prepayments, or (c) adjustments resulting from defects in the eligibility of the transferred receivables"—for example, defects in the legal title of the transferred receivables.

Under SFAS No. 77, a sale of receivables with recourse is recorded as a sale if *all* of the following three conditions are satisfied:

1. The seller surrenders control over the receivables; it has no option to repurchase receivables, and it cannot substitute new receivables for receivables previously sold except pursuant to the recourse provisions (that is, no call).

2. The seller's obligation under the recourse provisions can be reasonably estimated at the time of transfer.

3. The buyer cannot require the seller to repurchase the receivables except pursuant to the recourse provisions (that is, no put).

If all three conditions are satisfied, the transaction is accounted for as a full or partial sale, as discussed in the preceding two sections. In addition, the seller's estimated recourse obligation is recorded at the date of sale. A sale of receivables with recourse may follow any of the four forms discussed previously: whole receivables, undivided interests (for example, participations), principal or interest strips, or multiclass pass-throughs.

If any of the three conditions are not satisfied, the transaction is accounted for like a full recourse borrowing collateralized by receivables (as will be discussed).

With respect to conditions 1 and 3 above, SFAS No. 77 provides some additional guidance. First, the existence of a right of first refusal based on a bona fide offer by an unrelated party ordinarily will not preclude sale accounting. Further, some transfer agreements require or permit the seller to repurchase transferred receivables when the amount of outstanding receivables is minor to keep the cost of servicing those receivables from becoming unreasonable (a clean-up call). If those reversionary interests are not significant to the transferor—interpreted in practice as no more than 5 percent to 10 percent of the original balances (or participation interest) transferred—their existence alone does not preclude sale treatment. In 1989 the EITF reached a consensus that a clean-up call (or put) based solely on passage of time rather than on the uncollected balance would preclude sale accounting because of uncertainty concerning the amount of receivables outstanding at the time the call (or put) becomes exercisable unless the amount scheduled to be outstanding based on *contractual* maturities is not significant (EITF 89–2).

A put or call for any reason other than pursuant to the recourse provisions of the agreement or a clean-up call would violate the sale criteria in SFAS No. 77. For example, a repurchase option, even if at fair market value, is inconsistent with sale accounting. Further, a provision allowing the purchaser of the receivables to put the receivables back to the seller if the seller is not meeting certain defined servicing performance criteria would preclude sale accounting. A put triggered by declining creditworthiness of the *seller* or market value declines due to interest rate increases would also preclude sale accounting.

For a transaction to be covered by SFAS No. 77, the transaction must "purport to be a sale or participation." A discussion of this condition, as well as other implementation matters, follows.

Purport to Be a Sale

Because SFAS No. 77 is a fairly permissive accounting standard, sellers frequently desire to have the transaction covered by SFAS No. 77, particularly if the receivables are not "underwater" (or sale accounting would not otherwise give rise to loss recognition) and the objective is off-balance-sheet treatment. Off-balance-sheet treatment may be desired to improve reported debt/equity ratios, to avoid violating existing debt covenants, to address regulatory capital requirements, and for other reasons. If a transaction is covered by SFAS No. 77, sale accounting (with resulting gain or loss) is frequently not difficult to achieve. This is in contrast to the requirements of FTB No. 85–2 or other accounting literature, for example, in accounting for recourse debt securities. As a result, a frequent question—a scope question—is whether SFAS No. 77 applies.

Paragraph 3 of SFAS No. 77 states that "this Statement establishes standards of financial accounting and reporting by transferors for transfers of receivables with recourse that *purport* to be sales of receivables. It also applies to *participation agreements* (that is, transfers of specified interests in a particular receivable or pool of receivables) that provide for recourse, factoring agreements that provide for recourse, and sales or assignments with recourse of leases or property subject to leases that were accounted for as sales-type or direct financing leases" [emphasis added]. SFAS No. 77 "does not address accounting and reporting of loans collateralized by receivables, for which the receivables and the loan are reported on the borrower's balance sheet."

The FASB has provided limited additional guidance on the scope of SFAS No. 77. FTB No. 85–2 notes that its scope relates to *"bonds* secured by mortgage(s) . . . *structured* so that all or substantially all of the collections . . . are paid through to the holders. . . ."* [emphasis added]. In providing further background, FTB No. 85–2 notes that

> in specifying the scope of Statement 77, the phrase *purport to be sales* and all the transactions enumerated in paragraph 3 refer only to those transfers structured as sales agreements. As a result, the provisions of Statement 77 do not apply to CMOs because they are not structured as sales agreements; rather, CMOs are debt instruments collateralized by mortgage-backed securities or mortgage loans.

Questions arise as to whether a transaction must be a legal sale (a true sale for bankruptcy purposes) or a sale for tax purposes to be covered by SFAS No. 77. In practice, the answer generally is no. Each discipline has its own rules or guidelines in determining whether a transaction is a sale or a financing. For accountants, as indicated in FTB No. 85–2, the structure or form determines which accounting literature applies. In practice, disclosure document descriptions or other documentation of the transaction have typically been used to decide whether a transaction purports to be a sale (participation) or a borrowing. Descriptions such as "sale," "participation," or "transfer of rights, title and interest" typically indicate that the transaction purports to be a sale for accounting purposes.

However, representations by the parties to the agreement in the documentation that they will treat the transaction as a borrowing for tax purposes are troublesome to some accountants because those representations call into question what the transaction purports to be. In practice, this issue has usually been resolved by concluding that the tax representations do not change the financial reporting.

It is also possible that a transaction may represent a sale for tax purposes but a financing (borrowing) for financial reporting purposes because of the different criteria used to evaluate the transaction. This particularly may be the case for transactions involving real estate mortgages under the REMIC provisions of the tax law. In practice, accountants generally believe that this difference is less troublesome or not troublesome at all.

Forms of Recourse

Recourse in the transaction may take different forms. Determining whether recourse exists is important for two reasons. First, if it exists, the seller/issuer must be able to make a reasonable estimate of the obligation to achieve sale accounting. Second, if the recourse obligation can be estimated and sale accounting is achieved, the seller needs to record the estimated obligation. The amount of any such obligation should be determined based on the seller's normal practices for estimating the allowance for uncollectible accounts (and collection and repossession costs) for similar, wholly-owned assets taking into consideration the nature of and limits on the recourse and that the receivables are sold through their ultimate maturity.

Various forms of recourse are as follows:

Reimbursement In the most straightforward form of recourse, the seller makes cash payments to the buyer to reimburse the buyer for losses caused by debtor defaults or delinquencies. The buyer's recourse to the seller may be unlimited or capped. Under some recourse agreements, the buyer may be required to repossess any collateral before it can exercise its recourse rights.

Replacement Another form of recourse requires the seller to replace defaulted receivables with good receivables.

Holdback   Still another form of recourse is a holdback reserve. The buyer pays only part of the purchase price at the date of sale. The remainder is held back until the receivables are collected and is reduced by defaults on the receivables. After the receivables are collected, the balance remaining in the holdback reserve is paid to the seller. Until then, the estimated holdback is reflected by the seller as a receivable from the buyer and is adjusted periodically to reflect current estimates of the receivable's ultimate realizability.

Junior (subordinated) participation   The seller creates one or more senior and junior participation interests in a pool of receivables, sells the senior participations, and retains the junior participations. Defaults and other losses are charged first against the junior participations. The holders of the senior participations are protected against losses until the junior participations are completely eliminated. (Note that if the seller sells both the senior and junior participations, the sale would be in effect nonrecourse.)

Escrow account   Another form of recourse, which was developed to deal with certain regulatory constraints of financial institutions, involves depositing so-called *excess servicing fees* (excess of interest earned on the receivables transferred over the sum of interest passed through to investors and a servicing fee) in an escrow account. The recourse to the seller is limited to the amounts in the escrow account. The seller is entitled to any unused funds in the escrow account and may be able to withdraw funds from the escrow account before all receivables are collected if the account exceeds specified levels. This escrow account is also referred to as a *reserve fund* or *spread account*.

Many securitization transactions also involved third-party letters of credit, surety bonds, or cash collateral accounts that support the issuer's recourse obligations and provide additional assurances to the investors. Other than consideration of fees in gain or loss computations, the existence of third-party credit enhancement generally has no effect on the seller/issuer's accounting. Likewise, the seller/issuer may collateralize its promise under the recourse provisions (using other assets) without precluding sale accounting.

Estimating Losses under Recourse Provisions

With respect to meeting the second condition for sale accounting—ability to estimate the recourse obligation—SFAS No. 77 states that

> lack of experience with receivables with characteristics similar to those being transferred or other factors that affect a determination at the transfer date of the collectibility of the receivables may impair the ability to make a reasonable estimate of the probable bad debt losses and related costs of collections and repossessions. A transfer of receivables shall not be recognized as a sale if collectibility of the receivables and related costs of collection and repossession are not subject to reasonable estimation.

The ability to estimate just the maximum exposure is not sufficient to meet the condition. The seller must be able to make a reasonable estimate of the actual exposure.

It is not possible to state any single criterion to be used as a guideline to determine whether recourse obligations can be reasonably estimated. There are, however, a number of factors that bear on this determination. They include the following:

1. *Type of loan*   Transactions in the marketplace today involve a wide range of commercial or consumer receivables and loans. Consumer loans such as automobile and credit card receivables are common, and the related recourse provisions generally are more susceptible to loss estimation.

2. *Number of loans*   As the number of loans involved
   in a transaction increases, the ability to estimate
   losses on the portfolio as a whole also usually
   increases. In other words, the range of probable loss
   percentages typically is narrower in larger
   populations.

3. *Nature of the recourse obligation*   The nature of the
   formula for determining recourse is a factor in
   estimation. For example, recourse up to a stated
   ceiling may be easier to estimate than unlimited
   (100 percent) recourse, particularly if the ceiling is
   significantly less than the probable losses.

4. *Quality of the loans*   Generally, the better the
   quality of the loans, the easier it is to estimate
   losses. For example, loss estimation may be easier
   in the case of performing loans (versus
   nonperforming), third-party guaranteed receivables
   (versus unguaranteed loans), and low loan-to-value
   loans (versus high loan-to-value loans).

5. *Homogeneity*   Loss estimation is generally simpler
   for a transaction involving a large number of small-
   balance receivables when all of the receivables in
   the transaction have similar characteristics. On the
   other hand, diversity of exposures (industry,
   geographic, and so on) may be a positive factor for a
   large pool of commercial loans.

6. *Track record*   If the type of receivable involved in
   the transaction is well established in the
   marketplace, there may be significant track records
   with regard to past losses. Loss estimation is easier
   in this case than in a transaction in which the type
   of receivable is novel and little or no track record
   exists.

7. *Seasoning*   Loss estimation is typically easier for
   seasoned receivables as compared to new
   receivables.

If a transaction involves a large number of receivables of a common variety, and if a significant track record on losses exists for receivables of a type that is representative of the subject receivables, there generally should be no problem with regard to loss estimation under the recourse provisions for accounting purposes. Receivables in this category typically include pools of single-family mortgage loans, automobile loans, and credit card receivables. At the other end of the spectrum, a transaction involving a single commercial loan would infrequently qualify for sale accounting because the loss on a single loan may not be reasonably estimable. The preexistence of an allowance for credit losses does not automatically satisfy the requirements of No. 77.

Gain or Loss Computations—Recourse

SFAS No. 77 provides that if a transfer of receivables qualifies as a sale, all "probable adjustments" in connection with the recourse obligations to the seller should be accrued in accordance with FASB Statement No. 5, *Accounting for Contingencies* (1975).[1] Probable adjustments are defined as

> adjustments for (a) failure of the debtors to pay when due, for example, estimated bad debt losses and related costs of collections and repossessions accounted for in accordance with Statement 5, (b) estimated effects of prepayments, and (c) defects in the eligibility of the transferred receivables, for example, defects in the legal title of the transferred receivables.

The difference between (1) the sales price (adjusted for the accrual of probable adjustments) and (2) the net receivables (gross receivables plus accrued interest less unearned

---

1. SFAS No. 5 requires loss or expense recognition when both of the following conditions are met: (1) Information available prior to issuance of the financial statements indicates that it is probable that an asset had been impaired or a liability had been incurred at the date of the financial statement. (2) The amount of loss can be reasonably estimated.

finance and service charges and fees net of deferred origination costs) should be recognized as a gain or loss on the sale. Investment or commercial banking fees, legal fees, and so on incurred to consummate the transaction should be accrued as a reduction of the gain or increase in the loss.

Disclosure of Recourse

For transfers of receivables with recourse reported as sales, the transferor's financial statements should disclose (1) the sales proceeds to the transferor during each period for which an income statement is presented, (2) if the information is available, the balance of the receivables transferred that remain uncollected at the date of each balance sheet presented, and (3) the nature and amount of the recourse provisions.

Sales of Receivables with Seller Guarantee of Prepayment Experience

Some receivables transactions require the seller/transferor/debtor to make payments to the buyer/transferee/lender on a fixed schedule regardless of when the transferred receivables are collected. For example, the purported seller may directly or indirectly guarantee a specified prepayment pattern or a minimum or maximum prepayment pattern on the receivables because the investor does not want to assume the risk of prepayments. While the transactions are described as sales or participations in the legal documents, an issue arises as to whether a fixed payment schedule is consistent with the notion of a sale or participation. Part of the reason for this issue is that SFAS No. 77 defines "recourse" to include the "effects of prepayments," but never describes what those effects are. Does it include a seller guarantee of the timing of the collection of the receivables?

The resolution of this issue has been that a commitment by the seller to pay cash to the buyer on a fixed schedule indicates that either (1) the transfer is structured as a loan and falls outside the scope of SFAS No. 77, or (2) the transaction is covered by SFAS No. 77 but must be accounted for as a borrowing because the commitment represents an effective put or call option and thus violates the SFAS No. 77 criteria for sale accounting. As reaffirmed in EITF 89–2, this is the case even if the projections of prepayment experience approximately coincide with the guarantees. Stated differently, to achieve sale accounting the receivables should be sold through their maturity, whether that is earlier or later than anticipated or hoped for. Thus, while the seller can guarantee a yield or rate of return to the buyer, it cannot guarantee a maturity and achieve sale accounting.

Sale accounting is allowed if the seller pays a bona fide third party to provide a guarantee of the timing of payments to the investor, provided that the third party has no recourse to the seller and the seller will not finance the third party with regard to the guarantee.

Sales of Receivables with Seller Retention of Interest Rate Risk

Some sales or participations of fixed-rate receivables provide that the seller will pay a floating rate to the investors. Thus, if the fixed rate exceeds the floating pass-through rate, the seller retains the excess. If the floating pass-through rate exceeds the fixed rate, the seller makes up the deficiency. The converse, of course, is also possible; that is, the underlying receivables are floating rate, but the investors desire a fixed rate. Further, the interest rate on the underlying receivables may float based on one index (for example, prime), while the investors desire a rate that floats based on another index (for example, LIBOR).

SFAS No. 77 specifically indicates that a floating rate provision does not preclude sale accounting treatment if a transaction otherwise qualifies as a sale. This is true regardless of whether the floating rate provision is traditional or "inverted." The sale is recorded based on market interest rates in effect at the date of sale for receivables having the inherent characteristics of those sold. Thus, as described more fully at the bottom of this page, if fixed-rate receivables are sold to investors to yield a floating rate, the gain or loss on sale should be based on market rates for fixed-rate receivables. Subsequent changes in interest rates are accounted for as changes in the sales price, that is, recorded as current gains or losses as the negative or positive spread accrues.

Some sales or participations of fixed-rate receivables provide that the investors will receive a fixed rate of interest for a stated period and will receive a floating rate thereafter. Because SFAS No. 77 permits sale accounting treatment if the transaction provides for a floating rate beginning on the date of sale, sale accounting also would be permitted in a transaction in which the floating rate begins at a later date. As noted in the preceding paragraph, the sale is recorded based on market interest rates in effect at the date of sale; when the floating rate period begins, changes in interest rates are recorded as current gains or losses.

SFAS No. 77 also does not preclude sale accounting if the seller guarantees the buyer a yield. Such a guarantee, however, could impact gain or loss computations.

Gain or Loss Computations—Interest Rate Differentials

As noted at the top of this page, sometimes fixed-rate receivables are sold to investors to yield a floating rate, or vice versa. One aspect of the EITF 88–11 consensus is that the gain or loss on sale should be calculated using interest rate assumptions that market participants would use for similar financial instruments subject to interest rate risks. Thus, if fixed-rate receivables (for example, 10 percent) are sold to investors to yield a floating rate (for example, currently 8 percent), the gain or loss on sale should be based on market rates for fixed-rate receivables, *not* on the current excess spread of fixed rates over floating rates of 2 percent.

Sales of Receivables with Seller Retention of Foreign Exchange Risk

Questions have arisen about the acceptability of sale accounting if the receivables are denominated in one currency but are transferred to investors with the cash flows to be received by the investors as denominated in another currency; that is, the seller retains foreign exchange rate risk. Although SFAS No. 77 does not specifically address the issue, some view sale accounting as acceptable based on an analogy to interest rate changes. However, the staffs of the FASB and the SEC have concluded that retention of foreign currency risk goes beyond the intent of SFAS No. 77 and precludes sale accounting.

Securitization of Short-Term Receivables

Securitization of short-term receivables, such as credit card and trade receivables, generally is structured as a sale of ownership interests in the receivables (participation) or in a trust that owns the pool of receivables. These structures usually (1) provide for credit enhancement by a third party, (2) call for the originator to continue to service the receivables and (3) provide recourse to the seller through an escrow account arrangement (see page 155). Most of the accounting issues raised by these structures are covered in the preceding sections of this chapter.

These structures involve additional complications that arise from the revolving nature of the short-term receivables — that is, in a revolving receivables pool, customers are continually making new purchases and paying down old balances. As long as customers continue to meet the seller's credit criteria, they are entitled to make new purchases up to their credit limit. This revolving nature leads to the following transaction structure:

1. The transferor sells a participation in an existing pool of receivables (a selected closed group of accounts). Generally, more receivables balances are included than the investors' interest, with the transferor retaining an ownership interest in the excess. The additional amount provides a buffer so that the total receivables balance always exceeds the investors' interest in the receivables. In certain instances, additional accounts may be added to the pool at a later date and in certain instances accounts are deleted from the pool.

2. The investors receive an agreed pass-through rate of interest (fixed or variable) on their outstanding participation balance. Any difference between the finance charge paid by customers and the interest paid to the investors is retained by the transferor similar to other receivable sales with servicing retained.

3. For a specified period (the revolving period), the investors' participation principal balance does not amortize as payments are made on the receivables. Instead, principal payments received on the receivables are retained by the transferor on behalf of the investors to reinvest in additional undivided interests in new receivables (that is, new borrowings by the credit cardholders or trade customers). The length of the revolving period is selected by the transferor. During the revolving period, the investors maintain a constant dollar investment. However, because the total dollar balance in the pool may increase or decrease, the investors' *percentage* interest in the pool is constantly changing. The seller retains the remaining interest (100 percent less the investors' percentage interest).

4. Portfolio charge-offs will be passed through to the investors based upon the participation interest. However, the investors are typically protected against loss because there is recourse (a) directly to the transferor (including senior/subordinated structures), (b) to an escrow account (see page 155), and/or (c) to third-party credit enhancement.

5. At the end of the revolving period, the amortization period begins. During that period, principal repayments on the receivables are distributed to the investors.

The revolving period may end (and the amortization period begin) sooner than scheduled if certain events occur. These so-called *payout events* are intended to protect investors against severe deterioration in the credit quality or payment characteristics of the underlying assets. Payout events can include a large decline in portfolio yield, a significant increase in losses or changes in cardholder repayment or borrowing patterns that could adversely affect portfolio performance.

The accounting issues center around the revolving period, the amortization period, and gain or loss computations.

The Revolving Period

During the revolving period, the investors' *dollar* investment remains constant, but their *percentage* interest is constantly changing. For example, assume that a group of investors buys a $100 participation in a $400 pool of credit card receivables. During the first month, cardholders pay $100 on prior charges and incur $150 of new charges. The activity in the receivables pool is as follows:

	Total Pool	Investors' Share Amount	Investors' Share Percent
Beginning of Month 1	$400	$100	25.0%
Collections	(100)	(25)	25.0%
New charges	150	25*	16.7%
End of Month 1	$450	$100	22.2%

* Investors' share of collections is reinvested.

A recap of receivables at the end of Month 1 is as follows:

	Total Pool	Investors' Share before Substitution		Substitution of New for Old	Investors' Share after Substitution	
Old receivables	$300	$75	(25.0%)	$(8)	$67	(22.2%)
New receivables	150	25	(16.7%)	8	33	(22.2%)
	$450	$100	(100.0%)	$0	$100	(100.0%)

An issue arises as to whether, in effect, the investors are putting $8 of receivable interests back to the transferor or the transferor has a call to reacquire $8 of receivable interests. If so, the provisions of SFAS No. 77 for sale accounting would be violated, and off-balance-sheet treatment of the transaction, a frequent objective of structure 1, would not be achieved. During 1988 the EITF reached a consensus that sale accounting is not precluded (EITF 88–22). In part, the rationale is that the changing percentage interest in the pool occurs automatically. Neither the investors nor the transferor can control the extent to which customers make new purchases within their credit limits. Neither party has an option; both parties are locked into a particular course of action as defined at the outset of the transaction.

The EITF discussed a related issue in 1990 (EITF 90–18). Some securitization transactions contain a "removal of accounts" provision that allows the seller periodically, under certain defined conditions and with trustee approval, to withdraw individual accounts from the pool of receivables securitized. The issue is whether such a provision represents a seller option to reacquire receivables previously sold. The EITF reached a consensus that a "removal of accounts" provision does not preclude sale accounting provided that

> (1) removal of such individual accounts is within the specified terms of the securitization and cannot reduce the amount the investor has invested in the pool and (2) the seller's relative percentage interest in the pool is not decreased below that specified by the contractual terms of the securitization.

The Amortization Period

The amortization period also raises accounting issues. A number of formulas or liquidation methodologies have been devised to determine the amount of principal payments allocable to investors. One method (the *floating participation method*) calls for a continuation of the constantly changing percentage approach; that is, a portion of the monthly principal payments received on the entire pool will be passed through to the investors based on the percentage, at the beginning of the month, of their remaining participation balance to the entire pool balance. A second method (the *fixed participation method*) calls for fixing the percentage at the end of the revolving period based on the then-determined relationship of the investors' balance to the total balance of the pool. Principal collections on the pool are allocated to investors based on this fixed percentage until the investors' balance is reduced to zero. (Variations of this method that have similar economic effects are possible.) A third method (the *preset participation method*) calls for an arbitrary or formula-driven percentage or percentages (for example, 99 percent) of all principal payments of the pool to be allocated to investors even though their percentage ownership in the pool at the end of the revolving period is significantly lower.

In 1988 the EITF 88–22 concluded that the type of liquidation method specified in the short-term receivables securitization agreement should not affect the accounting for the transfer except when the percentage of principal payments allocated to the investors exceeds the investors' ownership interests in the receivables in the trust at the beginning of the liquidation period. Thus the first and second methods described above do not preclude sale accounting. In part, the rationale is that they attempt to approximate actual payments on the investors' balance in a cost-effective manner. However, under the third method, the transfer of receivables would not qualify as a sale under SFAS No. 77 because the investor (buyer of the receivables) would have, in effect, the ability to require the seller to repurchase some of the receivables. Stated differently, the preset participation method conflicts with the notion that the transaction is a pro rata participation in a pool of receivables, and thus sale accounting is inappropriate.

The consensus in EITF 88–22 also precludes sale accounting if the amortization involves any type of "sequential pay" or "fast pay/slow pay" structure in which the investors receive a share of principal collections that exceeds their share in the receivables pool under the floating or fixed participation method. Thus, sale accounting is not acceptable if the principal collections from ineligible receivables, which were not sold, are used during the amortization period to accelerate the paydown of the investor's interest. Similarly, a "turbo" feature in which the seller funds in the escrow account are used in the event of an early amortization to pay off a portion of the investor's interest in the receivables also would preclude sale treatment.

The Gain or Loss Computation

The third unique accounting issue involving short-term receivables sales is the gain or loss computation. As indicated in a previous section of this chapter, if the excess of the earnings on the pool over the pass-through rate to the investors exceeds a normal servicing fee, the present or fair value of the difference—assuming reliable estimates can be made—may be imputed as gain at the outset of the transaction (either directly or indirectly by allocating part of the recorded investment to excess servicing). These computations involve difficult estimates and, in some cases, no such upfront gain exists.

In those cases when such gain does exist, an issue arises for what period the difference can be computed. As described previously, during the revolving period, collections of principal balances on receivables existing at the time of sale are reinvested in new receivables on behalf of the investors. Some believe that the difference can be computed for the entire contemplated period of the transaction, including the total revolving and amortization periods. Others, however, believe that this position is inconsistent with what the transaction purports to be (that is, a purchase of a specified interest in the cash flows from a pool of existing and future receivables). They believe that any gain computed at the inception of the transaction should be limited to the gain (spread) on the receivables that then exist. Gain should not be imputed on receivables that do not yet exist. Any gain on yet-to-be-originated receivables should be recognized when those receivables arise and are sold to the investors via reinvestment. In the case of a partial sale, where excess servicing is recorded by allocating part of the recorded investment, it is clear that the excess is limited to the receivables that then exist.

For example, assume a bank sells a $100 participation in a pool of short-term receivables. The investors will reinvest their share of collections for 18 months. At the end of 18 months, the investors will begin to receive their share of collections. The pool at any point in time has a weighted average expected life of six months. Further, the excess spread is 4 percent per year. Under the first approach, the bank would estimate that investors will hold $100 of receivables for a weighted average of 24 months (18-month revolving period plus weighted average run off of six months). The gain from excess spread is $100 × 4 percent/year × 24 months = $8, all recognized at the date of the initial sale. Under the second approach, the $100 of receivables sold initially has a weighted average life of six months, so gain on the initial sale is computed as $100 × 4 percent/year × 6 months = $2. Additional gain would be computed as investors apply their share of collections to buy additional receivables.

EITF 88–22 reached a consensus on the issue that any gain on the sale of receivables should be limited to amounts related to those receivables that exist at the date of the sale and should not include amounts related to future receivables that are expected to be sold during the reinvestment period. Further, the EITF generally agreed that, based on their knowledge of certain transactions, the gain generally would not be significant due to the relatively short life of the receivables sold, the high cost of servicing credit card receivables as evidenced by industry statistics, and the yields currently required by investors in the current interest rate environment. EITF members noted that the terms of a transaction should be reviewed to determine whether a loss should be recognized for the costs expected to be incurred for all future servicing obligations, including costs for receivables not yet sold. Some EITF members observed that transaction costs relating to the sale of the receivables may be recognized over the initial and reinvestment periods in a rational and systematic manner unless the transaction results in a loss.

Collateralized Mortgage Obligation-Type Structures

As indicated previously, FTB No. 85–2 is the other major pronouncement of the FASB affecting securitization transactions. FASB developed the technical bulletin when CMO transactions began to grow in volume, but before securitization of other receivables became more common. Although the FASB had mortgage receivables in mind when it issued the technical bulletin, the FASB staff has since indicated that it is appropriate to apply FTB No. 85–2 to other types of receivables transactions by analogy.

CMO transactions are in form borrowings by the issuer (often a special-purpose subsidiary of the sponsor) secured (collateralized) by mortgage receivables. The borrowings (bonds) are structured so that all or substantially all of the collections of principal and interest from the underlying mortgage collateral are paid through to holders of the bonds. The CMOs are frequently nonrecourse to the general credit of the borrower; the holders may look only to the cash flow from the mortgage collateral for their interest and principal payments. The bonds are typically issued with two or more maturity or cash-flow classes (tranches); the actual maturity of each bond class may vary depending upon prepayment experience on the underlying mortgage collateral. One or more of the classes may provide a variable rate to investors even though the underlying receivables are fixed rate, and one or more of the classes may directly or indirectly guarantee a specified schedule of cash flows to investors in one or more other classes. Further, one of the classes may be a zero coupon bond. The sponsor of the CMO often retains the mortgage servicing rights.

Originators of receivables can participate in the issuance of the CMOs in two ways: (1) by sponsoring a CMO entity using only receivables previously originated or purchased by the company or (2) by participating with other independent enterprises who also contribute receivables into one overall bond issue.

Technical Bulletin No. 85–2.

FTB No. 85–2 provides that CMO transactions should be recorded as a liability and the mortgages should continue to be recorded as assets unless all of the following conditions are satisfied:

1. Neither the issuer nor its affiliates have the right or obligation to substitute collateral or to obtain it by calling the obligations.

2. The expected residual interest, if any, in the collateral is nominal.

3. The investor can look only to the issuer's assets or to third parties (insurers or guarantors) for repayment of both principal and interest on the obligation, and neither the sponsor nor its other affiliates are even secondarily liable.

4. There is no requirement to redeem the obligations before their stated maturity other than through normal pay-through of collections on the mortgage collateral.

If all four conditions are satisfied, the transaction is recorded as a sale of the mortgage collateral for the proceeds received on the obligations, with gain or loss recognized for the difference between the initial proceeds and the full carrying amount of the underlying collateral. If the issuer retains any residual interest, the residual interest is not recorded as an asset; instead the residual is recorded as it accrues to the benefit of the issuer.

If the CMO transaction does not qualify for sales accounting, offsetting of the assets and liabilities is not appropriate.

CMOs usually are issued by special-purpose corporations or trusts. The sponsor should consolidate its majority-owned special-purpose CMO entities. Thus, if the CMO transaction is recorded by the issuer as a borrowing, the mortgage assets and CMO liabilities are reflected on the sponsor's consolidated balance sheet. No gain or loss is recognized upon issuance of the CMO debt, assuming the issuer has both the intent and ability to hold the mortgage assets until maturity.

Some CMOs require or permit the issuer to call the obligation when the amount of the outstanding bonds is minor to keep the cost of servicing the underlying mortgage loans relative to their remaining outstanding balances from becoming unreasonable. With respect to condition 1 above, if the amount of reacquired collateral is expected to be minor (no more than 5 to 10 percent in practice), the existence of this type of call provision alone does not preclude sale accounting. Further, a provision calling for substitution of collateral in the event of faulty title for a limited period after inception of the transaction (for example, 90 days) typically would not preclude sale accounting.

With regard to condition 2, the expected residual is defined as the present value of all amounts expected to revert to the issuer or its affiliates (including reinvestment earnings). Excess (above normal) servicing fees and any overcollateralization should be considered to be part of the expected residual interest. In practice, "nominal" has been interpreted as 1 to 2 percent of the fair market value of the collateral. Further, condition 2 would not be met if an affiliate of the issuer retained one of the CMO tranches (even if the residual

cash flows are not retained). However, the retention of servicing rights does not, in itself, preclude sale accounting.

Prior to the introduction of the REMIC provisions of the
1986 Tax Reform Act, tax law constraints caused CMO transactions to be structured in such a way that they typically
failed the sale recognition criteria of FTB No. 85–2. With
REMIC, this has changed. However, REMIC may be applied
only to real estate mortgage transactions, not to other types
of receivables.

Sales of Interests

To avoid recording the mortgage collateral and the CMOs on
their consolidated balance sheets, sponsors sell either ownership interests in the CMO entity or residual interests in the
mortgage collateral. The sale of ownership interests typically
is accomplished by issuing CMOs through a trust. The sponsor creates a trust entity and deposits the underlying mortgage collateral into the trust. The trust then issues CMOs.
The issuance would be accounted for as a financing at the
trust level. The sponsor then sells ownership interests in the
trust to third-party investors currently or at a later date.

If the sponsor retains more than a 50 percent ownership
interest in the trust, consolidation of the trust (including
balance sheet presentation of all the mortgages and debt
payable) would generally be required under FTB No. 85–2, as
the trust is considered to be a conduit for the sponsor. If the
sponsor retains less than a 50 percent ownership interest in
the trust, the trust would generally not be consolidated (or
would be deconsolidated). Thus, the mortgages and debt would
not appear on the sponsor's consolidated balance sheet.

An issuer might sell the contractual right to residual
cash flows (for example, a residual bond), rather than selling
ownership interests. In such instances, if the issuer sells
sufficient residual cash flows to reduce its retained interest
in the residual cash flows to a nominal level and the other

conditions of FTB 85–2 are satisfied, the issuance of CMOs would be accounted for as a sale. The sale of the residual cash flows must occur at inception since that is the only time the original accounting—sale versus financing—is determined. A later sale of the contractual right to residual cash flows does not change the original accounting. (The fact that the value of the residual cash flows retained may decline to a nominal amount at a later date also does not change the accounting.)

Third-Party CMO Transactions

During 1986, the EITF addressed a transaction involving mortgages that could also be accomplished with other receivables (EITF 86–24). In the transaction, an enterprise sells receivables with (or without) recourse to an unrelated third party that then uses the receivables as collateral for debt issued through a special-purpose entity owned and controlled by the unrelated third party. The enterprise does not have the right to repurchase the receivables nor can the receivables be put back to the enterprise other than through the recourse provisions, if any. As part of the transaction, the enterprise acquires the right to receive a defined portion of the total payments received from the receivables in excess of the amount required to service the collateralized debt (the residual interest).

The accounting issue is whether SFAS No. 77 or FTB No. 85–2 applies to the enterprise—a scope question. (FTB No. 85–2 would apply to the third party.) The FASB and SEC staffs expressed concerns because the enterprise is in approximately the same economic position as if it sponsored its own debt issue, but the EITF reached a consensus that because there was a legal sale, the transaction should be accounted for in accordance with SFAS No. 77. Any gain or loss from the sale, including the fair value of the residual interest if it can be reliably estimated, should be recognized in the period in which the transaction occurs.

A third-party CMO transaction should be distinguished from a situation in which the enterprise that originated the receivables uses the special-purpose entity of an unrelated third party to obtain existing SEC registration rights but simultaneously the enterprise originating the receivables becomes the legal owner of the special-purpose entity. This transaction should be accounted for under FTB No. 85–2.

Consolidation

The rules that deal with consolidation of subsidiaries with their parent companies for financial reporting purposes are contained in the following pronouncements:

1. FASB Statement No. 94, *Consolidation of All Majority-Owned Subsidiaries*
2. Technical Bulletin No. 85–2
3. SEC Regulation S-X Rule 3A-02
4. Emerging Issues Task Force issues 85–28 and 90–15

SFAS No. 94

As part of its major project on consolidation and the reporting entity (as shall be discussed later), the FASB issued SFAS No. 94 in October 1987. The statement, which became effective for fiscal years ending after December 15, 1988, requires consolidation of all majority-owned subsidiaries unless

1. Control is expected to be temporary, *or*
2. Control does not rest with the majority owner (for example, a subsidiary in bankruptcy or a subsidiary subject to severe foreign exchange restrictions).

Although SFAS No. 94 specifically applies only to corporate subsidiaries, most accountants would apply the same rules to noncorporate entities (for example, trusts and partnerships) in which a parent company holds a controlling ownership interest.

SFAS No. 94 continues the requirement of providing summarized information about previously unconsolidated subsidiaries—specifically, summarized information about assets, liabilities, and results of operations (or separate statements) for each subsidiary or in groups, as appropriate.

Technical Bulletin No. 85–2

As indicated previously, FTB No. 85–2, which addresses collateralized mortgage obligations (but can be applied to other receivable transactions by analogy), concludes that a majority-owned entity formed to issue the CMO is merely a conduit for the sponsor and the financial statements of that entity should be consolidated with those of its sponsor.

If a controlling share of the ownership interest of the issuer is sold to independent third parties, the issuer's financial statements would generally not be consolidated with those of its original parent or sponsor. If a securitization transaction is consummated through a trust or other entity whose financial statements are consolidated by its parent or sponsor, the consolidated financial statements will contain the assets and liabilities of the issuer. However, if substantially all of the receivable interests are transferred to others in transactions accounted for as sales, consolidation will generally have minimal effect on the balance sheet of the parent or sponsor.

SEC Regulation S-X

The SEC's rules in Regulation S-X Rule 3A-02 generally are consistent with official promulgations of the FASB. In addition, the rule states that, in some situations, "consolidation of an entity, *notwithstanding the lack of technical majority ownership,* is necessary to present fairly the financial position and results of operations of the registrant, because of the existence of a parent–subsidiary relationship by means other than record ownership of voting stock" [emphasis added]. Thus, the SEC requires consideration of indications of control other than ownership of a majority interest in deciding whether a parent–subsidiary relationship exists requiring financial statement consolidation.

EITF Issue 85–28

The EITF addressed the issue of consolidation of 50 percent or more owned special-purpose CMO entities when ownership is considered to be temporary in nature. The transaction (EITF 85–28) involves a majority-owned entity (the "issuer") that is formed by a financial institution to issue collateralized mortgage obligations. The collateralized mortgage obligations are to be accounted for as borrowings and remain on the balance sheet of the issuer. The question is whether the financial institution is required to consolidate the issuer if a sale of ownership of the issuer is expected, although a specific sale has not yet been arranged. A consensus was reached that consolidation would always be required if the entity was formed by an institution that normally originates mortgages and then transfers those mortgages to the entity. Also discussed was the question of whether an investment banker that does not normally originate mortgages and that establishes a special-purpose entity to house the mortgages would be required to consolidate if control is likely to be temporary. There were mixed views on the latter question, and no consensus was reached.

EITF 90–15 and Special-Purpose Entities

As indicated earlier, some securitization transactions entail establishment of a special-purpose entity, for example, a corporation that is organized solely to issue debt and purchase receivables from its sponsor. The purpose is to isolate the receivables from bankruptcy concerns relating to the originator or to achieve some other objective (for example, regulatory). If these entities are owned by their sponsors, FTB No. 85–2 and SFAS No. 94 provide guidance—they should be consolidated by their parents.

If, however, these special-purpose entities are not owned by their sponsor but rather are owned by another party (so-called *orphan subsidiaries* or *nonsubsidiary subsidiaries*), the existing accounting literature is not clear. This other party might be a not-for-profit entity or an individual such as an employee of the investment banking organization hired to broker the transaction or another party. During a 1989 EITF meeting, the SEC observer made the following announcement with respect to this issue:

> The SEC staff is becoming increasingly concerned about certain receivables, leasing, and other transactions involving special-purpose entities (SPEs). Certain characteristics of those transactions raise questions about whether SPEs should be consolidated (notwithstanding the lack of majority ownership) and whether transfers of assets to the SPE should be recognized as sales. Generally, the SEC staff believes that for nonconsolidation and sales recognition by the sponsor or transferor to be appropriate, the majority owner (or owners) of the SPE must be an independent third party who has made a substantive capital investment in the SPE, has control of the SPE, and has substantive risks and rewards of ownership of the assets of the SPE (including residuals). Conversely, the SEC staff believes that nonconsolidation and sales recognition are not appropriate by the sponsor or transferor when the majority owner of the SPE makes only a nominal capital investment, the activities of the SPE are virtually all on the sponsor's or transferor's behalf, and the substantive risks and rewards of the assets or the debt of the SPE rest directly or indirectly with the sponsor or transferor.
>
> Also, the SEC staff recently has objected to a proposal in which the accounting for a transaction would change only because an SPE was placed between the two parties to the transaction. The SEC staff believes that insertion of a nominally capitalized SPE does not change the accounting for the transaction.
>
> The SEC staff is considering the issuance of a staff accounting bulletin setting forth guidelines on the accounting for transactions involving SPEs.

At a subsequent EITF meeting, the SEC observer indicated that the SEC staff was continuing to consider the issuance of a staff accounting bulletin, and until such time would consider transactions on a case-by-case basis. The SEC observer emphasized that the SEC staff views the issue of special-purpose entities to be primarily a consolidation issue.

Subsequently, the EITF discussed EITF 90–15, which addresses whether a lessee should consolidate a SPE lessor. Although EITF 90–15 specifically deals with leasing SPEs, the EITF consensus is now widely applied to other SPEs. The EITF reached a consensus that a lessee should consolidate a SPE lessor if all of the following conditions exist:

1. Substantially all of the activities of the SPE involve assets that are to be leased to a single lessee.

2. The expected substantive residual risks and substantially all the residual rewards of the leased asset(s) and the obligation imposed by the underlying debt of the SPE reside directly or indirectly with the lessee through such means as, for example,

   a. The lease agreement

   b. A residual value guarantee

   c. A guarantee of the SPE's debt

   d. An option granting the lessee the right to (1) purchase the leased asset at a fixed price or at a defined price other than fair value or (2) receive any of the lessor's sales proceeds in excess of a stipulated amount.

3. The owner(s) of record of the SPE has not made an initial substantive residual equity capital investment that is at risk during the entire term of the lease. The EITF Working Group responsible for Issue 90–15 concluded that 3 percent of total capitalization is the minimum acceptable investment for a leasing transaction.

For receivables transactions involving SPEs, consolidation by the sponsor is an issue only if the transaction is a borrowing in the financial statements of the SPE. (If the transaction is a sale in the financial statements of the SPE, then there is little on its balance sheet for the sponsor to consolidate.) For SPEs with borrowings—such as SPEs that buy receivables funded by issuing commercial paper, a full recourse loan—sponsors follow two approaches to avoid consolidation. The first approach is to form a SPE that buys receivables from many sellers. This transaction fails the first condition in the consensus in EITF 90–15. The second approach is to form a single-seller SPE that has substantive outside residual equity capital at risk, thereby failing the third condition in the consensus in EITF 90–15. As noted above, 3 percent of total capitalization is the minimum acceptable equity for leasing SPEs, and that is the safe minimum for receivables SPEs. In practice, however, many single-seller SPEs have been set up with equity equal to 1 percent or less of total capitalization, and so far the SEC staff has not challenged nonconsolidation.

INVESTORS' ACCOUNTING

Accounting by investors for interests in asset-backed securities raises three principal accounting issues: carrying amount (amortized cost versus fair value), recognition of interest income, and recognition of impairment. The accounting differs depending on whether the securities are like traditional bonds, with rights to interest and repayment of a fixed principal amount, or whether the securities are more exotic, for example, interest-only strips, principal-only strips, or residual securities.

This section of the chapter deals only with the accounting by investors unrelated to the seller/sponsor of the securitization transaction. Investments by the seller/sponsor should be accounted for in accordance with SFAS No. 77 or FTB No. 85–2 as discussed in the preceding section of the chapter.

Carrying Amount

Investments in asset-backed securities are covered by FASB Statement No. 115, *Accounting for Certain Investments in Debt and Equity Securities*. SFAS No. 115 addresses the accounting and reporting for investments in equity securities that have readily determinable fair values and for *all* investments in debt securities. Those investments are to be classified in three categories and accounted for as follows:

1. Debt securities that the enterprise has the positive intent and ability to hold to maturity are classified as held-to-maturity securities and reported at amortized cost.

2. Debt and equity securities that are bought and held principally for the purpose of selling them in the near term are classified as trading securities and reported at fair value, with unrealized gains and losses included in earnings.

3. Debt and equity securities not classified as either held-to-maturity securities or trading securities are classified as available-for-sale securities and reported at fair value, with unrealized gains and losses excluded from earnings and reported in a separate component of shareholders' equity.

SFAS No. 115 provides detailed guidance for accounting for transfers of investments from one category to another, with strict limitations on the ability to sell or transfer securities classified as held to maturity.

Asset-backed securities that are like conventional bonds may be classified in any of the three categories, depending on the investor's intentions. Similarly, principal-only strips may be classified in any of the three categories.

By contrast, many accountants believe that the held-to-maturity classification may be inappropriate for interest-only strips and residual interests that have no stated principal. The term *maturity* is not defined in SFAS No. 115 but is generally understood to mean the date on which the principal amount of a debt instrument becomes due and payable. Interest-only strips and many residual interests do not involve cash flows designated as principal. For those securities, some accountants believe the notion of maturity is irrelevant. Other accountants believe that the notion of maturity for those securities should be understood as the stated maturity dates of the interest cash flows—in other words, the dates that the interest coupons are due. Uncertainty exists as to whether the interest cash flows will be realized because of the possible prepayment of the underlying principal upon which the interest cash flows are based.

Those uncertainties, however, seem to have been resolved by the issuance of SFAS No. 125 which states:

> 14. Interest-only strips, loans, other receivables, or retained interests in securitizations that can contractually be prepaid or otherwise settled in such a way that the holder would not recover substantially all of its recorded investment shall be subsequently measured like investments in debt securities classified as available-for-sale or trading under Statement 115, as amended by this Statement.

Certain entities, for example, broker-dealers, investment companies, and employee benefit plans, use market value accounting as their fundamental accounting method. Those entities treat all investments in asset-backed securities as though they are trading securities under SFAS No. 115—mark-to-market with unrealized gains and losses included in income currently.

Recognition of Interest Income

The recognition of interest income on investments in loans and debt securities is governed by SFAS No. 91, *Accounting for Nonrefundable Fees and Costs Associated with Originating or Acquiring Loans and Initial Direct Costs of Leases.* Generally, interest income is recognized using the interest method, which is defined in SFAS No. 91 as follows:

> The objective of the interest method is to arrive at periodic interest income (including recognition of fees and costs) at a constant effective yield on the net investment in the receivable (that is, the principal amount of the receivable adjusted by unamortized fees or costs and purchase premium or discount). The difference between the periodic interest income so determined and the stated interest on the outstanding principal amount of the receivable is the amount of periodic amortization.

Applying the interest method is relatively simple for traditional bonds or for asset-backed securities with terms like traditional bonds. Applying the interest method becomes more complex if the securities are subject to prepayments (as is the case with many mortgage-backed securities) or have a floating interest rate. Interest-only strips and residual interest are subject to particularly severe swings in interest rates.

An illustration of applying the interest method with and without assumed prepayments is presented in the appendix to this chapter.

Prepayments

SFAS No. 91 provides that the interest method generally shall be applied assuming no prepayments, that is, assuming that collections of principal are received no sooner than contractually required. However, if the investor holds a large number of similar loans for which prepayments are probable and the timing and amount of prepayments can be reasonably estimated, the investor may consider estimates of future principal prepayments in the calculation of the constant effective yield necessary to apply the interest method. Mortgage-backed securities typically are backed by a pool of a large number of mortgages that meets these conditions, and accountants generally believe it is preferable for an investor to estimate prepayments when it is possible to do so.

If the investor anticipates prepayments in applying the interest method and a difference arises between the prepayments anticipated and actual prepayments received, SFAS No. 91 requires that the investor recalculate the effective yield to reflect actual payments to date and anticipated future payments. The net investment in the securities is adjusted to the amount that would have existed had the new effective yield been applied since the acquisition of the securities, with a corresponding charge or credit to interest income—that is, a cumulative catch-up for the effects of the change in estimate.

Floating Interest Rate

SFAS No. 91 provides the following guidance to apply the interest method when the stated interest rate is not constant throughout the term of the securities:

- If the stated interest rate increases (so that interest accrued under the interest method in early periods would exceed interest at the stated rate), interest income shall not be recognized to the extent that the net investment would increase to an amount greater than the amount at which the borrower could settle the obligation.

- If the security's stated interest rate decreases during the term of the security, the stated periodic interest received early in the term of the security would exceed the periodic interest income that is calculated under the interest method. In that circumstance, the excess shall be deferred and recognized in those future periods when the constant effective yield under the interest method exceeds the stated interest rate.

- If the security's stated interest rate varies based on future changes in an independent factor, such as an index or rate (such as the London Interbank Offered Rate [LIBOR] or the U.S. Treasury bill weekly average rate), the calculation of the constant effective yield necessary to recognize fees and costs shall be based either on the factor (the index or rate) that is in effect at the inception of the security or on the factor as it changes over the life of the security.

Interest-Only Strips and Certain Residual Interests

For interest-only strips and certain residual interests, the effects of changes in prepayments and changes in the yield are inextricably linked. Faster than expected prepayments reduce the number of interest payments to be collected, which causes the security's yield to fall. Slower than expected prepayments increase the number of interest payments to be collected, which causes the security's yield to rise. It was unclear which provision of SFAS No. 91 governed in this circumstance. As a result, the EITF addressed the problem in EITF 89–4.

The task force specifically discussed investments in CMO instruments, because CMO instruments represent the vast majority of asset-backed securities with significant prepayment risk. However, to the extent that nonmortgage asset-backed securities have similar characteristics, the consensuses in EITF 89–4 would apply to them as well. The EITF reached a consensus that the accounting for a purchased investment in a CMO instrument should generally be consistent with the form of the investment. If the instrument is in the form of a debt security, with defined interest, principal, or both, the investor should account for it as a debt security. Conversely, if the CMO instrument is in the form of equity (for example, beneficial interest in a trust, common stock, or partnership interest), it generally should be accounted for as an equity security: consolidation for a controlling interest, equity method for an interest with the ability to exercise significant influence, SFAS No. 115 for a marketable interest that lacks the ability to exercise significant influence, and lower of cost or impaired value for a nonmarketable interest that lacks the ability to exercise significant influence. The task force noted that some CMO instruments in the form of equity actually represent solely the purchase of a stream of future cash flows to be collected under preset terms and conditions. The EITF reached a consensus that a CMO instrument in equity form meeting *all* of the following criteria is required to be accounted for as a debt security, regardless of its legal form:

1. The assets in the issuing entity were not transferred to the issuing entity by the purchaser of the CMO instrument. (An investor in a CMO instrument who transferred assets to the issuing entity should follow the accounting established by SFAS No. 77 or FTB No. 85–2, as applicable.)

2. The assets of the issuing entity consist solely of a large number of similar high-credit-quality monetary assets.

3. The issuing entity is self-liquidating; that is, it will terminate when the existing assets are fully collected and the existing obligations of the issuing entity are fully paid.

4. Assets collateralizing the obligations of the issuing entity may not be exchanged, sold, or otherwise managed as a portfolio, and the purchaser has neither the right nor the obligation to substitute assets that collateralize the entity's obligations.

5. There is no more than a remote possibility that the purchaser would be required to contribute funds to the issuing entity to pay administrative expenses or other costs.

6. No other obligee of the issuing entity has recourse to the purchaser of the investment.

EITF reached a consensus that nonequity CMO instruments that have potential for loss of a significant portion of the original investment due to changes in (1) interest rates, (2) the prepayment rate of the assets of the CMO structure, or (3) earnings from the temporary reinvestment of cash collected by the CMO structure but not yet distributed to the holders of its obligations (reinvestment earnings) are high-risk CMO instruments and should be accounted for as described below. (Nonequity CMO instruments include all CMO instruments issued in debt form and those CMO instruments issued in equity form that meet all six criteria listed above.) CMO residuals and interest-only strips typically will meet these criteria to be considered, and accounted for, as high risk.

Nonequity CMO instruments that do not have the potential for loss of a significant portion of the original investment due to the factors enumerated above, such as principal-only certificates, are not high-risk CMO instruments. Premiums and discounts arising from the purchase of CMO instruments that are not high risk should be amortized in accordance with the provisions of SFAS No. 91.

EITF reached a consensus that in accounting for each purchased high-risk nonequity CMO instrument, the investor should allocate the total cash flows expected to be received over the estimated life of the investment between principal and interest in the following manner. At the date of purchase, an effective yield is calculated based on the purchase price and anticipated future cash flows. In the initial accounting period, interest income is accrued on the investment balance using that rate. Cash received on the investment is first applied to accrued interest with any excess reducing the recorded investment balance. At each reporting date, the effective yield is recalculated based on the amortized cost of the investment and the then-current estimate of future cash flows, reflecting current prepayment estimates. This recalculated yield is then used to accrue interest income on the investment balance in the subsequent accounting period.

Absent an impairment (see the section titled "Impairment" below), this procedure continues until all cash flows from the investment have been received. Absent an impairment, the amortized cost of the investment at the end of each period will equal the present value of the estimated future cash flows discounted at the newly calculated effective yield. Unrealized gain or loss is computed by comparing this amortized cost to the market or fair value of the security.

A simple example of recording yield for the first three years on a high-risk nonequity CMO security follows:

	Inception	End of Year 1	End of Year 2	Inception Hindsight 1	Inception Hindsight 2
Investment	$100				
Estimated cash flows					
Year 0	100			$100	$100
Year 1	(50)	$82		(45)	(45)
Year 2	(42)	(32)	$55	(32)	(34)
Year 3	(34)	(26)	(30)	(26)	(30)
Year 4	(26)	(20)	(23)	(20)	(23)
Year 5	(18)	(14)	(16)	(14)	(16)
Year 6	(9)	(7)	(8)	(7)	(8)
Year 7	—	—	(4)	—	(4)
Estimated yield	26.77%	8.63%	20.98%	15.91%	19.89%

	Year 1	Year 2	Year 3
Beginning investment	$100	$82	$55
Income recognized	27	7	12
Cash received	(45)	(34)	(30)
Ending investment	82	55	36

Impairment

Securities classified as trading under SFAS No. 115 are carried at market or fair value at all times with unrealized gains and losses included in earnings. No impairment test is necessary for them. For held-to-maturity and available-for-sale securities, SFAS No. 115 requires an investor to determine whether a decline in fair value below the amortized cost basis is other than temporary. For example, if it is probable that the investor will be unable to collect all amounts due according to the contractual terms of a debt security not impaired at acquisition, an other-than-temporary impairment has occurred. If the decline in fair value is judged to be other than temporary, the cost basis of the individual security is written down to fair value as a new cost basis and the amount of the write-down is included in earnings (that is, accounted for as a realized loss). The new cost basis may not be changed for subsequent recoveries in fair value.

For high-risk, nonequity CMO instruments covered by EITF 89–4, the task force reached a consensus that if the present value of estimated future cash flows discounted at a risk-free rate is less than the amortized cost basis of the instrument, an impairment loss should be recognized. That comparison should be made at each reporting date. The excess of the amortized cost basis over the instrument's fair value should be recognized as a realized loss in the income statement, thereby establishing a new cost basis for the security.

FUTURE ADOPTED AND PROPOSED ACCOUNTING STANDARDS

In June 1996 the FASB issued a new standard—Statement of Financial Accounting Standards 125, *Accounting for Transfers and Servicing of Financial Assets and Extinguishments of Liabilities*—which significantly changes the accounting described earlier in this chapter. The FASB had hoped to also issue a final statement on consolidation policy by June 30, 1996, but that has been deferred and is now planned for the last half of 1996. As discussed below, new consolidation rules could significantly affect the consolidation requirements for Special Purpose Entities (SPEs) formed in connection with many securitizations of financial assets.

New Standard on Transfers of Financial Assets

SFAS No. 125 provides a single approach for all transfers of financial assets whether they purport to be sales or borrowings and whether securities or other types of financial instruments are involved. Securitizations, participations, and pass-throughs are all accounted for in an identical manner. SFAS No. 125 supersedes both Statement No. 77 and Technical Bulletin 85–2, is effective for transactions occurring after December 31, 1996, and is to be applied prospectively; earlier or retroactive application is not permitted.[2]

The standard is based on a new model that the FASB calls *the financial components approach.* Under that approach, financial instruments and financial transactions are analyzed into their component parts, and the entity accounts for those component parts in accordance with their nature. The new standard eliminates the conflicting guidance existing under current accounting as discussed earlier in this chapter.

As applied to a transfer of receivables and other financial assets, the financial components approach leads a company to derecognize (remove from the balance sheet) those financial components that have been sold or transferred and to retain or recognize those components that have been retained or that are created as a result of the transaction.

A transfer of financial assets, regardless of form (sale or collateralized borrowing) is accounted for as a sale if the transferor surrenders control over the assets. Control is surrendered if all of the following three conditions are met:

1. The transferred assets have been isolated from the transferor—put preemptively beyond the reach of the transferor and its creditors, even in bankruptcy or receivership.

---

2. The new standard also deals with sales of securities with agreements to repurchase, servicing of financial assets, and extinguishments of liabilities—subjects which are beyond the scope of this discussion.

2. Either (a) each transferee obtains the right—free of conditions that effectively constrain it from taking advantage of that right—to pledge or exchange the transferred assets or (b) the transferee is a qualifying special-purpose entity and the holders of beneficial interests in that entity have the right—free of conditions that effectively constrain them from taking advantage of that right—to pledge or exchange their interests.

3. The transferor does not effectively maintain control over the transferred assets through (a) an agreement that both entitles and obligates the transferor to repurchase or redeem them before their maturity or (b) an agreement that entitles the transferor to repurchase or redeem transferred assets that are not readily obtainable. (SFAS No. 125, paragraph 9, references to other paragraphs omitted.)

If the three conditions are not met, the transaction is accounted for as a collateralized borrowing. Each of those three conditions requires some elaboration, which is provided in the following three sections.

Isolation from Transferor

Under the first condition, control is not surrendered until the transferred assets are *isolated* from the transferor, that is, are beyond the reach of the transferor and its creditors. This condition was derived from the Board's observation of common practice in designing SPEs for holding securitized financial assets. In order for the securities or participations issued by an SPE to receive a credit rating independent of the credit standing transferor, the rating agencies commonly insist that the transfer of the assets to the SPE qualify as a true sale at law. That is done to provide assurance that if the transferor becomes bankrupt, its creditors do not have any claim to the securitized assets.

SFAS No. 125 does not require that a transfer be a true sale at law to achieve the isolation needed to qualify as a sale for accounting purposes. The statement instead directs an evaluation of the facts and circumstances attending a transfer of assets in order to support the assertion that those assets are presumptively beyond the reach of the transferor and its creditors. SFAS No. 125 states:

> All available evidence that either supports or questions an assertion shall be considered. That consideration includes making judgments about whether the contract or circumstances permit the transferor to revoke the transfer. It also may include making judgments about the kind of bankruptcy or other receivership into which a transferor or special-purpose entity might be placed, whether a transfer of financial assets would likely be deemed a true sale at law, whether the transferor is affiliated with the transferee, and other factors pertinent under applicable law. Derecognition of transferred assets is appropriate only if the available evidence provides reasonable assurance that the transferred assets would be beyond the reach of the powers of a bankruptcy trustee or other receiver for the transferor or any of its affiliates other than qualifying special purpose entities designed to make remote the possibility that they would enter bankruptcy or other receivership. (Paragraph 23)

For securitizations that involve public sale of beneficial interests that are rated by independent rating organizations, no change from current practice is anticipated insofar as obtaining legal opinions as to compliance with true sale at law requirements. However, for unrated securitizations in which the investors do not insist on a specific legal opinion, the decision as to whether or not to incur the expense of obtaining one may prove troublesome. It is a matter that will require the exercise of judgment by the issuer and its auditors.

Sales of receivables with-recourse which are presently treated as sales under the provisions of SFAS No. 77 may not necessarily qualify as sales under SFAS No. 125. This follows because sales with-recourse depending upon the nature of the recourse may or may not meet the isolation requirements of SFAS 125. Here again, a decision as to whether or not to obtain a legal opinion in specific cases will require the exercise of judgment by the seller and its auditors. On the other hand, if the isolation requirement is met, the fact that various put or call options or forward agreements are created as part of a sale with-recourse does not negate sale treatment as is the case under SFAS No. 77.

Conditions That Constrain a Transferee

The second condition required to establish surrender of control by a transferor is that the transferee's right to pledge or exchange the transferred assets shall not be constrained by conditions imposed by the transferor or for other reasons.

Conditions cited in the statement (paragraph 25) that do not preclude a transfer from being accounted for as a sale are:

- A transferor's right of first refusal on a bona fide offer from a third party.

- A requirement to obtain the transferor's permission to sell or pledge that shall not be unreasonably withheld.

- A prohibition on sale to the transferor's competitor if the transferee is able to sell the transferred assets to a number of other parties.

If assets are transferred to a special-purpose entity, the above requirements relate to the holders of beneficial interests in that entity. For this purpose, *special-purpose entity* is restrictively defined as follows:

A qualifying special-purpose entity must meet both of the following conditions:

a. It is a trust, corporation, or other legal vehicle whose activities are permanently limited by the legal documents establishing the special-purpose entity to:

   (1) Holding title to transferred financial assets

   (2) Issuing beneficial interests (If some of the beneficial interests are in the form of debt securities or equity securities, the transfer of assets is a securitization.)

   (3) Collecting cash proceeds from assets held, reinventing proceeds in financial instruments pending distribution to holders of beneficial interests, and otherwise servicing the assets held

   (4) Distributing proceeds to the holders of its beneficial interests.

b. It has standing at law distinct from the transferor. Having standing at law depends in part on the nature of the special-purpose entity. For example, generally, under U.S. law, if a transferor of assets to a special-purpose trust holds all of the beneficial interests, it can unilaterally dissolve the trust and thereby reassume control over the individual assets held in the trust, and the transferor "can effectively assign his interest and his creditors can reach it." In that circumstance, the trust has no standing at law, is not distinct, and thus is not a qualifying special-purpose entity. (SFAS No. 125, paragraph 26, footnote references omitted)

That definition describes the special-purpose entity structure commonly used and should not therefore impact current practice.

Transferor Does Not Effectively Maintain Control

The third condition necessary to characterize a transfer as a sale quoted above was designed to allow most but not all transactions involving sales of securities with agreements to repurchase, usually referred to as *repos,* to be characterized as collateralized borrowings rather than as sales. A strict interpretation of the financial components approach could have led to the conclusion that most repos are sales because the transferee is able to sell or pledge the repoed securities during the term of the agreement. Since that provision does not impact securitizations it is not discussed further here.

ACCOUNTING FOR SALES TRANSACTIONS

If a transaction effecting the transfer of financial assets meets the three conditions discussed in the preceding section to be designated a sale, SFAS No. 125 requires the seller to:

1. Derecognize all assets sold
2. Recognize all assets obtained and liabilities incurred in consideration of proceeds of the sale, including cash, put or call options held or written (for example, guarantee or recourse obligations), forward commitments (for example, commitments to deliver additional receivables during the revolving periods of some securitizations), swaps (for example, provisions that convert interest rates from fixed to floating), and servicing liabilities if applicable.
3. Initially measure at fair value assets obtained and liabilities incurred in a sale or if it is not practicable to estimate the fair value of an asset or a liability, apply alternative measures.
4. Recognize in earnings any gain or loss on the sale. (Paragraph 11, references to other paragraphs omitted)

In many securitizations and sales of participations the seller retains a partial interest in the transferred assets. In those circumstances SFAS No. 125 directs the seller to:

1. Continue to carry in its statement of financial position any retained interests in the transferred assets, including if applicable, servicing assets, beneficial interests in assets transferred to a qualifying special-purpose entity in a securitization, and retained undivided interests.

2. Allocate the previous carrying amount between the assets sold, if any, and the retained interests, if any, based on their relative fair values at the date of transfer. (Paragraph 10, references to other paragraphs omitted)

The term undivided interests refers to sales of participations in a financial asset or a pool of financial assets or transactions involving SPEs where the beneficial interests are not in the form of securities. The requirement to value retained interests in transferred assets at an allocated portion of the total carrying amount of the assets before transfer is consistent with current practice. The requirement that the allocation be based on the relative fair values at the date of transfer represents a change, at least in theory, from preexisting practice. EITF 88–11, *Allocation of Recorded Investment When a Loan or Part of a Loan Is Sold,* provides in cases where a portion of a loan is sold that the seller—"should allocate the recorded investment in the loan between the portion of the loan sold and the portion retained based on the relative fair values of those portions on the date the loan was acquired, adjusted for payments and other activity from the date of acquisition to the date of sale. The task force acknowledged that it may not be practicable to determine fair values as of the date of acquisition. In that case allocation should be based on the relative fair values of the portion sold and the portion retained on the date of sale." Accordingly under the new statement, it is not necessary to consider fair values at the date of acquisition but only at the date of the transfer.

The definition of "fair value" in SFAS No. 125 is substantially the same as the one contained in SFAS No. 121, *Accounting for the Impairment of Long-Lived Assets and for Long-Lived Assets to Be Disposed Of,* issued in March 1995, and is as follows:

42.   The fair value of an asset (or liability) is the amount at which that asset (or liability) could be bought (or incurred) or sold (or settled) in a current transaction between willing parties, that is, other than in a forced or liquidation sale. Quoted market prices in active markets are the best evidence of fair value and shall be used as the basis for the measurement, if available. If a quoted market price is available, the fair value is the product of the number of trading units times market price.

43.   If quoted market prices are not available, the estimate of fair value shall be based on the best information available in the circumstances. The estimate of fair value shall consider prices for similar assets and liabilities and the results of valuation techniques to the extent available in the circumstances. Examples of valuation techniques include the present value of estimated expected future cash flows using a discount rate commensurate with the risks involved, option-pricing models, matrix pricing, option-adjusted spread models, and fundamental analysis. Valuation techniques for measuring financial assets and liabilities and servicing assets and liabilities shall be consistent with the objective of measuring fair value. Those techniques shall incorporate assumptions that market participants would use in their estimates of values, future revenues, and future expenses, including assumptions about interest rates, default, prepayment, and volatility. In measuring financial liabilities and servicing liabilities at fair value by discounting estimated future cash flows, an objective is to use discount rates at which those liabilities could be settled in arm's-length transaction.

44. Estimates of expected future cash flows, if used to
estimate fair value, shall be the best estimate
based on reasonable and supportable assumptions
and projections. All available evidence shall be
considered in developing estimates of expected
future cash flows. The weight given to the evidence shall be commensurate with the extent to
which the evidence can be verified objectively. If a
range is estimated for either the amount or
timing of possible cash flows, the likelihood of
possible outcomes shall be considered in determining the best estimate of future cash flows.

That board has decided to use the same wording to define
fair value in all of its statements and the Exposure Draft of
the Proposed Statement of Financial Accounting Standards,
*Accounting for Derivative and Similar Financial Statements
and for Hedging Activities,* also would adopt that wording and
would amend SFAS No. 107 and No. 115 to conform.

That newly worded definition is not substantively different from the definition in SFAS No. 107 taken together with
supplementary guidance. included in that statement which is
not amended by SFAS No. 125. Accordingly the guidance
included in Chapters 7 and 8 continues to be appropriate.

If Measurement Fair Value Is Not Practicable

The accounting prescribed by SFAS No. 125 that allows gain
recognition by a seller with continuing involvement presumes
that the fair value of any assets obtained or retained or
liabilities incurred is practicably measurable. However, it may
not be practicable to measure the fair value of those assets
or liabilities in some circumstances. The board did not want
to allow recognition of nonexistent gains or failure to recognize incurred losses resulting from undervalued liabilities or
overvalued assets. Accordingly, SFAS No. 125 prescribes
restrictive accounting in those circumstances:

45. If it is not practicable to estimate the fair values of assets, the transferor shall record those assets at zero. If it is not practicable to estimate the fair values of liabilities, the transferor shall recognize no gain on the transaction and shall record those liabilities at the greater of:

   a. The excess, if any, of (1) the fair values of assets obtained less the fair values of other liabilities incurred, over (2) the sum of the carrying values of the assets transferred

   b. The amount that would be recognized in accordance with FASB Statement No. 5, *Accounting for Contingencies,* as interpreted by FASB Interpretation No. 14, *Reasonable Estimation of the Amount of a Loss.*

Specific Securitization Provisions

Securitizations accomplished by transferring financial assets to an SPE in which the transferor-seller has no continuing involvement are to be accounted for under SFAS No. 125 as sales consistent with current practice. If the transferor does have continuing involvement with the SPE, sale accounting is dependent on complying with the provisions of paragraph 9 as discussed above.

A common approach utilized by securitizers involves two entities. The securitizer first sells financial assets without recourse to a first entity, often a limited-purpose wholly-owned subsidiary. That sale is designed to be a true sale at law so that creditors of the securitizer do not have any claim to the assets even in the event of the securitizer's bankruptcy. The first entity then transfers the assets to a qualifying SPE and retains a subordinated interest while the SPE sells the senior interests to third parties. The retained subordinated interest provides desired credit enhancement for the senior interests. The sale of the assets to the SPE by the limited-purpose subsidiary may not qualify as a true sale at law.

However, assuming that all of the provisions of paragraph 9, discussed above, are met, the transfer to the limited-purpose subsidiary would get sale treatment under SFAS No. 125 which is consistent with current practice. Also under current practice, although the limited-purpose subsidiary would be consolidated with the securitizer, the SPE would not be consolidated with the limited-purpose subsidiary. As a result the senior interests in the SPE sold to third parties would not be included in the securitizers consolidated assets. SFAS No. 125 does not deal with consolidation matters since those are to be covered in a separate statement as discussed in the following section.

Securitizations with revolving periods such as the typical securitizations of credit card receivables will continue under SFAS No. 125 to be treated as sales of receivables to the SPE. However, the agreement by the securitizer to sell additional receivables to the SPE during the revolving period is considered to be an implicit forward contract under the financial components approach adopted by SFAS No. 125. That contract would usually have no value at the initiation of the securitization but may have a positive or negative value subsequently arising from the difference between the agreed-upon rate of return to investors on their beneficial interests in the SPE and the market rates of return on similar investments. That positive or negative value must be recognized by the securitizer.

Another common securitization with revolving arrangements involves an originating entity transferring trade receivables to an SPE which finances such purchases by a combination of the sale of commercial paper for 97 percent of the required funding and the remaining three percent by equity investment from an entity independent of the of originator. The commercial paper is highly rated because of an implicit guarantee of the originator. Under current practice the transfer by the originator is accounted for as a sale. Under SFAS No. 125, however, such arrangements are likely to be accounted for as secured borrowings with pledge of collateral because it is unlikely that those transfers are true sales at law or would otherwise meet the isolation requirement.[3] The need for the originator to consolidate the SPE is discussed in the next section.

Consolidated Financial Statements Policy

The FASB issued an Exposure Draft, *Consolidated Financial Statements Policy and Procedures,* in October 1995 which proposes new standards to determine when a subsidiary or affiliate company should be consolidated. It would supersede Statement of Financial Accounting Standards 94, *Consolidation of All Majority-Owned Subsidiaries.* Under the ED, a parent company would consolidate all entities that it controls, unless control is temporary at the time it is achieved. Control is defined as power over the other entity's assets—power to use or direct the use of the other entity's assets as if the parent owned those assets directly. Control means that the parent can establish the controlled entity's policies and its capital and operating budgets and can hire, fire, and decide how to compensate its personnel.

The ED notes that control may be obtained in two ways: legal control or effective control. The requirement in SFAS No. 94 to own a majority of the voting common stock is a form of legal control, and all entities required to be consolidated under SFAS No. 94 would be required to be consolidated under the ED. Legal control also encompasses rights via contract or partnership agreement to appoint a majority of the controlled entity's governing board.

Effective control is a new, and much more subjective, concept. The ED lists six factors that create a presumption, absent evidence to the contrary, that effective control exists:

---

3. SFAS No. 125, paragraph 56.

1. Ownership of a large minority interest, for example, 40 percnt, with no other owner holding a significant interest.

2. Demonstrated ability to dominate the naming of members to the other entity's governing board or to cast a majority of votes in their elections.

3. Unilateral ability to obtain a majority voting interest in the other entity (through ownership of warrants or convertible securities).

4. "A relationship with an entity that it has established that has no voting stock or member voting rights and has provisions in its charter, bylaws, or trust instrument that (1) cannot be changed by entities other than its creator (sponsor) and (2) limit the entity, including the power of its board of directors or trustees, to activities that the creating entity can schedule (or initiate) to provide substantially all future net cash inflows or other future economic benefits to its creator." This is the provision of most relevance to securitization transactions, because it may require consolidation of SPEs that today are not required to be consolidated.

5. Unilateral ability to dissolve an entity and assume control of its individual assets.

6. Sole general partnership interest in a limited partnership.

In addition, the ED provides a list of other indicators of effective control that must be assessed to determine whether effective control exists. The ED also proposes significant changes to the mechanics of consolidating subsidiaries, but those changes generally are of limited relevance to securitization transactions and will not be covered here.

The ED appears to require the consolidation of many "orphan subsidiary" SPEs that are today not required to be consolidated. Today, under the consensus in EITF Issue 90–15, 3 percent equity at risk from an independent third party avoids consolidation. Under the ED, that level of independent third party equity often won't avoid consolidation because the sponsor rather than the equity owners will have effective control over the SPE. However, the impact on securitization transactions can only be assessed by considering the combined impact of the ED and SFAS No. 125. For example, consider a SPE that buys trade receivables under a revolving arrangement from one commercial entity and funds those purchases with 3 percent independent third-party equity and 97 percent commercial paper. Under today's accounting, the SPE is not consolidated by virtue of the third-party equity, but the SPE has all the receivables and commercial paper on its balance sheet. Under the ED, the SPE probably has to be consolidated, but the issuance of commercial paper through the SPE may or may not qualify as a sale of receivables by the sponsor.

The comment period ended in January 1996. The FASB was not able to complete a final statement by June 30, 1996, as had originally been planned. If issued in final form as proposed, the new standard would have been effective for financial statements for fiscal years beginning after December 15, 1996. However, since a final statement is unlikely before the end of 1996 a later effective date will no doubt be selected. The ED encourages that earlier application and financial statements of prior years would be retroactively restated.

Simplified Example of Applying the Interest Method with and without Assumed Prepayments

FACTS COMMON TO ALL CASES:

Initial principal	$100,000
Initial carrying amount of loans	$98,000
Contractual maturity	5 years
Annual contractual payments	$25,000
Contractual interest rate	7.93%
Initial yield assuming no prepayments	8.70%

| | Without Prepayment | | | With 6% Estimated Annual Prepayment | | | |
Year	Contractual Interest	Contractual Principal	Unpaid Principal	Contractual Interest	Contractual Principal	Prepayment at 6%	Unpaid Principal
1	$ 7,931	$ 17,069	$82,931	$ 7,931	$17,069	$ 6,000	$76,931
2	6,577	18,423	64,508	6,101	17,090	4,616	55,225
3	5,116	19,884	44,624	4,380	17,023	3,313	34,889
4	3,539	21,461	23,163	2,767	16,779	2,094	16,016
5	1,837	23,163	$ 0	1,270	16,016	0	$ 0
Total	$25,000	$100,000		$22,449	$83,977	$16,023	

CASE 1

Application of Interest Method Assuming No Prepayments

Year	Carrying Amount Beginning of Year	Interest Income[a]	Contractual Collections	Carrying Amount End of Year	Memo—Discount Amortization[b]	Cash Flows Used to Compute Interest Rates		
						Initial Yield Assuming No Prepayments	Contractual Yield	Yield with 6% Annual Prepayments
0						$-98,000	$-100,000	$-98,000
1	$98,000	$ 8,527	$ 25,000	$81,527	$ 596	$ 25,000	$ 25,000	$ 31,000
2	81,527	7,094	25,000	63,621	517	25,000	25,000	27,807
3	63,621	5,536	25,000	44,157	420	25,000	25,000	24,716
4	44,157	3,842	25,000	22,999	303	25,000	25,000	21,639
5	$22,999	2,001	25,000	$ 0	164	$ 25,000	$ 25,000	$ 17,287
Total		$27,000	$125,000		$2,000	8.70%	7.93%	8.78%

CASE 2

Application of Interest Method Assuming No Prepayments, but Full Prepayment Occurs at the End of Year 3

Year	Carrying Amount Beginning of Year	Interest Income[a]	Contractual Collections	Actual Prepayments	Carrying Amount End of Year
1	$98,000	$ 8,527	$25,000	$ 0	$81,527
2	81,527	7,094	25,000	0	63,621
3	$63,621	5,536	$25,000	$44,157	$ 0
Total		$21,157			

CASE 3

Application of Interest Method Based on Estimated Prepayment Patterns of 6% per Year

Year	Carrying Amount Beginning of Year	Principal Cash Collections	Discount Amortization[c]	Interest Income[d]	Remaining Principal	Unamortized Discount	Carrying Amount End of Year
1	$98,000	$ 23,069	$ 674	$ 8,605	$76,931	$1,326	$75,605
2	75,605	21,706	538	6,639	55,225	788	54,437
3	54,437	20,336	400	4,780	34,889	388	34,501
4	34,501	18,873	263	3,030	16,016	125	15,891
5	$15,891	16,016	125	1,395	$ 0	$ 0	$ 0
Total		$100,000	$2,000	$24,449			

CASE 4

Application of Interest Method Based on Estimated Prepayment Patterns of 6% per Year

Prepayment Rate in Year 3 Increases to 20%, Causing Lender to Change Estimated Prepayment Rate in Year 4 to 10%

Year	Carrying Amount Beginning of Year	Cash Collections	Discount Amortization[e]	Interest Income[f]	Remaining Principal	Unamortized Discount	Carrying Amount End of Year
1	$98,000	$ 23,069	$ 674	$ 8,605	$76,931	$1,326	$75,605
2	75,605	21,706	538	6,639	55,225	788	54,437
3	54,437	28,068	483	4,863	27,157	305	26,852
4	26,852	15,777	213	2,367	11,380	92	11,288
5	$11,288	11,380	92	995	$ 0	$ 0	$ 0
Total		$100,000	$2,000	$23,468			

With 6%, 20%, and 10%
Annual Prepayment

Year	Contractual Interest	Contractual Principal	Prepayment 6%, 20%, and 10%	Unpaid Principal	Cash Flows Used to Compute Yields Assuming 6%, 10% and 20% Prepayments
0					–98,000
1	$ 7,931	$17,069	$ 6,000	$76,931	$31,000
2	6,101	17,090	4,616	55,225	27,807
3	4,380	17,023	11,045	27,157	32,448
4	2,154	13,061	2,716	11,380	17,931
5	903	11,380	0	$ 0	12,283
Total	$21,468	$75,623	$24,377		8.81%

Notes:

a. Interest at 8.70%.

b. Ratio of interest income recognized for period to contractual interest *without* prepayments for the period.

c. Ratio of interest income recognized for period to contractual interest *with* prepayments for the period.

d. Interest at 8.78%.

e. Ratio of interest income recognized for period to contractual interest with 6%, 20%, and 10% prepayments for the period.

f. Interest at 8.78% for periods 1 and 2; at 8.81% for period 3 plus catch-up adjustment to bring cumulative interest for periods 1 and 2 to 8.81%; and at 8.81% for periods 4 and 5.

CHAPTER 6

Financial Statement Disclosures

Raymond E. Perry

The financial disclosure requirements for derivative financial instruments have been developed by the FASB over a number of years and are currently found in three different statements issued by the board, since 1991, some of which also apply to financial instruments that are not derivatives. The three statements are SFAS No. 105, *Disclosure of Information about Financial Instruments with Off-Balance-Sheet Risk and Financial Instruments with Concentration of Credit Risk (1990)*, SFAS No. 107, *Disclosures about Fair Values of Financial Statements (1991)*, SFAS No. 119, *Disclosures about Derivative Financial Instruments and Fair Value of Financial Instruments (1994)*. Each of the later statements also amends the earlier statements. Accordingly, reference to current requirements should be made to the *FASB's Current Text Accounting Standards, Volume I: General Standards,* Section F25 where all three statements are codified into a single presentation that gives effect to the later statements' amendments of the earlier statements. Even Section F25 is daunting because the current text approach uses all of the original language, including footnotes that include clauses for numerous specialized exceptions and nuances. The result is a quite complex presentation.

The purpose of this chapter is to present summary highlights of the disclosure requirements extracted from the text of Section F25 and SFAS No. 115 as they relate to derivatives (as broadly defined in Chapter 1). This chapter is not meant to be a substitute for the full text of Section F25 and SFAS No. 115, but it should help one navigate through them. Illustrative examples taken from practice are included at the end of this chapter.

The FASB defines derivative financial instruments narrowly as "future, forward, swap, or option contracts, or other financial instruments with similar characteristics" (SFAS No. 119, paragraph 5). Excluded are

> all on-balance-sheet receivables and payables, including those that "derive" values or contractually required cash flows from the price of some other security or index such as mortgage-backed securities, interest-only and principal-only obligations, and indexed debt instruments. It also excludes optional features that are embedded within an on-balance-sheet receivable or payable, for example, the conversion feature and call provisions embedded in convertible bonds. (SFAS No. 119, paragraph 7)

FASB's narrow definition was a result of the board's particular concern with the need for improved disclosures for derivatives with off-balance-sheet risk of loss as no authoritative pronouncement had covered them prior to the adoption of SFAS No. 105. An entity holding derivatives may be exposed to the risk of accounting loss because of counterparty default or adverse changes in market prices. For most on-balance-sheet financial instruments, the maximum exposure to such loss is usually evident from the carrying amount of the instrument. However that is not the case for most futures, forwards, swaps, options, and similar instruments because either no amount appears on the balance sheet or the amount recorded does not indicate the potential loss. Those instruments are referred to here as "off-balance-sheet derivatives." The following discussion covers first disclosures for off-balance-sheet derivatives and later other derivatives.

DISCLOSURES FOR OFF-BALANCE-SHEET DERIVATIVES

For each category of off-balance-sheet derivatives,[1] distinguishing those held for trading purposes (those measured at fair value with gains and losses recognized in earnings) from those held for purposes other than trading requires the following disclosures:[2]

Nature and Amount

1. The face or contract amount (or notional amount if there is no face or contract amount).

2. The nature and terms, including as a minimum, a discussion of (1) the credit and market risk, (2) cash requirements, and (3) related accounting policies.

3. If subject to off-balance-sheet risk of loss

   - The amount of accounting loss the entity would incur if any party to the financial instrument failed completely to perform according to the terms of the contract and the collateral or other security, if any, for the amount due proved to be of no value.

---

1. The following disclosure requirements also relate to purchased options even though they do not usually entail off-balance-sheet risk.
2. This discussion is based on quotes from FASB's *Current Test Accounting Standards, Volume 1: General Standards,* Section F25, 112–115. Repetitive text and some of the transitional phrases have been omitted.

- The entity's policy of requiring collateral or other security to support financial instruments subject to credit risk, information about the entity's access to that collateral or other security, and the nature and a brief description of the collateral or other security supporting those financial instruments.

Concentrations

1. All significant concentrations of credit risk whether from an individual counterparty or groups of counterparties. *Group concentrations* of credit risk exist if a number of counterparties are engaged in similar activities or activities in the same region or have similar economic characteristics that would cause their ability to meet contractual obligations to be similarly affected by changes in economic or other conditions—for example, concentrations of credit risk resulting from highly leveraged transactions. Disclose about each significant concentration any information about the (shared) activity, region, or economic characteristic that identifies that concentration including maximum accounting loss and policy on collateral as described with nature and amount disclosures.

Fair Values

1. Disclose, either in the body of the financial statements or in the accompanying notes, the fair value of all financial instruments[3] for which it is practicable to estimate that value. Additionally,

---

3. No disclosure is required for trade receivables and payables if carrying value approximates fair value which normally is the case.

- Fair value disclosed in the notes shall be presented together with related carrying amount in a form that makes it clear whether the fair value and carrying amount represents assets or liabilities and how the carrying amounts relate to what is reported in the statement of financial position.

- If disclosed in more than a single note, one of the notes shall include a summary table. The summary table shall contain the fair value and related carrying amounts and cross-references to the location(s) of the remaining fair value disclosures.

- Disclose the method(s) and significant assumptions used to estimate the fair value.

Derivatives for Trading   For derivatives held or issued for *trading* purposes the following additional disclosures are required:

1. The average fair value during the reporting period, presented together with the related end-of-period fair value, distinguishing between assets and liabilities.

2. The net gains or losses (often referred to as net trading revenues) arising from trading activity during the reporting period disaggregated by class, business activity, risk, or other category that is consistent with the management of those activities and where those net trading gains or losses are reported in the income statement. If the disaggregation is other than by class, also describe for each category the classes of derivative financial instruments, other financial instruments, and

nonfinancial assets and liabilities from which net trading gains and losses arose.

Derivatives for Other Than Trading For derivatives held or issued for *other than trading* purposes the following additional disclosures are required:

1. A description of the entity's objectives for holding or issuing the derivative financial instruments, the context needed to understand those objectives, and the entity's strategies for achieving those objectives, including the classes of financial instruments used.

2. A description of how each class of derivative financial instrument is reported in the financial statements including the policies for recognizing (or reasons for not recognizing) and measuring the derivative financial instruments held or issued; and when recognized, where those instruments and related gains and losses are reported in the statements of financial position and income.

3. For derivative financial instruments that are held or issued and accounted as hedges of anticipated transactions (both firm commitments and forecasted transactions for which there is no firm commitment) the following disclosures are required:

   - A description of the anticipated transactions whose risks are hedged, including the period of time until the anticipated transactions are expected to occur.

   - A description of the classes of derivative financial instruments used to hedge the anticipated transactions.

   - The amount of hedging gains and losses explicitly deferred.

- A description of the transactions or other event
  that result in the recognition in earnings of gains
  and losses deferred by hedge accounting.

DISCLOSURES FOR OTHER DERIVATIVES

For derivatives that do not come within the FASB's definition
of derivatives, such as the cash securities with embedded
derivatives discussed in Chapter 4 and mortgage-backed
securities discussed in Chapter 5, the disclosures described
above relating to fair value apply in addition to disclosures
prescribed by SFAS No. 115. However, SFAS No. 115 applies
to all investments in debt securities and certain equity securities and requires disclosure as follows:

1. For each major security type and distinguishing
   between securities classified as held-to-maturity and
   those classified as available-for-sale—fair value,
   gross unrealized holding gains, gross unrealized
   holding losses, and amortized cost.
2. Information about contractual maturities combined
   in appropriate groupings.

For financial institutions:

1. Required major security types as a minimum are
   equity securities, debt securities issued by the U.S.
   Treasury and other U.S. government corporations
   and agencies, debt securities issued by states of the
   United States and political subdivisions of the
   states, debt securities issued by foreign
   governments, corporate debt securities, mortgage-
   backed securities, and other debt securities.
2. At least four maturity groupings (a) within one
   year, (b) after one year through five years, (c) after
   five years through 10 years, and (d) after 10 years.

In addition, all the disclosure requirements described in the preceding section that relate to concentrations of credit risk and fair values also apply to all financial instruments.

Disclosure If Measurement of Fair Value Not Practicable

Although SFAS No. 107 allows considerable latitude in measuring fair values of derivatives and other financial instruments provision is made for circumstances where measurement is not practicable as follows:

14. If it is not practicable for an entity to estimate the fair value of a financial instrument or a class of financial instruments, the following shall be disclosed:

a. Information pertinent to estimating the fair value of that financial instrument or class of financial instruments, such as the carrying amount, effective interest rate, and maturity

b. The reasons why it is not practicable to estimate fair value.

15. In the context of this statement, *practicable* means that an estimate of fair value can be made without incurring excessive costs. It is a dynamic concept: what is practicable for one entity might not be for another; what is not practicable in one year might be in another. For example, it might not be practicable for an entity to estimate the fair value of a class of financial instruments for which a quoted market price is not available because it has not yet obtained or developed the valuation model necessary to make the estimate, and the cost of obtaining an independent valuation appears excessive considering the materiality of the instruments to the entity. Practicability, that is, cost considerations, also may affect the required precision of the estimate; for example, while in many cases it might seem impracticable to estimate fair value on an individual instrument basis, it may be practicable for a class of financial instruments in a portfolio or on a portfolio basis. In those

cases, the fair value of that class or of the portfolio should be disclosed. Finally, it might be practicable for an entity to estimate the fair value only of a subset of a class of financial instruments; the fair value of that subset should be disclosed.

In practice, use of the practicability exception has been rare. None were reported in an analysis prepared by the FASB staff.

ENCOURAGED DISCLOSURES

The FASB encourages, but does not require, entities to disclose quantitative information about interest rate, foreign exchange, commodity price, or other market risks pertaining to derivatives consistent with the way the entity manages those risks. Examples of disclosures that may be appropriate for some entities cited by the FASB are more details about current positions and perhaps activity during the period; the hypothetical effects on equity or on annual income of several possible changes in market prices; a gap analysis of interest rate repricing or maturity dates; duration of financial instruments; the entity's value at risk from derivative financial instruments at the end of the reporting period; and the average value at risk during the year.

In practice, few entities have made those encouraged but not required disclosures. However, the SEC has proposed requirements that would mandate additional disclosures for companies under its jurisdiction. They are briefly discussed in the next section.

ADDITIONAL DERIVATIVES DISCLOSURES PROPOSED BY THE SEC

On December 28, 1995, the Securities and Exchange Commission issued proposed rules that would require additional detailed disclosures about accounting policies relating to derivatives as well as both qualitative and quantitative information about market risk. Comments were requested by May 21, 1996. After a review of the comments received, the SEC may decide to adopt the proposed rules, possibly with changes, or to defer the matter for further consideration and possibly issue a revised proposal.[4]

The proposed disclosure requirements are intended to clarify and expand upon those required by the FASB. Distinguishing between derivatives used for trading and other derivatives, the proposals would require disclosure of:

- Each method used to account for derivatives (fair value accounting, deferral accounting, and accrual accounting).
- Types of derivatives accounted for under each method.
- The criteria required to be met for each accounting method.
- The accounting method used if the specified criteria are not met.
- The accounting for the termination of derivatives designated as hedges or used to affect directly or indirectly the terms, fair values, or cash flows of a designated item.
- The accounting for derivatives if the designated item matures or is sold, extinguished, terminated, or if related to an anticipated transaction, is not likely to occur.
- Where and when derivatives and their related gains and losses are reported in the statements of financial position, cash flows, and results of operations.

---

4. On July 24, 1996, an SEC staff person reported that the staff was in the process of reviewing and summarizing the more than 100 comment letters received on the proposal.

Additionally, the proposed rules would require disclosure outside the financial statements of extensive quantitative and qualitative information relating to derivatives market risk—basically requiring the information that is suggested but not required by FASB statements. The additional disclosures that would be required under the SEC proposal focus on forward-looking information whereas the disclosures required by the FASB relate to historical information.

Illustrations
from Practice

The following appendix contains excerpts from the 1994 financial reports of Merck & Co., Dow Chemical Company, Intel Corporation, and Nations Bank that present their disclosures about derivative financial instruments. The disclosures are primarily from the notes to financial statements, but the case of Merck also includes pertinent data from the financial review, and for Nations Bank has data from management's discussion and analysis. The industrial companies chosen make extensive use of derivatives and the scope of their disclosures are greater than would be the case for a typical company. The excerpts from Nations Bank show how especially extensive disclosures can be for financial institutions.[5]

---

5. A detailed analysis of disclosures about derivatives is contained in Jeffrey P. Mahoney and Yoshinori Kawamura, *Special Report, Review of 1994 Disclosures about Derivative Financial Instruments and Fair Value of Financial Instruments,* published by the Financial Accounting Standards Board.

EXCERPTS FROM MERCK & CO. INC. 1994 ANNUAL REPORT

Financial Review: Analysis of Liquidity and Capital Resources[6]

A significant portion of the Company's cash flows are denominated in foreign currencies. The Company relies on sustained cash flows generated from foreign sources to support a long-term commitment to U.S. dollar-based research and development. To the extent the dollar value of cash flows is diminished as a result of a strengthening dollar, the Company's ability to fund research and other dollar-based strategic initiatives at a consistent level may be impaired. To protect against the reduction in value of foreign currency cash flows, the Company has instituted balance sheet and revenue hedging programs to partially hedge this risk.

The objective of the balance sheet hedging program is to protect the U.S. dollar value of foreign currency denominated net monetary assets from the effects of volatility in foreign exchange that might occur prior to their conversion to U.S. dollars. To achieve this objective, the Company will hedge foreign currency risk on monetary assets and liabilities where hedging is cost beneficial. The Company seeks to fully hedge exposure denominated in developed country currencies, such as those of Japan, Europe, and Canada, and will either partially hedge, or not hedge at all, exposure in other currencies, particularly exposure in hyperinflationary countries where hedging instruments may not be available at any cost. The Company will minimize the effect of exchange on unhedged exposure principally by managing operating activities and net asset positions at the local level. The Company manages its net asset exposure principally with forward exchange contracts. These contracts enable the Company to buy and sell

---

6. Merck & Co. Inc. 1994 Annual Report, pp. 36–37.

foreign currencies in the future at fixed exchange rates. On net monetary assets hedged, forward contracts offset the consequences of changes in foreign exchange on the amount of U.S. dollar cash flows derived from the net assets. Contracts used to hedge net monetary asset exposure have average maturities at inception of less than one year. The cash flows generated from these forward contracts are reported as arising from operating activities in the Statement of Cash Flows. The balance sheet hedging program has significantly reduced the volatility of U.S. dollar cash flows derived from foreign currency denominated net monetary assets.

The objective of the revenue hedging program is to reduce the potential for longer-term unfavorable changes in foreign exchange to decrease the U.S. dollar value of future cash flows derived from foreign currency denominated sales. To achieve this objective, the Company will partially hedge forecasted sales that are expected to occur over its planning cycle, typically no more than three years into the future. The Company will layer in hedges over time, increasing the portion of sales hedged as it gets closer to the expected date of the transaction. The portion of sales hedged is based on assessments of cost-benefit profiles that consider natural offsetting exposures, revenue and exchange rate volatilities and correlations, and the cost of hedging instruments. The Company manages its forecasted transaction exposure principally with purchased local currency put options. On the forecasted transactions hedged, these option contracts effectively reduce the potential for a strengthening U.S. dollar to decrease the future U.S. dollar cash flows derived from foreign currency denominated sales. Purchased local currency put options provide the Company with a right, but not an obligation, to sell foreign currencies in the future at a pre-determined price. If the value of the U.S. dollar weakens relative to other major currencies when the options mature, the options would expire unexercised, enabling the Company to benefit from favorable movements in exchange, except to the extent of premiums paid for the contracts. Over the last three years the program has had a minimal cumulative effect on cash flows, principally because of the prevailing weakness in the U.S. dollar compared with other major currencies. However, the program has prevented a loss in value of cash flows during interim periods of relative strength in the U.S. dollar for the portion of revenues hedged. The cash flows associated with these contracts are reported as arising from operating activities in the Statement of Cash Flows.

Selected Notes to Financial Statements

4. Financial Instruments and Related Disclosures

Summarized below are the carrying values and fair values of the Company's financial instruments at December 31, 1994 and 1993. Fair values were estimated based on market prices, where available, or dealer quotes.

(In millions)	1994 Carrying Value	1994 Fair Value	1993 Carrying Value	1993 Fair Value
Assets				
Cash and cash equivalents	$1,604.0	$1,604.0	$ 829.4	$ 829.4
Short-term investments	665.7	665.9	712.9	714.4
Long-term investments	1,416.9	1,405.8	1,779.9	1,908.3
Purchased currency options	97.6	42.5	132.1	136.2
Forward exchange contracts	27.2	27.2	—	—
Interest rate swaps	—	—	—	2.2
Liabilities				
Loans payable	$ 146.7	$ 143.4	$1,736.0	$1,735.5
Long-term debt	1,145.9	1,114.0	1,120.8	1,137.7
Written currency options	0.5	0.5	6.4	5.8
Forward exchange contracts and currency swap	45.2	45.2	25.4	25.4
Interest rate swaps	—	9.4	—	—

The Company has established revenue and balance sheet hedging programs to protect against reductions in value and volatility of future foreign currency cash flows caused by changes in foreign exchange rates. The objectives and strategies of these programs are described in the Analysis of Liquidity and Capital Resources section of the Financial Review.

The Company hedges forecasted revenues denominated in foreign currencies with purchased currency options. When the dollar strengthens against foreign currencies, the decline in the value of future foreign currency cash flows is partially offset by the recognition of gains in the value of purchased currency options designated as hedges of the period. Conversely, when the dollar weakens, the increase in the value of future foreign currency cash flows is reduced only by the recognition of the premium paid to acquire the options designated as hedges of the period. Market value gains and premiums on these contracts are recognized in Sales when the hedged transaction is recognized. The carrying value of purchased currency options is reported in Prepaid Expenses and Taxes, or Other Assets.

The Company continuously reviews its portfolio of purchased options and will adjust its portfolio to accommodate changes in exposure to forecasted revenues. The most cost-effective means of decreasing coverage provided by purchased options is to write options with terms identical to purchased options that are no longer necessary. Deferred gains or losses that accumulate on purchased options prior to writing an offsetting position will remain deferred and are recognized when the hedged transaction occurs. Subsequent changes in the market value of the written options and related purchased options are recorded in earnings. Because the changes in market value of the purchased and written options equally offset, there is no net impact on earnings. The carrying value of written currency options is reported in Accounts Payable and Accrued Liabilities, or Deferred Income Taxes and Noncurrent Liabilities.

Deferred gains and losses on currency options used to hedge forecasted revenues mounted to $3.2 million and $58.3 million at December 31, 1996, and $22.9 million and $18.2 million at December 31, 1993, respectively.

The Company also hedges certain exposures to fluctuations in foreign currency exchange rates that occur prior to conversion of foreign currency denominated monetary assets and liabilities into U.S. dollars. Prior to conversion to U.S. dollars, these assets and liabilities are translated at spot rates in effect on the balance sheet date. The effects of changes in spot rates are reported in earnings and included in Other (Income) Expense, Net. The Company hedges its exposure to changes in foreign exchange with forward contracts. Because monetary assets and liabilities are marked to spot and recorded in earnings, forward contracts designated as hedges of the monetary assets and liabilities are also marked to spot with the resulting gains and losses similarly recognized in earnings. Gains and losses on forward contracts are included in Other (Income) Expense, Net and offset losses and gains on the net monetary assets and liabilities hedged. The carrying value of forward exchange contracts is reported in Accounts Receivable, Other Assets, Accounts Payable and Accrued Liabilities, or Deferred Income Taxes and Noncurrent Liabilities.

At December 31, 1994 and 1993, the Company had contracts to exchange foreign currencies, principally the Japanese yen, French franc and Deutschemark, for U.S. dollars in the following notional amounts:

(In millions)	1994	1993
Purchased currency options	$1,793.8	$1,604.5
Written currency options	114.6	122.0
Forward sale contracts	1,463.6	1,350.7
Forward purchase contracts	404.5	400.5

The Company uses interest rate swaps contracts on certain borrowing and investing transactions. Interest rate swap contracts are intended to be an integral part of borrowing and investing transactions and, therefore, are not recognized at fair value. Interest differentials paid or received under these contracts are recognized as adjustments to the effective yield of the underlying financial instruments hedged. Interest rate swap contracts would only be recognized at fair value if the hedged relationship is terminated. Gains or losses accumulated prior to termination of the relationship would be amortized as a yield adjustment over the shorter of the remaining life of the contract or the remaining period to maturity of the underlying instrument hedged. If the contract remained outstanding after termination of the hedged relationship, subsequent changes in market value of the contract would be recognized in earnings. The Company does not use leveraged swaps and, in general, does not use leverage in any of its investment activities that would put principal capital at risk.

At December 31, 1994, the Company had an interest rate swap contract with a notional amount of $82.0 million to convert a portion of its variable rate investments to fixed rates. This contract matures in two years. The Company also had three interest rate swap contracts outstanding with a combined notional amount of $370.6 million to convert fixed rates on debt issues to floating rates slightly below commercial paper rates. The maturities of these contracts coincide with the maturities of the underlying debt instruments hedged. The debt issues include $55 million in medium-term notes, $200 million in zero coupon euronotes and 200 million in Swiss franc eurobonds. Concurrent with the issuance of the Swiss franc eurobonds, the Company entered into an interest rate and currency swap. The currency swap is accounted for similar to forward exchange contracts. (See Note 6 for further information.)

The interest rate and currency swaps on the debt issues described above essentially provide the Company with variable rate, U.S. dollar denominated debt at rates of interest lower than rates the Company could otherwise obtain had it actually issued variable rate U.S. dollar debt.

As part of its ongoing control procedures, the Company monitors concentrations of credit risk associated with financial institutions with which it conducts business. Credit risk is minimal as credit exposure limits are established to avoid a concentration with any single financial institution. The Company also monitors the credit worthiness of its customers to which it grants credit terms in the normal course of business. Customers for human health products and services include drug wholesalers and retailers, hospitals, clinics, governmental agencies, corporations, labor unions, retirement systems, insurance carriers, managed health-care providers such as health maintenance organizations, and other institutions. Customers for the Company's animal health/crop protection products include veterinarians, distributors, wholesalers, retailers, feed manufacturers, veterinary suppliers, and laboratories. Concentrations of credit risk associated with these trade receivables are considered minimal due to the Company's diverse customer base. Bad debts have been minimal. The Company does not normally require collateral or other security to support credit sales.

Effective January 1, 1994, the Company adopted the provisions of Statement No. 115, Accounting for Certain Investments in Debt and Equity Securities, which requires certain investments to be recorded at fair value or amortized cost. In accordance with this statement, the Company has classified its investments as available-for-sale and held-to-maturity. Available-for-sale investments are carried at fair value with unrealized gains and losses recorded, net of tax and minority interests, in Stockholders' Equity: Held-to-maturity investments are carried at amortized cost. Prior to 1994, these investments were carried at the lower of cost or market. Adoption of this (SFAS No. 115) did not materially impact the results. At January 1, 1994, the unrealized gain associated with available-for-sale investments of $37.5 million, net of tax and minority interests, was included in Retained Earnings.

At December 31, 1994, available-for-sale investments include debt and equity securities carried at their fair values of $926.3 million ($474.5 million of which mature within one year) and $507.4 million, respectively. Gross unrealized gains and losses amounted to $2.3 million and $22.8 million for debt securities and $201.7 million and $65.9 million for equity securities, respectively. Held-to-maturity investments are carried at amortized cost of $648.9 million ($183.5 million of which mature within one year) and have a fair value of $638.0 million.

6. Loans Payable and Long-Term Debt

Loans payable at December 31, 1994, included $76.2 million of unsecured parent company borrowings. The remainder of the 1994 balance was principally borrowings by foreign subsidiaries. The weighted average interest rate for these borrowings was 5.3% and 3.4% at December 31, 1994 and 1993, respectively. Loans payable decreased in 1994 primarily as a result of the repayment of commercial paper borrowings funded by operating cash flows and proceeds received from Astra on the sale of an interest in a joint venture.

Long-term debt at December 31 consisted of:

(In millions)	1994	1993
5.3% euronotes due 1998	$ 252.4	$ 253.0
7.8% notes due 1996	249.6	249.2
Zero coupon euronotes due 1997	170.9	—
5.4% Swiss franc eurobonds due 1997	153.5	—
6.0%–7.7% medium term notes due 1996–1997	139.8	139.7
6.7% convertible subordinated debentures due 2001	74.8	316.4
Floating rate notes due 1995	—	54.9
Other	104.9	107.6
	$1,145.9	$1,120.8

The face values of the convertible subordinated debentures due 2001 are comprised of the following components: $28.7 million issued by Medco (on which Merck has become a co-obligor); and $34.2 million issued by Medical Marketing Group, Inc. (MMG), a subsidiary of Medco (on which Merck has also become co-obligor). Prior to maturity, each $1,000 Medco debenture can be redeemed for approximately 25 Merck shares and $533 in cash, and each $1,000 MMG debenture can be redeemed for $681 in cash. $159.5 million carrying value ($118.6 million face value) of these debentures were converted in 1994.

At December 31, 1994, the Company had an interest rate swap contract to convert the 6.1% fixed rate on the zero coupon euronotes to a variable rate slightly below commercial paper rates. In addition, the Company entered into an interest rate and currency swap concurrent with the issuance of the Swiss franc eurobonds. The contract converts the fixed rate on the eurobonds to a variable rate slightly below commercial paper rates, payable in U.S. dollars, and enables the Company to buy 200 million Swiss francs at maturity at a fixed exchange rate. Accordingly, any exchange gain or loss on these bonds will be entirely offset by the change in the carrying value of the contract.

EXCERPTS FROM DOW CHEMICAL COMPANY 1994 ANNUAL REPORT

Notes to Financial Statements

A. Summary of Significant Accounting Policies

Financial Instruments   Interest differentials on swaps and forward rate agreements designated as hedges of exposures to interest rate risk are recorded as adjustments to interest expense over the contract period. Premiums for early termination of derivatives designated as hedges are amortized as adjustments to interest expense over the original contract period. Interest derivatives not designated as hedges are marked-to-market at the end of each accounting period.

The Company calculates the fair value of financial instruments using quoted market prices whenever available. When quoted market prices are not available, the Company uses standard pricing models for various types of financial instruments (such as forwards, options, swaps, etc.) which take into account the present value of estimated future cash flows.

Investment in debt and equity securities are classified as either Trading, Available-for-Sale or Held-to-Maturity. Investments classified as Trading are reported at fair value with unrealized gains and losses included in income. Investments classified as Available-for-Sale are reported at fair value with unrealized gains and losses recorded in a separate component of stockholders' equity. Investments classified as Held-to-Maturity are recorded at amortized cost.

The cost of investments sold is determined by specific identification.

J. Financial Instruments

Fair Value of Financial Instruments at December 31

(In millions, except for share amounts)	1994				1993			
	Cost	Gain	Loss	Fair Value	Cost	Gain	Loss	Fair Value
Nonderivatives								
Interest-bearing deposits	$ 92	—	—	$ 92	$ 105	—	—	$ 105
Marketable equity and debt securities:								
Trading	414	$20	—	434	433	$ 7	—	440
Available-for-Sale								
Debt securities	824	3	$(22)	805	732	38	$ (3)	767
Equity securities	454	64	(45)	473	489	205	(22)	672
Held-to-Maturity	408	1	(1)	408	177	3	(3)	177
Other	337	—	(7)	330	357	—	(4)	353
Total investments	$ 2,529	$88	$(75)	$ 2,542	$ 2,293	$253	$ (32)	$ 2,514
Long-term debt	$(5,303)	$33	—	$(5,270)	$(5,902)	—	$(391)	$(6,293)
Derivatives relating to:								
Foreign currency	—	$52	$(70)	$ (18)	—	$ 9	—	$ 9
Interest	—	37	(45)	(8)	—	176	$(130)	46
Cross-currency swaps	—	15	(93)	(78)	—	—	—	—

The cost approximates the fair value for all other financial instruments.

Investments   Total investments at December 31, 1994 and 1993, included cash equivalents of $455 and $362, marketable securities and interest-bearing deposits of $565 and $430, and other investments of $1,529 and $1,726, respectively.

The proceeds from sales of Available-for-Sale securities were $981 for 1994. These sales resulted in gross realized gains of $55 and losses of $26.

Maturities for most debt securities ranged from 1 to 10 years for the Available-for-Sale classification and one to five years for the Held-to-Maturity classification at December 31, 1994.

Foreign Currency Risk Management   The Company's global operations require active participation in the foreign exchange markets. The Company enters into foreign exchange forward contracts and options to hedge various currency exposures or create desired exposures. Exposures primarily relate to (a) assets and liabilities denominated in foreign currency in Europe, Asia, and Canada; (b) bonds denominated in foreign currency; and (c) economic exposure derived from the risk that currency fluctuations could affect the dollar value of future cash flows at the operating margin level. The primary business objective of the activity is to optimize the U.S. dollar value of the Company's assets, liabilities, and future cash flows with respect to exchange rate fluctuations. Hedging is done on a net exposure basis, namely, assets and liabilities denominated in the same currency are netted and only the balance is hedged.

At December 31, 1994 and 1993, the Company had forward contracts outstanding with various expiration dates (primarily in January of the next year) to buy, sell, or exchange foreign currencies with a U.S. dollar equivalent of $6,573 and $3,664, respectively. The unrealized gains or losses on these contracts, based on the foreign exchange rates at December 31, 1994 and 1993, were a loss of $18 and a gain of $9, respectively, and were included in income in "Net gain (loss) on foreign currency transactions."

Interest Rate Risk Management   The Company enters into various interest rate contracts with the objective of lowering funding costs, diversifying sources of funding or altering interest rate exposure. In these contracts, the Company agrees with other parties to exchange, at specified intervals, the difference between fixed and floating interest amounts calculated on an agreed upon notional principal amount.

The notional principal on all types of interest derivative contracts at December 31, 1994 and 1993 totaled $4,264 and $9,302, with a weighted average remaining life of 3.3 and 3.8 years, respectively. The $37 in gains and $45 in losses in 1994 related to interest derivatives were not recognized in income as they represented hedges of debt-related exposures. The $15 in gains and $93 in losses in 1994 related to cross-currency swaps were primarily recognized in income in "Net gain (loss) on foreign currency transactions" and offset the gains and losses from the assets and liabilities being hedged. In 1993, there were $176 in gains and $130 in losses related to cross-currency swaps and interest derivatives. Of these amounts, $142 in gains and $103 in losses had not been recognized in income as they represented hedges of debt-related exposures.

Interest Derivatives at December 31, 1994

	Notional Amount	Maturities	Weighted Average Rate	
			Receive	Pay
Cross-currency swaps	$1,427	1995–1999	—	—
Receive Fixed Hedge	1,630	1995–2005	6.1%	5.5%
Receive Floating Hedge	1,024	1996–2005	5.5%	6.8%
Other	183	1995–1998	—	—

The Company's risk management program for both foreign currency and interest rate risk is based on fundamental, mathematical, and technical models that take into account the implicit cost of hedging. Risks created by derivative instruments and the mark-to-market valuations of positions are strictly monitored at all times.

Financial Instruments The Company uses portfolio sensitivities and stress tests to monitor risk. Because the counterparties to these contracts are major international financial institutions, credit risk arising from these contracts is not significant and the Company does not anticipate any such losses. The net cash requirements arising from risk management activities are not expected to be material. The Company's overall financial strategies and impacts from using derivatives in its risk management program are reviewed periodically with the Finance Committee of the Company's Board of Directors and revised as market conditions dictate.

The Company's global orientation in diverse businesses with a large number of diverse customers and suppliers minimize concentrations of credit risk. No concentration of credit risk existed at December 31, 1994.

EXCERPTS FROM INTEL CORPORATION 1994 ANNUAL REPORT

Notes to Financial Statements[7]

Put Warrants

In a series of private placements from 1991 through 1994, the Company sold put warrants that entitle the holder of each warrant to sell one share of common stock to the Company at a specified price. Activity during the past three years is summarized as follows:

---

7. Intel Corporation 1994 Annual Report, pp. 19–21.

(In millions)	Cumulative Premium Received (Paid)	Put Warrants Outstanding	
		Number of Warrants	Potential Obligation
December 28, 1991	$ 14	7.0	$140
Sales	43	14.0	373
Repurchases	(1)	(5.2)	(104)
Expirations	—	(1.8)	(36)
December 26, 1992	56	14.0	373
Sales	62	10.8	561
Expirations	—	(10.0)	(246)
December 25, 1993	118	14.8	688
Sales	76	12.5	744
Exercises	—	(1.0)	(65)
Expirations	—	(13.8)	(623)
December 31, 1994	$194	12.5	$744

The amount related to Intel's potential repurchase obligation has been reclassified from stockholders' equity to put warrants. The 12.5 million put warrants outstanding at December 31, 1994, expire on various dates between February 1995 and December 1995 and have exercise prices ranging from $55 to $63 per share. There was no effect on earnings per share for the periods presented. During 1994, in connection with the exercise of 1.0 million put warrants, the Company repurchased and retired 1.0 million shares of common stock at a cost of $65 million (see "Stock Repurchase Program").

Borrowings

Short-Term Debt   Short-term debt and weighted average interest rates at fiscal year-ends are as follows:

(In millions)	1994		1993	
	Balance	**Weighted Average Interest Rate**	**Balance**	**Weighted Average Interest Rate**
Borrowed under lines of credit	$ 68	3.2%	$ 85	5.8%
Reverse repurchase agreements	99	8.0%	197	7.9%
Notes payable	5	4.7%	2	3.4%
Short-term portion of long-term debt	179	11.8%	—	—
Drafts payable	166	N/A	115	N/A
Total	**$517**		**$399**	

At December 31, 1994, the Company had established foreign and domestic lines of credit of approximately $1,040 million. The Company generally renegotiates these lines annually. Compensating balance requirements are not material.

The Company also borrows under commercial paper programs. Maximum borrowings reached $700 million during both 1994 and 1993. This debt is rated A1+ by Standard and Poor's and P1 by Moody's. Proceeds are used to fund short-term working capital needs.

Long-Term Debts   Long-term debt at fiscal year-ends is as follows:

(In millions)	1994	1993
Payable in U.S. dollars:		
AFICA bonds due 2013 at 4%	$110	$110
Zero coupon notes due 1995 at 11.8%, net of unamortized discount of $8 ($27 in 1993)	179	160
8$^{1}/_{8}$% notes due 1997	—	98
Other U.S. dollar debt	4	6
Payable in other currencies:		
Irish punt due 2008–2024 at 6%–12%	228	146
Greek drachma due 2001	46	—
Other foreign currency debt	4	4
(Less short-term or redeemable portion)	(179)	(98)
Total	**$392**	**$426**

The Company has guaranteed repayment of principal and interest on the AFICA Bonds which were issued by the Puerto Rico Industrial, Medical and Environmental Pollution Control Facilities Financing Authority (AFICA). The bonds are adjustable and redeemable at the option of either the Company or the bondholder every five years through 2013 and are next adjustable and redeemable in 1998. The $8^{1}/_{8}$ percent notes were called and repurchased by the Company during 1994 for $98 million. The Irish punt borrowings were made in connection with the financing of a factory in Ireland, and Intel has invested the proceeds in Irish punt denominated instruments of similar maturity to hedge foreign currency and interest rate exposures. The Greek drachma borrowings were made under a tax incentive program in Ireland, and the proceeds and cash flows have been swapped to U.S. dollars.

In 1993, the Company filed a shelf registration statement with the SEC. When combined with previous registration statements, this filing gave Intel the authority to issue up to $3.3 billion in the aggregate of common stock, preferred stock, depositary shares, debt securities and warrants to purchase the Company's common stock, preferred stock and debt securities, and, subject to certain limits, stock index warrants and foreign currency exchange units. In 1993, Intel completed an offering of step-up Warrants (see "1998 Step-Up Warrants") and may issue up to $1.4 billion in additional securities under open registration statements.

As of December 31, 1994, aggregate debt maturities are as follows: 1995—$187 million; 1996—none; 1997—none; 1998—$110 million; and thereafter—$282 million.

Investments

The Company's policy is to protect the value of the investment portfolio by minimizing principal risk and earning returns based on current interest rates. All hedged equity and a majority of investments in the long-term fixed-rate debt securities are swapped to U.S. dollar LIBOR-based returns.

The currency risks of investments denominated in foreign currencies are hedged with foreign currency borrowings, currency forward contracts, or currency interest rate swaps (see "Derivative Financial Instruments"). Investments with maturities of greater than one year are classified as long term. There were no material proceeds, gross realized gains, or gross realized losses from sales of securities during the year.

Investments with maturities of greater than six months consist primarily of A/A2 or better rated financial instruments and counterparties. Investments with maturities of up to six months consist primarily of A1/P1 or better rated financial instruments and counterparties. Foreign government regulations imposed upon investment alternatives of foreign subsidiaries or the absence of A/A2 rated counterparties in certain countries result in some minor exceptions. Intel's practice is to obtain and secure collateral from counterparties against obligations whenever deemed appropriate. At December 31, 1994, investments were placed with approximately 100 different counterparties, and no individual security, financial institution, or issuer exceeded 10 percent of total investments.

Investments at December 31, 1994, are comprised of the following:

(In millions)	Cost	Gross Unrealized Gains	Gross Unrealized Losses	Estimated Fair Value
Securities of foreign governments	$ 518	$ 2	$ (7)	$ 513
Floating rate notes	488	1	(1)	488
Corporate bonds	440	12	(14)	438
Loan participations	200	6	(2)	204
Collateralized mortgage obligations	170	—	(4)	166
Fixed rate notes	167	1	(2)	166
Commercial paper	134	—	—	134
Other debt securities	439	—	(5)	434
Total debt securities	2,556	22	(35)	2,543
Hedged equity	431	—	(58)	373
Preferred stock and other equity	368	20	(16)	372
Total equity securities	799	20	(74)	745
Swaps hedging debt securities	—	22	(14)	8
Swaps hedging equity securities	—	60	—	60
Currency forward contracts hedging debt securities	—	1	—	1
Total available-for-sale securities	$3,355	$125	$(123)	$3,357

At December 31, 1994, the Company also holds $930 million of available-for-sale investments in other debt securities that are classified as cash and equivalents on the balance sheet.

The amortized cost and estimated fair value of investments in debt securities at December 31, 1994, by contractual maturity, are as follows:

(In millions)	Cost	Estimated Fair Value
Due in 1 year or less	$1,144	$1,144
Due in 1–2 years	515	512
Due in 2–5 years	642	635
Due after 5 years	255	252
Total investments in debt securities	$2,556	$2,543

Derivative Financial Instruments

As part of its ongoing asset and liability management activities, the Company enters into derivative financial instruments to reduce financial market risks. These instruments are used to hedge foreign currency, equity market, and interest rate exposures of underlying assets, liabilities, and other obligations. These instruments involve elements of market risk which offset the market risk of the underlying assets and liabilities they hedge. The Company does not enter into derivative financial instruments for trading purposes.

Notional amounts for derivatives at fiscal year-ends are as follows:

(In millions)	1994	1993
Swaps hedging investments in debt securities	$1,080	$809
Swaps hedging investments in equity securities	$ 567	$260
Swaps hedging debt	$ 155	$110
Currency forward contracts	$ 784	$620
Currency options	$ 10	$ 28

While the contract or notional amounts provide one measure of the volume of these transactions, they do not represent the amount of the Company's exposure to credit risk. The amounts potentially subject to credit risk (arising from the possible inability of counterparties to meet the terms of their contracts) are generally limited to the amounts, if any, by which the counterparties' obligations exceed the obligations of the Company. The Company controls credit risk through credit approvals, limits and monitoring procedures. Credit rating criteria for off-balance-sheet transactions are similar to those for investments.

Swap Agreements   The Company enters into swap agreements to exchange the foreign currency, equity market, and fixed interest rate exposures of its investment and debt portfolios for a floating interest rate. The floating rates on swaps are based primarily on U.S. dollar LIBOR and reset on a monthly, quarterly, or semiannual basis.

Weighted average pay and receive rates, average maturities, and range of maturities on swaps at December 31, 1994, are as follows:

	Weighted Average Pay Rate	Weighted Average Receive Rate	Weighted Average Maturity	Range of Maturities
Swaps hedging investments in U.S. dollar debt securities	6.7%	6.0%	1.2 years	0–4 years
Swaps hedging investments in foreign currency debt securities	10.8%	8.2%	1.8 years	0–3 years
Swaps hedging investments in equity securities	N/A	5.5%	2.1 years	0–3 years
Swaps hedging debt	6.1%	5.2%	4.9 years	4–7 years

Pay rates on swaps hedging investments in debt securities generally match the yields on the underlying investments they hedge. Payments on swaps hedging investments in equity securities generally match the equity returns on the underlying investments they hedge. Receive rates on swaps hedging debt generally match the expense on the underlying debt they hedge. Maturity dates of swaps generally match those of the underlying investment or debt they hedge. There is approximately a one-to-one matching of investments and debt to swaps. Swap agreements generally remain in effect until expiration. Income or expense on swaps is accrued as an adjustment to the yield of the related investments or debt they hedge.

Other Foreign Currency Instruments   Intel transacts business in various foreign currencies, primarily Japanese yen and certain European currencies. The Company enters into currency forward and option contracts to hedge foreign exchange risk. The Company also periodically enters into currency option contracts to hedge certain anticipated revenue and purchases for which it does not have a firm commitment. The maturities on most of these foreign currency instruments are less than 12 months. Any gains or losses on these instruments are recognized in accordance with SFAS Nos. 52 and 80. Deferred gains or losses attributable to foreign currency instruments are not material.

Fair Values of Financial Instruments

The estimated fair values of financial instruments at fiscal year-ends are as follows:

(In millions)	1994 Carrying Amount	1994 Estimated Fair Value	1993 Carrying Amount	1993 Estimated Fair Value
Cash and cash equivalents	$1,180	$1,180	$1,659	$1,659
Short-term investments	1,230	1,230	1,477	1,477
Long-term investments	2,058	2,058	1,416	1,412
Swaps hedging investments in debt securities	8	8	—	—
Swaps hedging investments in equity securities	60	60	—	—
Short-term debt	(517)	(517)	(399)	(399)
Long-term debt	(392)	(364)	(426)	(436)
Swaps hedging debt	—	(12)	—	—
Currency forward contracts	1	5	—	9
Currency options	—	—	—	—
Total	$3,628	$3,628	$3,727	$3,722

Concentrations of Credit Risk

Financial instruments that potentially subject the Company to concentrations of credit risk consist principally of investments and trade receivables. Intel places its investments with high-credit-quality counterparties and, by policy, limits the amount of credit exposure to any one counterparty. A majority of the Company's trade receivables are derived from sales to manufacturers of microcomputer systems, with the remainder spread across various other industries. The Company keeps pace with the evolving computer industry and has adopted credit policies and standards to accommodate the industry's growth and inherent risk. Management believes that any risk of accounting loss is significantly reduced due to the diversity of its products, end customers, and geographic sales areas. Intel performs ongoing credit evaluations of its customers' financial condition and requires collateral, such as letters of credit and bank guarantees, whenever deemed necessary.

EXCERPTS FROM NATIONS BANK 1994 ANNUAL REPORT

Management's Discussion and Analysis[8]

Interest Rate Risk Management

The Corporation's asset and liability management process is utilized to manage the Corporation's interest rate risk through structuring the balance sheet and off-balance-sheet portfolios to maximize net interest income while maintaining acceptable levels of risk to changes in market interest rates. While achievement of this goal requires a balance between profitability, liquidity, and interest rate risk, there are opportunities to enhance revenues through controlled risk.

---

8.   Nations Bank 1994 Annual Report, pp. 45–50.

Interest rate risk is managed by the Corporation's Finance Committee which formulates strategies based on a desirable level of interest rate risk. In setting desirable levels of interest rate risk, the Finance Committee considers the impact on earnings and capital of the current outlook on interest rates, potential changes in the outlook on interest rates, world and regional economies, liquidity, business strategies, and other factors.

To effectively measure and manage interest rate risk, the Corporation uses computer simulations which determine the impact on net interest income of various interest rate scenarios, balance sheet trends, and strategies. These simulations incorporate assumptions about balance sheet dynamics, such as loan and deposit growth, loan and deposit pricing, changes in funding mix, and asset and liability repricing and maturity characteristics. Simulations based on numerous assumptions are run under various interest rate scenarios to determine the impact on net interest income and capital. From these scenarios, interest rate risk is quantified and appropriate strategies are developed and implemented. The overall interest rate risk position and strategies are reviewed on an ongoing basis by executive management.

Additionally, duration and market value sensitivity measures are selectively utilized where they provide added value to the overall interest rate risk management process.

In implementing strategies to manage interest rate risk, the primary tools used by the Corporation are the discretionary portfolio, which is comprised of the securities portfolio and interest rate swaps, and management of the mix, rates, and maturities of the wholesale and retail funding sources of the Corporation.

The investment securities portfolio serves a primary role in positioning the Corporation based on the long-term interest rate outlook. Securities available for sale serve as a key tool for near-term interest rate risk management and can be utilized to take advantage of market opportunities that are medium-term in nature. Interest rate swaps allow the

Corporation to adjust its interest rate risk position without exposure to risk of loss of principal and funding requirements, as swaps do not involve the exchange of notional amounts, only net interest payments. The interest payments can be based on a fixed rate or a variable index.

The Corporation uses nonleveraged generic swaps, index amortizing swaps, and collateralized mortgage obligation (CMO) swaps. Generic swaps involve the exchange of fixed and variable interest rates based on the contractual underlying notional amounts. Index amortizing and CMO swaps also involve the exchange of fixed and variable interest rates; however, their notional amounts decline and their maturities vary based on certain interest rate indices in the case of index amortizing swaps, or mortgage prepayment rates in the case of CMO swaps. Such instruments are subjected to the same credit risk management policies and procedures as trading instruments . . .

In light of the economic momentum in the U.S. economy and the associated tightening of credit by the Federal Reserve Bank through increases in interest rates, the Corporation shifted, in the latter half of 1994, its interest rate risk position from one postured to benefit modestly from stable to declining rates to a more neutral position. The actions taken by the Corporation to shift its position included reduction of the net swap position, reduction of fixed-rate assets, and extension of maturities of fixed-rate deposits and borrowings.

In the third quarter of 1994, in order to reduce the net swap position, the Corporation entered into two-year maturity, pay fixed interest rate swaps with a notional amount of $8.0 billion. As a result, the Corporation's net receive fixed position on December 31,1994, was $8.9 billion, compared to $13.5 billion on December 31, 1993. Exhibit 1 summarizes the notional contracts and the activity for the year ended December 31, 1994, of asset and liability management interest rate swaps (ALM swaps). The interest rate swap transactions entered into during 1994 increased the gross notional amount of the Corporation's ALM swaps program on December 31,

1994, to $26.0 billion with the Corporation receiving fixed on $17.5 billion, converting variable-rate commercial loans to fixed rate and receiving variable on $8.5 billion, fixing the cost of certain variable-rate liabilities, primarily market-based borrowed funds.

Secondly, the Corporation adjusted its interest rate risk position by reducing the level of fixed-rate securities. As securities matured in 1994, the Corporation did not fully reinvest these proceeds. Additionally, during the fourth quarter, approximately $1.5 billion of securities were sold, without reinvestment of those proceeds. These actions give the Corporation the flexibility to reinvest as deemed appropriate.

The third action taken to adjust the interest rate risk position was extension of the maturities of market-based funds, primarily bank notes and foreign time deposits.

In addition to these efforts, the acquisition of approximately $3.9 billion of customer-based deposits from California Federal Savings Bank in 1994 helped adjust the interest rate risk sensitivity of the Corporation's liabilities, as approximately one-half of these deposits are not rate sensitive and are longer-term.

The above actions shifted the Corporation's interest rate position from one postured to benefit modestly from stable to declining interest rates to a more neutral position. On December 31, 1994, the impact of a gradual 100-basis point rise in interest rates over the next 12 months was estimated to have an insignificant impact on net income when compared to stable rates.

Exhibit 2 summarizes the maturities, average pay and receive rates, and the market value on December 31, 1994, of the Corporation's ALM swaps. The weighted average interest receive rate was 4.98 percent and pay rate was 6.10 percent as of December 31, 1994. Net interest receipts and payments have been included in interest income and expense on the underlying instruments. Deferred gains and losses relating to any terminated contracts are insignificant.

EXHIBIT 1

Asset and Liability Management Interest Rate Swaps Notional Contracts

Dollars in millions	Generic		Index Amortizing	CMO		Total		
	Receive Fixed	Pay Fixed	Receive Fixed	Receive Fixed	Pay Fixed	Receive Fixed	Pay Fixed	Total
Balance on December 31, 1993	$6,500	$ —	$6,150	$1,076	$182	$13,726	$ 182	$13,908
Additions	320	8,469	2,300	2,000	—	4,620	8,469	13,089
Maturities	(292)	(23)	—	(572)	(85)	(864)	(108)	(972)
Balance on December 31, 1994	$6,528	$8,446	$8,450	$2,504	$ 97	$17,482	$8,543	$26,025

EXHIBIT 2

Asset and Liability Management Interest Rate Swaps

(Dollars in millions, Average maturity in years)	Market Value	Total	Maturities						Average Maturity
			1995	1996	1997	1998	1999	After 1999	
Asset Conversion Swaps									
Receive fixed generic	$(188)								1.14
Notional value		$ 6,528	$3,137	$ 2,705	$ 575	$ 3	—	$108	
Weighted average receive rate		4.52%	4.30%	4.63%	4.45%	6.58%	—	8.25%	
Weighted average pay rate		5.84							
Receive fixed amortizing	(619)								2.61
Notional value		$ 8,450	$ 110	$186	$6,140	$2,014	—	—	
Weighted average receive rate		4.92%	5.73%	5.69%	4.85%	5.01%	—	—	
Weighted average pay rate		6.02							
Receive Fixed CMO	(149)								2.25
Notional value		$ 2,504	$708	$488	$349	$474	$485	—	
Weighted average receive rate		5.12%	5.12%	5.10%	5.11%	5.07%	5.21%	—	
Weighted average pay rate		6.10							
Total asset conversion swaps	$(956)								2.01
Notional value		$17,482	$3,955	$ 3,379	$7,064	$2,491	$485	$108	
Weighted average receive rate		4.80%	4.49%	4.76%	4.83%	5.02%	5.21%	8.25%	
Weighted average pay rate		5.96							

Liability Conversion Swaps

	Fair Value	Total							
Pay fixed generic	$223								1.69
Notional value		$8,446	$110	$8,037	$125	$100	—	$74	
Weighted average pay rate		6.39%	6.64%	6.44%	4.52%	5.12%	—	5.37%	
Weighted average receive rate		5.35							
Pay fixed CMO	7								2.08
Notional value		$97	$24	$19	$14	$40	—	—	
Weighted average pay rate		4.44%	4.44%	4.44%	4.44%	4.44%	—	—	
Weighted average receive rate		6.19							
Total liability conversion swaps	$230								1.69
Notional value		$8,543	$134	$8,056	$139	$140	—	$74	
Weighted average pay rate		6.37%	6.25%	6.44%	4.51%	4.93%	—	5.37%	
Weighted average receive rate		5.35							
Total	$(726)								
Notional value		$25,025	$4,089	$11,435	$7,203	$2,631	$485	$182	
Weighted average receive rate		4.98%							
Weighted average pay rate		6.10							

Floating rates represent the last repricing and will change in the future based on movements in one, three or six month LIBOR rates.

Maturities are based on interest rates implied by the forward curve on December 31, 1994, and may differ from actual maturities, depending on future interest rate movements and resultant prepayment patterns.

In addition to the above asset and liability management interest rate swaps, on December 31, 1994, the Corporation had approximately $1.2 billion notional of net receive fixed generic interest rate swaps associated primarily with the credit card securitization. On December 31, 1994, these positions had an unrealized market value of negative $115 million. The weighted average receive rate is 5.19 percent and the pay rate on December 31, 1994 was 6.94 percent.

The unrealized depreciation in the estimated value of the ALM swap portfolio should be viewed in the context of the overall balance sheet. The value of any single component of the balance sheet or off-balance-sheet position should not be viewed in isolation. For example, the value of core deposits and other fixed-rate longer-term liabilities increased as interest rates rose, offsetting the decline in value of swaps and other fixed-rate assets. The overall impact of a 100-basis point parallel increase in interest rates from December 31, 1994, levels is estimated to have an insignificant impact on the market value of equity.

Exhibit 3 (pages 254 and 255) represents the Corporation's interest rate gap position on December 31, 1994. Based on contractual maturities or repricing dates, or anticipated dates where no contractual maturity or repricing date exists, interest sensitive assets and liabilities are placed in maturity categories. The Corporation's negative cumulative interest rate gap position in the near term reflects the strong customer-deposit gathering franchise which provides a relatively stable core deposit base. These available funds have been deployed in longer-term interest-earning assets including certain loans and securities. A gap analysis is limited in its usefulness as it represents a one-day position which is continually changing and not necessarily indicative of the Corporation's position at any other time. Additionally, the gap analysis does not consider the many factors accompanying interest rate movements.

Trading Activities

The Corporation maintains trading positions in a variety of cash and derivative financial instruments. The Corporation offers a number of products to customers, as well as enters into transactions for its own account. In setting trading strategies, the Corporation manages these activities to maximize trading revenues while at the same time taking controlled risk.

Capital markets activities are managed in the Capital Markets Group and are conducted in two principal divisions, NationsBanc Capital Markets, Inc. (NCMI) and NationsBanc-CRT. Major trading sites include Charlotte, Chicago, New York, and London.

NCMI underwrites, trades, and distributes debt and equity securities. Its business activities include both customer and proprietary trading activities. Additionally, NCMI is a primary dealer in U.S. government securities.

NationsBanc-CRT manages the Corporation's derivatives and foreign exchange business activities. Interest rate derivatives are the primary component of NationsBanc-CRT's customer-based and proprietary derivative products. Other derivative products consist primarily of commodity-based transactions.

Note 4 to the consolidated financial statements details the individual components of the Corporation's trading assets and liabilities. Additionally, Exhibit 4 (page 256) provides information on the Corporation's derivative dealer positions.

Credit Risk—Within the Corporation's Credit Policy organization, a group is dedicated to managing credit risks associated with trading activities. The Corporation maintains trading positions in a number of markets and with a variety of counterparties or obligors (counterparties). To limit credit exposure arising from such transactions, the Corporation evaluates the credit standing of counterparties, establishes limits for the total exposure to any one counterparty, monitors exposure against the established limits and monitors trading portfolio composition to manage concentration.

The Corporation's exposure to credit risk from derivative financial instruments is represented by the fair value of instruments. Credit risk amounts represent the replacement cost the Corporation could incur should counterparties with contracts in a gain position completely fail to perform under the terms of those contracts and any collateral underlying the

EXHIBIT 3

Interest Rate Gap Analysis
December 31, 1994

(Dollars in millions)	Interest Sensitive					Over 12 Months and Noninterest-Sensitive	Total
	30-Day	3-Month	6-Month	12-Month	Total		
Earning assets							
Loans and leases, net of unearned income	$45,946	$ 9,243	$ 4,713	$ 6,343	$ 66,245	$36,122	$102,367
Securities held for investment	49	88	222	4,485	4,844	12,956	17,800
Securities available for sale	523	1,844	407	152	2,926	5,099	8,025
Loans held for sale	318	—	—	—	318	—	318
Time deposits placed and other short-term investments	1,530	572	52	3	2,157	2	2,159
Other earning assets	21,053	—	—	—	21,053	—	21,053
Total	69,419	11,747	5,394	10,983	97,543	54,179	$151,722

Interest-bearing liabilities

Savings	9,037	—	—	—	9,037	—	$9,037
NOW and money market deposit accounts	21,881	—	—	—	21,881	7,871	29,752
Consumer CDs and IRAs	3,212	3,785	4,992	4,881	16,870	8,070	24,940
Negotiated CDs, public funds, and other time deposits	776	725	614	345	2,460	298	2,758
Foreign time deposits	5,754	1,542	3,513	1,794	12,603	—	12,603
Borrowed funds and trading account liabilities	39,614	1,449	2,188	2,304	45,555	—	45,555
Long-term debt and obligations under capital leases	552	1,605	2	565	2,724	5,764	8,488
Total	80,826	9,106	11,309	9,889	111,130	22,003	133,133
Noninterest-bearing, net	—	—	—	—	—	18,589	18,589
Total	80,826	9,106	11,309	9,889	111,130	40,592	$151,722
Interest rate gap	(11,407)	2,641	(5,915)	1,094	(13,587)	13,587	
Effect of asset and liability management interest rate swaps, futures and other off-balance-sheet items	(6,289)	(198)	(2,306)	2,662	(6,131)	6,131	
Adjusted interest rate gap	$(17,696)	$ 2,443	$ (8,221)	$ 3,756	$(19,718)	$19,718	
Cumulative adjusted interest rate gap	$(17,696)	$(15,253)	$(23,474)	$(19,718)			

E X H I B I T   4

Derivatives-Dealer Positions
December 31

| December 31 | 1994 | | 1993 | |
(Dollars in millions)	Contract/ Notional	Credit Risk Amount*	Contract/ Notional	Credit Risk Amount*
Interest Rate Contracts				
Swaps	$ 45,179	$ 531	$15,758	$185
Futures and forwards	124,620	30	32,503	—
Written options	114,928	—	58,499	—
Purchased options	118,839	481	55,616	129
Foreign Exchange Contracts				
Swaps	470	—	258	7
Spot, futures and forwards	26,987	221	12,516	106
Written options	13,398	—	8,058	—
Purchased options	13,507	167	8,051	134
Commodity Contracts				
Swaps	570	74	1,470	51
Futures and forwards	1,984	1	1,661	31
Written options	12,608	—	6,696	—
Purchased options	11,591	309	7,339	313
		$1,814		$956

* Represents the replacement cost the Corporation could incur should counterparties with contracts in a gain position to the Corporation completely fail to perform under the terms of those contracts. Amounts include interest.

contracts proves to be of no value to the Corporation. Counterparties are subject to the credit approval and credit monitoring policies and procedures of the Corporation. Certain instruments require the Corporation or the counterparty to maintain collateral for all or part of the exposure. Generally, such collateral is in the form of cash or other highly liquid instruments. Limits for exposure to any particular counterparty are established and monitored. In certain jurisdictions, counterparty risk is also reduced through the use of legally enforceable master netting arrangements which allow the Corporation to settle positions with the same counterparty on a net basis. The contract or notional amounts associated with the Corporation's dealer derivative positions are reflected in Exhibit 4. The notional or contract amounts indicate the total volume of transactions and significantly exceed the amount of the Corporation's credit or market risk associated with these instruments. The credit risk amount for the instruments reflected in Exhibit 4 is measured by the Corporation as the positive replacement cost on December 31, 1994 and 1993. Of the credit risk amount reported in Exhibit 4, $354 million and $343 million relates to exchange-traded instruments for 1994 and 1993, respectively. Because exchange-traded instruments conform to standard terms and are subject to policies set by the exchange involved, including counterparty approval, margin requirements and security deposit requirements, the credit risk to the Corporation is minimal.

Market Risk—Market risk arises due to fluctuations in interest rates and market prices that may result in changes in the values of trading instruments. The Corporation manages its exposure to market risk resulting from trading activities through a risk management function. Each major trading site is monitored by these risk management units.

Daily earnings at risk limits, which have been approved by the Corporation's Finance Committee, are generally allocated to the business units. In addition to limits placed on these individual business units, limits are imposed on the risks certain individual traders may take. Risk positions are monitored by line, risk management function personnel and senior management on a daily basis.

Daily earnings at risk measures the rate of loss for a one-day, three-standard deviation movement in market prices if traders are unable to rehedge. In addition to these daily earnings at risk simulations, portfolios which have significant option positions are stress tested continually to simulate the potential loss that might occur due to unexpected market movements in each market. Limits are also established by product for losses which could result in these stress scenarios.

Notes to Financial Statements[9]

Note 4. Trading Account Assets and Liabilities

The market values on December 31 and the average market values for the year ended December 31, 1994, of the components of trading account assets and liabilities were (dollars in millions):

	1994	1993	1994 Average
Securities owned			
U.S. Treasury securities	$ 5,968	$ 8,084	$ 7,713
Securities of other U.S. government agencies and corporations	1,185	885	1,322
Certificates of deposit, bankers' acceptances, and commercial paper	371	703	409
Corporate debt	581	194	722
Other securities	259	165	285
Total securities owned	8,364	10,031	10,451
Derivatives-dealer positions	1,577	579	1,158
Total trading account assets	$ 9,941	$10,610	$11,609
Short sales			
U.S. Treasury securities	$ 9,352	$ 7,542	$ 9,840
Securities of other U.S. government agencies and corporations	182	224	550
Corporate debt	278	—	134
Other securities	—	2	2
Total short sales	9,812	7,768	10,526
Derivatives-dealer positions	1,614	531	1,063
Total trading account liabilities	$11,426	$ 8,299	$11,589

9. Ibid, pp. 66, 74, and 75.

A discussion of the Corporation's trading activities is presented . . . including Exhibit 4. An analysis of the revenues associated with the Corporation's trading activities is presented in the table in the noninterest income section [not here included].

The net change in the unrealized gain or loss on trading securities held on December 31, 1994, included in noninterest income for 1994, was a loss of $3 million.

Derivatives-dealer positions presented in the exhibit above represent the market values of interest rate, foreign exchange, and commodity products including swap, futures, forward, and option contracts associated with the Corporation's trading derivatives activities.

A swap contract is an agreement between two parties to exchange cash flows based on specified underlying notional amounts and indices. A futures or forward contract is an agreement to buy or sell a quantity of a financial instrument or commodity at a predetermined future date and rate or price. An option contract is an agreement that conveys to the purchaser the right, but not the obligation, to buy or sell a quantity of a financial instrument or commodity at a predetermined rate or price at a time in the future.

These agreements can be transacted on an organized exchange or directly between parties.

Note 14. Fair Values of Financial Instruments

Statement of Financial Accounting Standards No. 107, *Disclosures About Fair Value of Financial Instruments* (SFAS No. 107), requires the disclosure of the estimated fair value of financial instruments. The fair value of a financial instrument is the amount at which the instrument could be exchanged in a current transaction between willing parties, other than in a forced or liquidation sale. Quoted market prices, if available, are utilized as estimates of the fair values of financial instruments. Because no quoted market prices exist for a significant part of the Corporation's financial instruments, the fair values of such instruments have been derived based on management's assumptions with respect to future economic conditions, the amount and timing of future cash flows, and estimated discount rates. The estimation methods for individual classifications of financial instruments are more fully described below. Different assumptions could significantly affect these estimates. Accordingly, the net realizable values could be materially different from the estimates presented below.

In addition, the estimates are only indicative of individual financial instruments' values and should not be considered an indication of the fair values of the combined Corporation. The provisions of SFAS No. 107 do not require the disclosure of nonfinancial instruments, including intangible assets. The value of the Corporation's intangibles such as franchise, credit card and trust relationships, and mortgage servicing rights, is significant.

Short-Term Financial Instruments   The carrying value of short-term financial instruments, including cash and cash equivalents, federal funds sold and purchased, resell and repurchase agreements, and commercial paper and short-term borrowings, approximate the fair value. These financial instruments generally expose the Corporation to limited credit risk and have no stated maturities, or have an average maturity of less than 30 days and carry interest rates that approximate market.

Financial Instruments Traded in the Secondary Market with Quoted Market Prices or Dealer Quotes Securities held for investment, securities available for sale, loans held for sale, trading account instruments, and long-term debt which are actively traded in the secondary market have been valued using quoted market prices.

Loans Fair values were estimated for groups of similar loans based upon type of loan, credit quality, and maturity. The fair value of fixed-rate loans was estimated by discounting estimated cash flows using corporate bond rates adjusted by credit risk and servicing costs for commercial and real estate commercial and construction loans; and for consumer loans, the Corporation's December 31 origination rate for similar loans. Contractual cash flows for consumer loans were adjusted for prepayments using published industry data. For variable-rate loans, the carrying amount was considered to approximate fair value. Where credit deterioration has occurred, cash flows for fixed- and variable-rate loans have been reduced to incorporate estimated losses. Where quoted market prices were available, primarily for certain residential mortgage loans, such market prices were utilized as estimates for fair values.

Deposits The fair value for fixed-rate deposits with stated maturities was calculated by discounting the difference between the cash flows on a contractual basis and current market rates for instruments with similar maturities. For variable-rate deposits, the carrying amount was considered to approximate fair value.

The book and fair values of financial instruments on December 31 were (dollars in millions):

	1994		1993	
	Book Value	**Fair Value**	**Book Value**	**Fair Value**
Financial Assets				
Cash and cash equivalents	$ 9,582	$ 9,582	$ 7,649	$ 7,649
Time deposits placed and other short-term investments	2,159	2,159	1,479	1,479
Securities held for investment	17,800	17,101	13,584	13,604
Securities available for sale	8,025	8,025	15,470	15,470
Loans held for sale	318	318	1,697	1,697
Trading account assets	9,941	9,941	10,610	10,610
Federal funds sold and securities purchased under agreements to resell	11,112	11,112	7,044	7,044
Loans, net of unearned income				
Commercial and foreign	46,649	46,375	41,786	41,812
Real estate commercial and construction	10,330	10,227	11,495	11,072
Residential mortgage	17,244	16,251	12,689	12,898
Credit card	4,753	4,782	3,728	3,839
Other consumer and home equity	20,511	20,328	19,326	19,413
Allowance for credit losses	(2,186)	—	(2,169)	—
Financial Liabilities				
Deposits				
Noninterest-bearing	21,380	21,380	20,723	20,723
Savings	9,037	9,037	8,784	8,784
NOW and money market deposit accounts	29,752	29,752	30,881	30,881
Consumer CDs	19,369	19,001	17,850	17,970
Other time deposits	20,932	20,721	12,875	13,014
Federal funds purchased and securities sold under agreements to repurchase	25,970	25,970	28,371	28,371
Commercial paper	2,519	2,519	2,056	2,056
Other short-term borrowings	5,640	5,640	5,522	5,522
Trading account liabilities	11,426	11,426	8,299	8,299
Long-term debt	8,464	8,199	8,325	8,774

Off-Balance-Sheet Financial Instruments   For a presentation of the fair value of the Corporation's derivative-dealer positions, see Note 4. The fair value of the Corporation's asset and liability management and other interest rate swaps is presented in Exhibit 2.

The fair value of liabilities on binding commitments to lend is based on the net present value of cash-flow streams using fee rates currently charged for similar agreements versus original contractual fee rates, taking into account the creditworthiness of the borrowers. The fair value was a liability of $92 million and $111 million on December 31, 1994 and 1993, respectively.

CHAPTER 7

Valuation—Concepts[1]

John T. Smith

Determining the fair value of derivatives as well as other financial instruments is crucial in applying currently applicable financial accounting standards. In many cases, fair value is the basis required for recording derivatives as discussed in Chapters 3, 4, and 5. In those cases where derivatives are recorded at amounts other than fair value in the basic financial statements, disclosure of fair values in the accompanying footnotes is required as discussed in Chapter 6. Fair values are also important in managing and controlling derivative positions as discussed in Chapter 9.

In recent years, the Financial Accounting Standards Board (FASB) has defined fair value in several different statements relating to different aspects of accounting. In Statement No. 107, *Disclosures about Fair Values of Financial Instruments,* (1991) the board said that

---

1. This chapter is adopted with permission from *Financial Instruments: Fair Value Considerations* (Wilton, CT: Deloitte & Touche, LLP, 1992).

the fair value of a financial instrument is the amount at which the instrument could be exchanged in a current transaction between willing parties, other than in a forced liquidation sale. If a quoted market price is available for an instrument, the fair value to be disclosed for that instrument is the product of the number of trading units of the instrument times the market price. [Paragraph 6]

Substantially the same definition is used by the board in other statements, including SFAS No. 115, *Accounting for Certain Investments in Debt and Equity Securities* (1993); SFAS No. 121, *Accounting for the Impairment of Long-Lived Assets and for Long-Lived Assets to Be Disposed Of* (1995); and SFAS No. 122, *Accounting for Mortgaging Servicing Rights* (1995). That definition is also included in a proposed statement, *Accounting for Transfers and Servicing of Financial Assets and Extinguishment of Liabilities* (1995). Accordingly, most accountants view the above definition to be generally accepted.

A problem arises, however, in determining the fair value of derivatives for which quoted market prices are not available. In SFAS No. 107 the board said:

Quoted market prices, if available, are the best evidence of the fair value of financial instruments. If quoted market prices are not available, management's best estimate of fair value may be used based on the quoted market price of a financial instrument with similar characteristics or on valuation techniques (for example, the present value of estimated cash flows using a discount rate commensurate with the risks involved, option pricing models, or matrix pricing models) . . . [Paragraph 11]

Similar provisions are included in the other statements mentioned above. SFAS No. 107, in addition in its Appendix A provides additional guidance in the form of examples for estimating fair value for financial instruments for which quoted market prices are not available.

In issuing SFAS No. 107 requiring disclosure of fair values of all financial instruments, the FASB recognized the concern by many of its constituents that estimating fair values in the absence of quotes in active trading markets could be difficult and perhaps impossible in some instances. The FASB had been interested in encouraging entities to make their best efforts in disclosing fair values. Accordingly, Appendix A to SFAS No. 107 allows consideration of several alternatives in estimating fair values. These include both entrance values (current acquisition cost) and exit values (current disposition proceeds).[2]

Recently adopted SFAS No. 125[3] defines "fair value" by repeating most of the wording contained in the SFAS No. 107 definition but does not repeat the Appendix A guidance and includes the following wording which does not appear in SFAS No. 107—"In measuring financial liabilities at fair value by discounting estimated future cash flows, an objective is to use discount rates at which those liabilities could be settled in an arm's-length transaction." (Paragraph 44). Thus SFAS No. 125 can be read to adopt an exclusive exit value approach, thus ruling out entrance values in measurement and recognition of assets and liabilities created in securitizations and other transfers of financial assets with continuing involvement by the seller.

Guidance in Appendix A of SFAS No. 107, which presumably remains appropriate for fair value disclosures, includes, among others, the following guidelines, based on entry values for valuing liabilities:

> Using an entity's current incremental rate of borrowing for a similar liability. (Paragraph 28)
>
> The discount rate could be the current rate offered for similar deposits with the same remaining maturity. (Paragraph 29)

---

2. SFAS No. 107 also allows exception to disclosure of fair value for those financial instruments for which fair value can not be practicably measured, as discussed in Chapter 6.
3. See discussion in Chapter 5.

And the following guidance among others for valuing loans held:

Current prices for similar loans in the entity's own lending activities. (Paragraph 26)

When estimating fair values of liabilities by discounting expected future cash flows, SFAS No. 107 allows the use of "the rate that an entity would have to pay to acquire essentially risk-free assets to extinguish the obligation in accordance with the requirements of Statement 76." (Paragraph 25.) That approach is no longer available after December 31, 1996, because SFAS No. 125, which rescinds the insubstance defeasance provisions of SFAS No. 76, deletes the quoted wording from SFAS No. 107 to conform.

The guidance on determining fair values contained in this chapter and in Chapter 8 was prepared in the context of the requirements of SFAS No. 107. Accordingly, the author does not believe the guidance describing the use of entry values (including replacement cost) is appropriate for measuring assets and liabilities in connection with SFAS No. 125. Nor does SFAS No. 125 provide a practicability exemption. Furthermore, whether entry values will continue to be appropriate for disclosures under SFAS No. 107 is questionable. However, at the date this was written, practice has not yet settled on what is acceptable.

In June, 1996, the FASB issued an Exposure Draft of a Proposed Statement of Financial Accounting Standards, *Accounting for Derivative and Similar Financial Instruments and for Hedging Activities*. The draft proposes to amend the definition of "fair value" in SFAS No. 107 to conform with SFAS No. 125, but it would leave the guidance in Appendix A intact. In proposing those amendments to SFAS No. 107, the FASB's intention is unclear. There is an apparent inconsistency between a definition that requires settlement value for liabilities while continuing the entrance values guidance of Appendix A. That matter may be clarified before a final statement is issued.

In the balance of this chapter discussion of valuation techniques focuses primarily on exit values. Discussion about the use of entry values and replacement costs to approximate fair values and of the practicability exemption are made solely in the context of disclosures under SFAS No. 107, and without consideration of any possible amendments.

Although not all financial instruments are derivatives, accounting for derivatives requires knowledge about valuation of most financial instruments. Therefore, this chapter discusses valuation of those financial instruments.

MARKET CONSIDERATIONS

The Markets

The markets in which derivatives and other financial instruments are traded can be distinguished as the following four principal types. Each of these markets is a source for obtaining fair values.

Exchange Markets

Exchange or "auction" markets, which provide visibility, liquidity, and order to the trading of a particular financial instrument, will provide much of the data needed to implement the statement. Listed stocks, options, some futures contracts, and many fixed-income securities are available on public exchanges from which closing prices and volume levels are available.

Dealer Markets

Some dealer markets, such as the NASDAQ–National Market Issues, function similar to exchanges, and closing prices and volumes are reported. Other dealer markets also exist for commercial and industrial loans, loans to less developed countries, mortgage-backed securities, asset-backed securities, corporate bonds, and municipal and federal securities. Market quotations for these securities are principally in the form of bid and ask amounts, between which there may be a sizable difference, that would be negotiated by the market participants. This adds an element of uncertainty to the concept of fair valuation for these securities. Generally, these quotations will be the best indication of a financial instrument's fair value; however, if there is evidence that suggests that the instrument in question is significantly mispriced by a dealer or there is a wide range of price estimates from different dealers (as might be the case for a junk bond that is not actively traded), the entity may choose to use another indicator in the determination of fair value. An internally developed model may be appropriate in these circumstances.

An additional complication exists when an entity holds a block of such securities that is large enough to dilute the price of a security if it were to be traded as a unit.

Brokered Markets

Brokered markets, in which intermediaries attempt to match buyers and sellers but do not trade for their own accounts, generally provide less data than either of the above markets. Parties on either side of a transaction are generally unaware of the other side's price requirements, although prices of comparable completed transactions may be available.

Principal-to-Principal Markets

In principal-to-principal transactions, transactions are conducted independently, with no intermediary and little if any public information available to estimate market price. Interest rate swaps between principals are an example of a financial instrument that is available only in principal-to-principal markets.

Market Indicators

There are a number of different approaches that can be used to obtain fair value estimates. The more significant market indicators are discussed below.

Market Quotations

Market quotations are, in reality, just estimates. A market is determined only when an actual exchange takes place. The price of the most recent exchange does not necessarily mean the next transaction will settle for the same amount. An active market, however, generally will provide a good indication of market value and, if it exists, the FASB requires it to be used.

Financial instruments that are actively traded in exchange markets have readily available closing prices and volume levels that can be used for valuing financial instruments. Clearly, quoted market prices in an active market are the best evidence of the fair value of financial instruments. Financial instruments that trade in dealer markets generally have bid and ask prices, which are available to potential purchasers.

The FASB definition of fair value requires that market quotations be used if they are available. Market quotations can generally be obtained from the exchange markets, the dealer markets, and the broker markets. It may be difficult, however, to obtain quotations from the principal-to-principal markets. In many instances quotations will not be available for a particular instrument or may not be considered reliable. In SFAS No. 107, paragraph 22, the FASB recognizes that quotations may not always be reliable and permits the use of other estimates of value in these circumstances, stating in part: "For financial instruments that do not trade regularly, or that trade only in principal-to-principal markets, an entity should provide its best estimate of fair value."

It may also be difficult to estimate the fair value of financial instruments that trade only in brokered markets. In some cases, financial instruments are custom-tailored for a particular entity. For these instruments, there may not be a consensus view of fair value and it may be necessary to use indicators other than market quotations to determine fair value. An entity should select the method that provides the best estimate of fair value to the extent practicable. Some of the more common indicators most likely to be relevant when market quotations are not available or reliable are discussed next.

Comparable Quoted Market Prices of Similar Financial Instruments

If no quoted market price exists for a particular category of financial instruments, the price of a similar instrument that is traded—with adjustments for differences in credit risk, interest rate, maturity, and prepayment risk as applicable—might be the best indicator. The methodology for estimating fair value based on adjusted prices of similar instruments is sometimes referred to as matrix pricing.

As an alternative to quoted market prices of similar instruments, which is an exit value approach, an entity could estimate fair value on entrance prices under SFAS No. 107. A bank, for example, could value its loans by basing the prices on similar instruments that it currently offers as part of its own lending activities.

Independent Appraisals and Valuations

Another approach that can be used when quoted market prices are not available is to obtain valuations from appraisers or specialist firms that offer pricing services for investments. A variation of this approach would be to obtain information about market data from a database service. Such data could be used as a basis for making a computation of fair value.[4]

---

4. There is a cost for database services, and if the fair value determination is solely for disclosure purposes the cost-benefit should be considered under the practicability provision of SFAS No. 107 relating to such required disclosures as discussed in Chapter 6.

Calculations

There are also different models and formulas that can be used to calculate fair values.

Present Value or Discounted Cash Flow Methods   For many financial instruments, particularly loans and notes that are originated by the entity itself and not purchased on an exchange market, the net present value of the future expected cash flows may be an appropriate (and, possibly, the only) indicator of fair value. Present value models require an assessment of cash flows, interest rates, and risks that affect the timing and amount of cash flows. This assessment involves considerable judgment because there are many different variables that must be used in present value models.

Options Pricing Methods   There are a number of models that can be used to price financial instruments with options characteristics. A key factor used in these models is the estimate of volatility. Other factors that are required to estimate value include the interest rate level, the relationship of an option's strike price to the underlying stock's price, and the time remaining before an option contract expires.

Replacement Value   Under this method available under SFAS No. 107, estimated fair value is determined based on an alternative use of funds. For example, instead of making credit card loans, an entity could invest in federal funds. The federal funds rate would have to be adjusted, however, for operating costs and ancillary income related to the credit card receivables, credit losses, and risk of prepayments to arrive at an equivalent replacement rate.

In some situations, replacement cost might be determined without making a computation. An entity might be able to obtain outside estimates from investment bankers of what it would cost to enter into a similar arrangement. Interest rate swaps and foreign currency contracts are typically custom-tailored financial instruments for which there may be no readily available market price, and an outside assessment of what it would cost to enter into a similar arrangement may be necessary.

Other Methods   There are also other methods that could be used to estimate fair value. For example, fair value could be based on a subsequent sale close to the report date or on a firm commitment to sell financial instruments at a specified price in the near future.

MODELING CONSIDERATIONS

For derivatives and other financial instruments that are not actively traded estimated fair values will, in many instances, be calculated by use of a model. Because any number of approaches could be used to estimate fair value, it will be necessary for the entity to understand the alternatives that are available in order to select appropriate assumptions and techniques to provide the best estimate of value. A number of decisions must be made when using models to estimate value. Such decisions involve the selection of methods, formulas, and assumptions. Each of those decisions requires judgment and will vary depending upon the particular instrument and the selected market reference.

Although the models used to estimate the value of financial instruments differ depending on the type of instrument being valued, most market valuation techniques are founded on arbitrage arguments, which are based on the premise that a risk-free profit cannot occur in the marketplace. Stated simply, if risk-free arbitrage profits cannot occur, the theoretical value of a financial instrument must be equal to the value of an equivalent alternative investment. As conceptual arbitrage arguments are an essential part of the foundation of almost all models, such arguments are identified throughout this section to provide a fuller understanding of the fundamental valuation concepts.

Most of the models that are used to compute the theoretical value of financial instruments are founded on just a few fundamental economic valuation principles, which are as follows:

- **Yield curve considerations** are a key factor in valuing virtually all financial instruments. An understanding of interest rate or yield curve mechanics is essential to an understanding of valuation techniques.

- **Present value methods** are also an important consideration in most valuation models because they provide for the time value of money.

- **Foreign exchange models** consider both exchange rates and relative forward interest rates in the valuation of foreign currency instruments.

- **Options pricing theories** are essential in the valuation of almost all instruments that contain options characteristics.

Present value models and options pricing models are commonly used to value various instruments directly. The results that ordinarily would be produced from each of these fundamental methods usually require adjustment or modification for other market factors such as credit and liquidity. Futures, forward, and foreign exchange valuations are based on present values. They must also consider forward interest rates and, for foreign exchange, relative interest rates in the domestic and foreign country. There are a number of different models that are used indirectly or used in part to value financial instruments. Such other models include yield curve models, prepayment models, and volatility models, which produce data to be used in present value and options pricing models, as applicable.

Models can produce results that range from very precise to rather imprecise estimates depending on the sophistication of the model and the use of simplifying assumptions that facilitate computation. Models can be used to make computations individually or on a portfolio or some other aggregate basis. The accuracy of computations made on an aggregate basis varies depending on the characteristics of the instruments aggregated.

Numerous complex factors must be considered in developing and using models to estimate fair value. Market data must be analyzed, assumptions must be made about future events, and methods to compute estimates must be selected. All of these factors must be understood to make appropriate decisions.

Recognize that no model is a perfect substitute for values evidenced by market transactions, and all models must be adjusted to comprehend the unique characteristics of the instrument being modeled. There is a trade-off between simple, inexpensive models that are easy to use, and complex, sophisticated models that are difficult to use. Regardless of the level of sophistication, a model produces only a theoretical representation of market value. The effectiveness of any model must be judged based on the necessity of obtaining some specified level of precision.

INTEREST RATE MECHANICS

Interest Rates

Before undertaking a discussion of interest rate mechanics, it is important to provide some understanding, from a broad macroeconomic perspective, of the factors that influence the level of interest rates. Interest rates indicate the market's assessment of what a fair return for a cash investment should be, given the current supply and demand for funds. This assessment includes an evaluation of the risk associated with a particular investment alternative at a given point in time, as well as a prediction of what effect various micro- and macroeconomic factors will have on that investment alternative in future periods.

The most basic level of risk associated with a financial transaction is the risk of default. The market evaluates this risk through a variety of mechanisms (such as the rating agencies Moody's and Standard & Poors) that assess the creditworthiness of borrowers and, in effect, the likelihood of default. This rating is translated into a financial cost to the borrower (and return to the holder) by the market and is expressed as a "spread over" (premium to) the risk-free rate that is given only to U.S. government securities (Treasury bills, notes, and bonds). Because Treasury securities are the benchmark used by the market for evaluating credit risk, the Treasury yield curve is the framework used by the market in assigning cost to particular instruments at a given time and over particular time periods.

The Treasury yield curve is a graphic representation of the relationship between Treasury interest rates and time to maturity and is also referred to as the term structure of interest rates. The shape of the Treasury yield curve as it extends out in time is influenced by the market's expectations about the future. The principal component of these expectations is inflation and its likely impact on the real value of an instrument's future cash flows. These expectations include the market's assessment of future political policy, the attractiveness and availability of funds both domestically and abroad, and the future impact of current economic trends. These factors are assessed in the marketplace where buy and sell orders bring the price of an instrument into equilibrium.

Using the Treasury yield curve as a starting point, the market constructs similar yield curves that reflect the risk-adjusted term structure for a particular instrument. In the case of corporate debt securities, this would be a sound theory-based approach to valuation. However, in some cases it may not be possible or desirable to construct a particular yield curve, because of liquidity or information constraints.

Key Interest Rate Concepts

Interest rates are an essential part of any model used to compute an estimate of the fair value of future cash flows. In the absence of an active market for the instrument being valued, the selection of an appropriate interest rate requires considerable judgment and must be founded, in part, on an understanding of interest rate mechanics.

Knowledge of the following concepts is essential to an understanding of interest rate mechanics:

Yield to Maturity

This is the internal rate of return, also referred to as the *accounting rate of return,* which is the rate of interest that equates the estimated periodic future cash flows of an instrument with its cost at acquisition.

Spot Rate

This refers to the prevailing rate of interest for a given maturity. *Spot price* in the market refers to immediate, as opposed to future, delivery. The spot rate for a particular maturity is used to determine the present value of any cash flow in the corresponding future period. The *spot rate* is the yield on a pure discount or zero coupon bond. In mathematical terms, the spot rate at a particular point in time is the geometric mean of consecutive forward rates through that point in time.

Forward Rate

This refers to a future rate of interest. It is the marginal yield between two successive spot rates. The forward rate is sometimes referred to as the implied forward rate because it is computed from, or implied by, spot rates. The forward rate is used to compute the theoretical spot rate for periods in which an actual security does not exist.

The relationship between spot rates (SR) and forward rates (FR) is a function of the following formula (where t = time period):

$$\text{FR}_{t} = \left[\frac{(1 + \text{SR}_{t+1})^{t+1}}{(1 + \text{SR}_{t})^{t}} \right] - 1$$

Yield Curve

Yield curve refers to the relationship between interest rates and time to maturity. The yield curve is also referred to as the *term structure of interest rates*. It is actually the graph of the relationship between the yield on Treasury securities or some other homogeneous group of securities and the time to maturity. The spot rate term structure or spot rate yield curve is a set of spot rates arranged by maturity.

Yield curves could be constructed for many different interest-bearing instruments. However, because of volume and liquidity constraints and lack of availability and other limitations on market information, it may not be possible or desirable to construct a particular yield curve. Perhaps the best known and most widely referred to yield curve is the U.S. Treasury yield curve. It shows the yields or spot rates of various U.S. Treasury bonds maturing over a long period of time. The curve is derived from the market prices of zero coupon Treasury securities and includes coupon-bearing securities, appropriately adjusted. In constructing the curve, *on-the-run* issues, which are current issue Treasury securities, should be used because they have greater liquidity than *off-the-run,* which are older issues and require higher yields because of their lower liquidity. In deriving the Treasury yield curve, adjustments must also be made to factor in the various points on the curve for which there is no corresponding Treasury instrument. Such adjustments are based on the implied forward rates. The Treasury yield curve is frequently used as a starting point in the selection of a discount rate because it is considered to be a risk-free rate. To arrive at a market rate, adjustments must be made to it to comprehend credit and other risks that may be inherent in a particular financial instrument.

The shape of the yield curve is influenced by risk and expectations. The theories that attempt to explain the shape of the curve are beyond the scope of this discussion. Recognize, however, that the shape of the curve at a point in time is an important factor in estimating value at that point in time.

Applying Interest Rate Concepts

For illustrative purposes, a spot yield curve is shown in Figure 7–1 based on rates shown in Table 7–1.

FIGURE 7–1

Spot Yield Curve

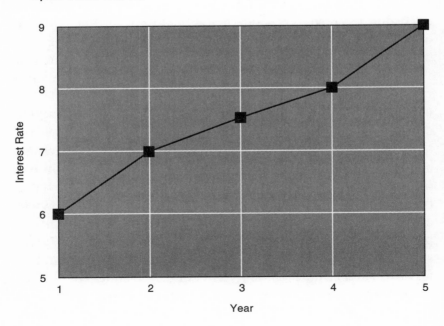

TABLE   7 – 1

Rates and Present Value Factors

			Present Value Factor	
Period	Spot Rate	Forward Rate	Spot	Forward
1	0.0600	0.06000	0.94340	0.94340
2	0.0700	0.08009	0.87344	0.85719
3	0.0750	0.08507	0.80496	0.78276
4	0.0800	0.09514	0.73503	0.69522
5	0.0900	0.13093	0.64993	0.54052

Each point depicted on the spot yield curve shown in Figure 7–1 represents the rate corresponding to the time periods shown in Table 7–1. The table also shows the corresponding present value factors for each series of interest rates. These present value factors are presented because they are used later in computations to help clarify differences between coupon or stated rates, spot rates, and forward rates.

Most accountants are familiar with the mechanics of computing present values and with the concept of the time value of money. They are generally not familiar, however, with concepts discussed previously that are used to measure value. These concepts can be best understood by example.

Assume that a zero coupon bond, a coupon bond, and an amortizing bond each have a five-year life and a nine percent annual stated interest rate, and are not subject to prepayment or credit risk. The cash flows associated with each bond are shown in Table 7–2 along with their present values, each computed to be $100,000 using the stated interest rate.

In the example, the term to maturity, stated interest rate, and present values using the stated interest rate are the same for each bond. The fact that all of these factors are equal does not suggest that the economic values or fair values also

TABLE 7-2

Cash Flows (Based on a 9 Percent Interest Rate)

Period	Zero Coupon	Coupon Bond	Amortizing Bond
1	$ 0.00	$ 9,000.00	$ 25,709.24
2	0.00	9,000.00	25,709.24
3	0.00	9,000.00	25,709.24
4	0.00	9,000.00	25,709.24
5	153,862.39	109,000.00	25,709.24
Present value @ 9%	$100,000.00	$100,000.00	$100,000.00

are equal. Value is not determined by computing a present value using the stated interest rate. To estimate value, the timing of the cash flows must be considered in relation to the spot rates in the corresponding time periods.

Assuming that the yield curve shown in Figure 7–1 represents the current risk-free interest rates or spot rates at the time the bonds are sold, the market prices of the bonds will be determined by such rates. Discounting the cash flows using such spot rates results in different values or market prices for each of the bonds. The results shown in Table 7–3 indicate that, given the term structure of interest rates specified in Table 7–1, the cash flows for the amortizing bond are the most valuable followed by the cash flows for the coupon bond. The reason for the difference in value is simply that the spot rates shown favor early payments over later payments. Said another way, in a normal (positive sloping) yield curve environment, cash flows received in early periods are present value weighted above cash flows received in later periods.

Table 7–3 also shows the yield to maturity or internal rate of return calculated by equating the market values computed using the spot rates with the future cash flows. Each bond shows a different yield to maturity. The yield to maturity

TABLE 7-3

Cash Flows (Based on a 9 Percent Interest Rate)

Period	Zero Coupon	Coupon Bond	Amortizing Bond
1	$ 0.00	$ 8,490.57	$ 24,254.00
2	0.00	7,860.95	22,455.45
3	0.00	7,244.65	20,694.92
4	0.00	6,615.27	18,897.06
5	$100,000.00	70,842.52	16,709.24
Market value @ spot rate	$100,000.00	$101,053.95	$103,010.67
Yield to maturity	9.00%	8.73%	7.87%

and spot rate are the same only for the zero coupon bond because its duration is equivalent to its life (that is, there is a single cash flow at maturity). The yield to maturity for the amortizing bond and the coupon bond differ from the spot rate at maturity because their yields are weighted by the different rates that are present when their cash flows are due.

In the example, the differences between the yield to maturity and the spot rate at the five-year point on the yield curve do not represent a spread to the curve. All of the yield to maturity rates are computed based on the average spot rates weighted by the cash flows. Therefore, in this example it is not possible to have a spread to the yield curve.

From a valuation perspective, yield to maturity is a difficult statistic to interpret. It is a better indicator of value than the stated rate or coupon rate because it equates price with future cash flows. Yield to maturity is deficient as a valuation tool, however, because it represents an average return on each cash flow computed without consideration of the term structure of interest rates. As an average, it has no direct relationship to any point on the yield curve. It can be used, however, to determine a spread to the yield curve. If there were a spread to the yield curve in the examples presented, the prices would have been different. In such instances, the spread to the yield curve can be determined by computing the yield to maturity based on price and comparing it to the yield to maturity based on the risk-free spot rates.

This is a rather simple example in which the impact of the yield curve can be computed rather easily. The impact on the valuation of ignoring the yield curve becomes much more difficult to assess when additional complexity is introduced by aggregating a large number of different instruments, particularly when the instruments contain options characteristics and there is a history of variable credit loss.

Intuition and Arbitrage Arguments

The previous discussion focused on the use of unique period spot rates as a starting point in determining a discounting rate to estimate fair value. That approach can be reasoned intuitively when each cash flow, be it contractual interest or contractual principal due, is viewed as a separate financial instrument. From this perspective it only makes sense that a five-year instrument should be valued using a five-year rate and a three-month instrument should command a three-month rate. The intuitive justification for the use of unique period spot rates is validated by basic arbitrage arguments.

Forward rates and spot rates are related by the formula presented previously. If the relationship did not hold, arbitrage opportunities would be present. As an example, assume an investor is seeking to lend funds for a two-year period. Using the rates in Table 7–1, the investor could lend for two years at 7.00 percent or lend for one year at 6.00 percent and for the second year, using the forward rate, at 8.01 percent. If an investor could make an alternative investment decision and borrow below the two-year forward rate or lend above the two-year forward rate, a risk-free incremental profit could be obtained. If the forward rate were 7.01 percent instead of 8.01

percent, the investor would borrow for one year at the one-year rate, borrow for the second year by writing a one-year forward contract at 7.01 percent, and then invest in the two-year contract at 7.00 percent. If instead the forward rate were 9.01 percent, the investor would borrow for two years at 7.00 percent and lend or invest in the one-year and one-year forward rate.

The investor's return on $100,000 for each of these scenarios would be as follows:

Forward Rate	7.01%	8.01%	9.01%
At two-year rate of 7%	$14,490.00	$(14,490.00)	$(14,490.00)
At one-year rate of 6.00%	(6,000.00)	6,000.00	6,000.00
At forward rate above	(7,430.60)	8,490.60	9,550.60
Arbitrage profit	$ 1,059.40	$ 0.60	$ 1,060.60

In theory, the imbalance between spot and forward rates would cause market participants to enter into arbitrage transactions that would change supply and demand dynamics and cause the rate differential to disappear. The arbitrage argument could be extended to all future periods, validating the theoretical relationship between spot and forward rates.

Although, from a theoretical viewpoint, the use of period spot rates provides a better estimate of value than yield to maturity rates, the arbitrage opportunities identified by the spot rate/forward rate dynamics may not be realizable in the marketplace. Particularly when considering cash flows over a long period of time, there may not be market opportunities to buy and sell cash at specific periods of time in the long run to take advantage of theoretical arbitrage benefits. Accordingly, the spot rate, although theoretically superior, will not always be a true indicator of value.

From this discussion it should be clear that unique period spot rates generally are preferable to a yield to maturity rate or a single spot rate, although the use of a single discount rate generally does not represent the best estimate of value. When the life of the instrument being valued is relatively short—for example, less than five years—the use of a single spot rate may not make a significant impact on the valuation. For longer periods of time, however, the difference generally will be more apparent. It should also be recognized that prices are frequently quoted as a spread to a single Treasury rate. This convention facilitates price quotations but would be viewed as a rather naive approach to valuation.

The use of period spot rates off the U.S. Treasury yield curve is only a starting point in selecting a discount rate. Adjustments must be made to those risk-free rates to consider credit and prepayment risk. Although such adjustments could be based on empirical data—such as a comparison of sales prices with risk-free prices as discussed previously—considerable judgment is required in establishing an appropriate spread to Treasury.

PRESENT VALUE MODELS

Present values refer to discounted future cash flows. As a proxy for fair value, the computation requires an estimate of expected cash flows and a selection of a market discount rate or rates. These factors are influenced by each other. The process of estimating cash flows and selecting the discount rate involves considerable judgment. The computation also requires the selection of a time period and interval of time. Each of these processes is discussed below.

Estimating Cash Flows

Estimating expected future cash flows to be used in present value computations can be done easily if there is no uncertainty surrounding the timing and amount of the cash flows. Most financial instruments, however, have some uncertainty relating to defaults, prepayments, and other options. In many instances, adjustments to contractual cash flows can be made for each of these factors to provide an estimate of expected cash flows. If there is a large population of homogeneous items, those adjustments can usually be based on historical patterns and known trends as well as any unique aspects of the group of financial instruments.

The use of historical data alone, however, may not be sufficient to comprehend uncertainties relating to cash flows if such data contains considerable volatility. In such instances these risks are usually comprehended by also adjusting the discount rate. If, for example, loan loss defaults have been extremely volatile, an adjustment to arrive at expected cash flows based on average historical loan loss experience generally will not fully comprehend the risk. If there is no homogeneous population or if there is no reliable history of prepayments and/or credit losses, it may not be possible to estimate cash flows with reasonable precision. In these instances, adjustments for these uncertainties are also generally made through the discount rate.

Cash-Flow Adjustments versus Rate Adjustments

Valuations based on historical averages are meaningful only in terms of some tolerance or volatility consideration. Such volatility can be comprehended in cash-flow estimates, in the discount rate, or in both of these factors.

There is no standard or guidance that defines the point at which the discount rate should be adjusted instead of adjusting cash flows, and any number of approaches could be used. Theoretically, a number of alternative computations could be made to produce the same valuation. Mechanically, the computation can be made by adjusting the amount and timing of estimated future cash flows, by adjusting the discount rate component, or by adjusting both of these factors in combination. Some of the alternatives for financial instruments having prepayment and/or default risk follow:

If:	*Then:*
Contractual cash flows are used	Use highest discount rate
Adjustments are made for probable prepayments and credit losses	Reduce discount rate
Adjustments are made for reasonably possible prepayments and credit losses	Reduce discount rate further
Adjustments are made for all possible losses including a volatility factor	Use lowest possible or risk-free discount rate

From a theoretical point of view, at one extreme no adjustments for prepayments and credit losses would be made to contractual cash flows, but the discount rate would be adjusted upward to provide the estimated market value. At the other extreme all possible adjustments would be included in estimated future cash flows, and the discount rate would be reduced to a risk-free rate. These factors cannot be adjusted in isolation. All factors must be considered in relation to each other to ensure that the fair value is computed appropriately.

As a practical matter, if historical and other data provide a reasonable basis for estimating prepayments, credit losses, and other factors that affect cash flows, such data should be used to adjust the cash flows. The likelihood of the adjusted cash flows being realized will determine the extent to which additional adjustments of the discount rate are warranted. Because volatility is an indicator of the extent of dispersion around an average, it is difficult to adjust cash flows for the risk of such dispersion. Volatility is usually comprehended by an adjustment of the discount rate.

Selecting the Discount Rate

Discount rates that approximate market can be obtained in a number of ways. They can be constructed by building each component of the rate, starting with the risk-free rate. They also can be obtained directly or developed from market interest rates of comparable instruments. Discount rates are developed by isolating the risk premium of the comparable instrument and adding it to the applicable risk-free rate. The risk premium can be isolated by computing the embedded spread to Treasury or the implied options adjusted spread.

Constructing the Discount Rate

The discount rate could be constructed based on an alternative use of funds concept. Under this approach, the impact of making an alternative investment in a risk-free instrument is quantified for each of the various factors that would be affected by making such an alternative risk-free investment. For example, for funds that are currently invested in mortgage loans, a discount rate would be determined as follows:

1. Use the risk-free Treasury rate for the applicable maturity.

2. Add adjustment for losses and prepayments that would have been anticipated based on historical patterns that are now avoided under the alternative risk-free investment. Alternatively, such estimates could be used to adjust cash flows.

3. Add adjustment for expenses that would have been incurred that are now avoided. Such adjustment should be based on internal cost allocations and generally would require a cost accounting system.

4. Add adjustment for volatility relating to credit and prepayments.

5. Add adjustment for liquidity considerations.

6. Deduct any ancillary benefit of owning the instrument that would be foregone. (For example, had the entity invested in credit card receivables, the credit card fee that provides additional revenue would necessitate an adjustment.)

Each of the factors mentioned above can be derived from historical data and from an analysis of operations. Volatility can be measured by computing the standard deviation based on historical prepayments, defaults, and losses. However, there is no standard that converts the standard deviation to a rate adjustment. To add further complications, the standard deviation does not fully account for these risks. Historical relationships change over time. As a measurement tool, the standard deviation does not differentiate an active, efficient market from an illiquid market and does not consider relationships as they change over time. Accordingly, considerable judgment is required to arrive at volatility adjustment factors. The liquidity adjustment is also highly judgmental. It is based primarily on preference and the needs of the particular entity.

Obtaining Rates Directly from Comparable Instruments

A rather simple yet effective approach in selecting a discount rate is to base the rate on rates being used in the marketplace for the same or similar financial instruments. The discount rate could be selected by reference to coupons or stated interest rates for current issues of the object financial instrument. For example, if single-family 30-year mortgage loans are being made at a 10 percent interest rate, it might be appropriate under SFAS No. 107 to use that rate for recent loans. Linking the discount rate to current issues can be based on the recent borrowing and lending rates of the entity or on rates charged by its competition. This approach is appropriate for current borrowing and lending activities and short-term investments.

Entities are frequently refinancing debt and borrowing or issuing new debt. By reference to current transactions, replacement rates can be used as a basis for determining a discount rate for existing debt instruments of comparable maturity.

Current Instruments versus Seasoned Instruments

The fact that there is a known market interest rate for current transactions of a particular instrument does not automatically mean that it can be used for a seasoned instrument of the same type. If the remaining maturities for the current issues and seasoned instruments differ, the use of the interest rate of the current issues for seasoned instruments will be inappropriate, unless the yield curve is flat. Different maturities require different discount rates. In these circumstances, instead of using the interest rate for the current transaction, it would be more appropriate to select a discount rate based on a spread to the Treasury or some other yield curve, using the points on the yield curve that correspond to the cash flows expected over the remaining life of the instrument being valued. When using a spread to the Treasury, however, it must be recognized that spreads do not remain constant. Therefore, a relationship that was appropriate in the past will not necessarily be representative of the market currently.

Developing Interest Rates from Comparable Instruments

Use of a Treasury or another yield curve may be necessary as a starting point in constructing a discount rate when market quotations are not available for the instrument being valued and there are no similar or comparable instruments in the marketplace that can be referenced.

Use of the Treasury or some other yield curve requires that a proven relationship exist between the instrument being valued and the movement of the yield curve. For example, pricing high-yield bonds off the Treasury yield curve may not make sense if, as a result of credit concerns, the value of the bonds does not change with changes in the yield curve.

Which Curve?   Because interest rates are changing constantly, the date selected to generate the yield curve will impact the market value computation. Ordinarily, the yield curve should be constructed based on rates in effect at the balance sheet date because such rates represent the market at that point in time.

Use of projected or forecasted rates, however, results not in market values or fair market values but in projected values or "what-if" values, and such an approach generally is not considered to be appropriate.

Risk Adjustments Whenever the Treasury curve is used to establish a discount rate, it must be adjusted for risk. There are a number of factors that contribute to the risk premium. Some of these factors, including credit and prepayment risk and the related volatility, have been discussed briefly and are discussed in more detail later in this chapter. Volatility of interest rates is also a factor in assessing risk.

Liquidity or the ability to dispose of or liquidate the instrument in a timely fashion in an efficient orderly market also may be a risk. Adjustments for these factors can be determined by reference to the risk factors implied by other similar instruments or by estimating the risk premium required for each of the factors individually.

Spread to Treasury This refers to the risk adjustment that is typically determined by computing the difference between market rate for a particular security and the risk-free rate. Frequently the price of a similar type of instrument can be determined, but it may not have the same maturity as the instrument being valued. In such instances the spread to Treasury can be computed for the similar instrument and used to adjust the Treasury rate for the comparable maturity of the instrument being valued.

Options Adjusted Spread, or OAS Options adjusted spread refers to the use of a simulation to quantify the value of embedded call options, typically relating to mortgage products. OAS is an extension of the basic present value approach. However, instead of using the rates from a single yield curve, a large number of possible yield curves or interest rate paths are used. Interest paths over the term of the security are generated based on a level of volatility. Prepayment models are used to obtain cash-flow estimates for each interest rate generated in each interest rate path. The OAS is the spread or incremental amount that must be added to each of the interest rates generated to arrive at a discount rate that equates the average of the present values for each path with the market price of the security.

Time Periods and Time Intervals

An important but less complicated requirement of a present value model is the selection of the time period and time interval over which cash flows are estimated and discounted. The time period usually corresponds with the life of the instrument, although a weighted average life may be used when instruments are valued on an aggregate basis.

The time interval refers to the compounding periods (the selection of the period in which interest is discounted [computed] on a simple interest basis). There is no requirement to use any particular period, but monthly compounding or discounting on a monthly basis is usually a better proxy for market value than the use of a longer period. Just as there is a trade-off between adjusting the discount rate and adjusting the cash flows, there is also a trade-off between compounding on a monthly basis and adjusting the discount rate to comprehend discounting on a quarterly, semiannual, or annual basis.

FUTURES, FORWARDS, AND FOREIGN EXCHANGE VALUATION

Foreign exchange valuation encompasses both forward interest rates and relative interest rates in domestic and foreign countries. Relative rates are based on interest rate parity considerations, which are explained in this section. The use of forward interest rates for valuation was explained in the section on interest rates. Since the use of forward rates is applicable to the valuation of forward and futures contracts, the methodology for valuation of such contracts is included in this section to provide a foundation for a better understanding of foreign exchange valuation.

Futures and Forward Contracts Valuation

Futures and forward contracts are agreements for a purchase and sale in the future based on prices established today. These instruments are discussed in more detail in Chapter 8, Valuation—Specific Types of Instruments.

At any given point in time, an investor has the choice between investing in a futures or a forward contract or purchasing the security. Theoretically, any difference between these alternatives will permit risk-free arbitrage profits to occur. Therefore, there should never be a difference between the alternatives. From this perspective, the price of an economic bundle made up of the underlying securities and the benefits derived from holding them should be equivalent to the price of opening and maintaining a futures position in the indexed item. There are essentially three theoretical components to valuing a futures or a forward contract.

Price of the Underlying Instrument The value of a futures or a forward contract is primarily determined by the value of the underlying instrument. The relationship, however, is not one for one because of the existence of investment opportunities that can be undertaken with the proceeds not invested ("tied up") in the underlying instruments themselves. For example, in the case of a futures position where Treasury securities must be held in a margin account as collateral for the futures contract, the rate of change is one plus the prevailing interest rate on those securities. This results from the opportunity to invest the amount of the contract at the riskless Treasury rate.

Time Remaining Until Contract Expiration   The more time remaining until a contract's expiration, the higher the value of the contract if the rate of return that can be earned (from Treasury securities held in a margin account or from alternative investments) is greater than the cash flow stream from a direct investment in the underlying securities.

Comparative Yields on Alternative Strategies   An investment in a futures or a forward contract provides the opportunity to earn a return on the money held by delaying payment until some future date. This is usually the risk-free interest rate on Treasury securities. At the same time, the return on the securities that could have been earned had they been purchased for immediate delivery is given up. When the risk-free rate exceeds the return on the underlying securities, the contract trades at a premium to their price. The higher the risk-free rate, the higher the premium. When the risk-free rate is lower than the return on the underlying securities, the contract will trade at a discount to their price. If the risk-free rate of return is equal to the yield on the underlying securities, the price of the contract will be equivalent to the price of the underlying securities.

The value of a futures or forward contract can be determined by applying the following formula:

Estimated fair value =
[Index price × (1 + Interest rate)] – Dividends

For example, assume the SOP 500 Index is 260 and the futures contract expires in three months. The underlying "basket" of securities, if purchased outright, would pay dividends of $3.25, and Treasury bills also maturing in three months would yield two percent (eight percent annualized, uncom-pounded). The value for that futures contract would be calculated as follows:

Estimated fair value = (260 × 1.02) – $3.25 = $261.95

The fact that these values are not always in equilibrium results in arbitrage opportunities. With state-of-the-art technology designed to spot and act upon pricing discrepancies, program traders have been able to take advantage of profit opportunities that arise when the futures and the cash markets are not in balance.

Foreign Exchange

Before beginning a discussion about how foreign exchange instruments are modeled, a general overview is presented of some of the more significant factors that affect foreign exchange rates.

Foreign exchange rates depend on the demand for and supply of currencies. Factors influencing demand and supply are determined both internationally and domestically. From an international perspective, a country's balance of trade is the most significant long-run factor that affects foreign exchange rates today. The price of a country's currency strengthens with the demand for its currency. When exports exceed imports the demand for a country's currency increases. Other supply and demand factors include capital investments in foreign countries and short-term capital flows related to interest rate differentials. The price of a country's currency is also influenced by the level of monetary reserves available to meet international obligations, which is somewhat akin to a credit factor.

On the domestic side, a number of different factors may affect foreign exchange rates depending on the relative conditions in the applicable foreign countries. The strength of the domestic economy, relative to other countries, impacts the value of a country's currency. The rate of steady real economic growth indicates the health of an economy. Inflation, however, erodes purchasing power and may indicate a weakening of the economy and, therefore, the currency. The relative price level affects the demand for imports and exports, which in turn affects the demand and supply of a country's currency. Finally, government activities such as trade agreements and import/export taxes also affect the relative exchange rates.

Foreign Exchange Valuation

Interest rates and forward exchange rates in one country are related to interest rates and forward exchange rates in another country through arbitrage. There is generally a high correlation between changes in interest rates and exchange rate movements in different countries. The valuation of foreign exchange instruments is based on arbitrage arguments, and valuation models assume that there is no potential for arbitrage in the marketplace. This assumption is valid only if there is a free flow of funds between countries. Trade barriers and other controls on the movement of funds, as well as an expectation of a devaluation or revaluation of a currency, preclude arbitrage profits; accordingly, in such circumstances the normal relationships between interest rates and exchange movements will not be valid.

Economic and political factors determine the spot rates or current exchange rates. Forward foreign exchange rates are determined by the foreign exchange spot rates and the country's interest rates. This means that the currency of the country with the higher interest rate should be trading at a forward rate discount to the currency of a country with lower interest rates. If interest rate differentials are not comprehended in the forward foreign exchange rates, arbitrage opportunities exist.

The relationship between currency spot rates and currency forward rates is expressed by the following formula:

$$FX = Spot \; \frac{1 + FX_{1t}}{1 + FX_{2t}}$$

where,

FX	=	Future foreign exchange price (FX_1/FX_2)
Spot	=	Spot foreign exchange price (FX_1/FX_2)
FX_{1t}	=	Interest rate for country 1 in period t
FX_{2t}	=	Interest rate for country 2 in period t

If this relationship did not hold, arbitrage opportunities would be present. As an example, assume the following interest rates for 90-day Treasury instruments:

	U.S.	Japan
Annual rate	3.91%	5.24%
Quarterly rate	0.98%	1.31%
Spot rate	124.85¥/US$	

Given these assumptions, the forward foreign exchange rate at the end of the first quarter must be:

$$FX = 124.85 \times \frac{1.0131}{1.0098} = 125.26 \ ¥/US\$$$

If the forward foreign currency rate is higher or lower than 125.26 yen/US$, an investor could make alternative investment decisions and obtain a risk-free incremental profit. Consider the following alternative investments:

	US Dollars	Yen
Alternative investments	$100,000	¥12,485,000
Quarterly interest:		
Dollars 0.98%	980	
Yen 1.31%		163,554
Total	$100,980	¥12,648,554

If the forward foreign exchange rate differed from the rate computed of 125.26 yen/US\$, an investor could earn a risk-free profit by entering into a forward market transaction to buy or sell the foreign currency at the exchange rate specified and make a loan or investment, as applicable, in the domestic currency as follows:

Invest (borrow) yen	¥12,485,000	¥12,485,000	¥(12,485,000)
Interest income (cost) @ 1.31%	163,554	163,554	(163,554)
Total yen	¥12,648,554	¥12,648,554	¥(12,648,554)
Forward exchange rate scenario yen/US\$	106.47	125.26	144.05
Convert to US\$ (domestic currency) at forward rate	\$118,798	\$100,980	\$(87,807)
Invest (borrow) US\$	(100,000)	(100,000)	100,000
Interest income (cost) @ 0.98%/90 days	(980)	(980)	980
Total dollars	(100,980)	(100,980)	100,980
Arbitrage profit US\$	\$17,818	\$0	\$13,173

Just as arbitrage arguments dictate the relationship between forward foreign exchange prices and interest rates, these relationships must also hold true for prices among countries. If parity does not exist for interest and spot price differentials among all currencies, there exists an opportunity for arbitrage. Accordingly, any imbalances are eliminated because there is an inherent equalizer that keeps all forward foreign exchange rates in balance with each country's interest rates. As a result, prices for any three currencies must be consistent with the following relationship:

$$\frac{DM}{Yen} = \frac{DM}{US\$} \times \frac{US\$}{Yen}$$

This relationship can be illustrated by the following example of 90-day forward rates:

If the US$ price per DM is DM 0.6511,

And the Yen per US$ is $125.26,

Then the Yen per DM must be DM 81.56.

In theory, any imbalance between the currency spot and currency forward rates would be corrected by market participants entering into arbitrage transactions. Just as yield curve arbitrage arguments can be extended to all future periods, in theory foreign currency arbitrage arguments also can be extended to all future periods. However, unlike domestic interest rates, it may be difficult to obtain spot rates beyond five years on most foreign government securities.

From this discussion, it is clear that the current exchange rate or spot rate is not necessarily the only variable necessary to value foreign exchange instruments. In addition to the spot rate, the term structure of interest rates in the applicable countries must be developed and used in the valuation of foreign exchange cash flows that will not be received or paid until future periods.

OPTIONS PRICING

In order to discuss option valuation techniques, it is necessary to define some of the terms that relate to options. The term *option* is defined in the AICPA Issues Paper 86–2, *Accounting for Options,* (March 6, 1986), as follows:

> An option is a contract allowing, but not requiring, its holder to buy (call) or sell (put) a specific or standard commodity or financial or equity instrument at a specified price during a specified time period. The principal difference between an option and a futures contract is that exercise of an option is optional but exercise of a futures contract is mandatory.

A financial option is defined in the FASB's November 18, 1991, Discussion Memorandum entitled *Recognition and Measurement of Financial Instruments,* as a contract that

a. Imposes on one entity—the option writer—an obligation to exchange other financial instruments with a second entity—the option holder—on potentially unfavorable terms if an event within the control of the holder occurs.

b. Conveys to the option holder a right to exchange other financial instruments with the option writer on potentially favorable terms if an event within the control of the holder occurs.

There are many different types of options. A *call option* gives the holder the right but not the obligation to buy the indexed instrument at a specified price. A *put option* gives the holder the right but not the obligation to sell the indexed instrument at a specified price. The *writer* of an option is obligated to sell (for call options) or buy (for put options) the underlying indexed instrument at a specified price during a specified period of time. The price specified by the option contract is referred to as the *strike price.* Options are differentiated based on how they can be exercised. *European options* can be exercised only at a particular point in time, at the expiration date of the option. *American options* can be exercised at any point in time up through the expiration date of the option. Some options, referred to as *deferred* or *forward options,* can be exercised at any time prior to maturity but only after a specified period of time has elapsed. There are options on almost all types of financial instruments. There are options on options, options to extend or contract the life of an instrument, and options embedded in financial instruments. Sometimes it is not easy to recognize the option feature embedded in an instrument.

An option is *at-the-money* when the strike price of an option equals the market value of the underlying indexed instrument. A call option is *in-the-money* when the market value of the underlying indexed instrument exceeds the strike price of the option. A put option is in-the-money when the strike price exceeds the market value of the underlying indexed instrument. When the option is in-the-money, the difference between the strike price and market value of the underlying indexed instrument is referred to as the *intrinsic value* of the option. The difference between the market value of an option and its intrinsic value is referred to as *time value*.

The valuation of financial options is more subjective than the valuation of financial instruments that can be valued based on discounting cash flows. Present value models require an estimate of cash flows and market interest rates. This data is also required for options valuation models. However, as the market value of the underlying indexed instrument provides the basis for the value of an option, it must be determined or modeled in order to value the option. Options valuation models also require an estimate of the volatility of the underlying indexed instrument during the life of the option. *Volatility* refers to the susceptibility to change. In mathematical terms, it refers to the standard deviation of the price underlying the indexed instrument. Volatility is generally the most important factor in determining the value of at-or near-the-money options. Options pricing models also require the use of complex mathematics. Although the models used to price options are complex, recognize that they only provide an estimate of value. No model is perfect in all situations. Therefore, regardless of the theoretical sophistication and complexity of the model, actual market transactions may differ significantly from the results indicated by the model.

Options Models

There are a number of well-known models that can be used to value options. Two of the most prominent models are the Black–Scholes model and the Cox–Ross–Rubinstein model which is also known as the "binomial model." The Black–Scholes model, which was introduced in 1973, is perhaps the best known option pricing model. It is based on a complex formula that computes the value of an option on a continuous basis over time. Its application is limited, however, because it contains a number of highly limiting assumptions. Some of the more significant of such assumptions include the following:

- Future prices are randomly distributed in a "log-normal" fashion.

- Volatility is constant over time.

- No dividends or interest is paid during the option period.

- The option is exercisable only on the expiration date.

As a result of these and other restrictive assumptions, the Black–Scholes options pricing model does not accurately price certain types of options.

The Black–Scholes model is described technically as a limiting case of the binomial model. Many of the restrictive assumptions of the Black–Scholes options pricing model can be avoided by use of the binomial model. It is based on less complex mathematics but requires a great many computations to simulate a continuous time span yet comprehend changes in volatility, interest, or dividend payments during the life of the option, and the possibility of early exercise. As an example, because the binomial model computes the value of an option at discrete time periods over the life of the option, it provides a more accurate valuation of certain American options, which can be exercised at any discrete point in time through the maturity of the option.

The value of an option depends on the following basic mechanisms:

- Strike price

- Risk-free interest rate

- Market value of the underlying instrument
- Volatility
- Expiration date of the option
- Dividends or interest payments

Just as arbitrage arguments are key to the valuation of interest-sensitive instruments, they are also key to options pricing. The Black–Scholes model and the binomial model assume an efficient marketplace. Accordingly, the potential for arbitrage is presumed to eliminate mispricing in the marketplace.

Inherent in the options pricing models are certain rules or postulates that provide a framework for constructing mathematical relationships and tests to ensure that the valuations are consistent with economic decision-making based on an arbitrage-free environment. One such rule, for example, requires that at immediate expiration the value of an option can never be less than its intrinsic value or zero. There are other restrictions or rules including restrictions based on the relationship between puts and calls, referred to as put–call parity relationships. A complete list of these restrictions or rules can be found in most textbooks on options.

Although the derivation of the Black–Scholes formula is rather complex, its underlying mathematical concepts are contained in the binomial model, which is much easier to understand. Based on the value and volatility of the underlying instrument, the binomial model computes the expected payoff structure of an option immediately before expiration. Commencing with the value at expiration and working backward, the amounts so computed are related algebraically to an equivalent investment. The equivalent investment is valued as of the inception date, which, given the arbitrage-free assumption, must also be the value of the option.

This procedure is illustrated for a call option using the basic binomial model (Base Model) and the following assumptions:

Strike price	$198
Risk-free interest rate (quarterly)	2.00%
Market value of the underlying security	$200
Volatility (quarterly)	8.00%
Expiration date of the option	90 days

At expiration, the value of the underlying security is expected to increase or decrease by eight percent, which will result in an expected value of $216 or $184. The expected values of the underlying security are used to determine the expected payoff at expiration, which must be either $18 or $0, the difference between the expected value of the underlying security and the strike price but not less than zero.

The expected payoff can be related to an equivalent alternative investment in some combination of shares or units in the underlying security and an amount of debt. The equivalent alternative investments are related to each other, and the value of the call is determined algebraically by solving for the unknown variables using simultaneous equations as follows:

$$S \times M_u - [D + (D \times I)] = C_u$$
$$S \times M_d - [D + (D \times I)] = C_d$$

where,

S = Shares or units

M = Current market price of the indexed security

M_u = Expected increased market price of the indexed security

M_d = Expected decreased market price of the indexed security

D = Debt

I = Risk-free interest rate

C = Price of the call option

C_u = Price of the call option if the price of the indexed security increases

C_d = Price of the call option if the price of the indexed security decreases

Substituting these variables for the known amounts in the example produces the following equations:

$$216S - (D + D \times I) = 18$$
$$184S - (D + D \times I) = 0$$

Solving for S

Equating the formulas:

$$216S - (D + D \times I) = 18 + 184S - (D + D \times I)$$

Simplifying:

$$216S = 18 + 184S$$
$$S = 0.5625$$

Solving for D

Substituting the computed value for S:

$$216 \times 0.5625 - (D + 0.02D) = 18$$

Simplifying:

$$121.5 - 1.02D = 18$$
$$1.02D = 103.5$$
$$D = \$101.47$$

Proof

$$216S - (D + D \times I) = 18$$

Substituting:

$$216 \times 0.5625 - (101.47 + 101.47 \times 0.02) = 18$$

Simplifying:

$$121.5 - 103.5 = 18$$

And

$$184S - (D + D \times I) = 0$$

Substituting:

$$184 \times 0.5625 - (101.47 + 101.47 \times 0.02) = 0$$

Simplifying:

$$103.5 - 103.5 = 0$$

The value of the call option must then be equal to the value of the alternative investment, which is

$$C = S \times M - D$$

Substituting:

$$C = 0.5625 \times 200 - 101.47$$

Simplifying:

$$C = \$11.03$$

The model assumes, however, that there are only two outcomes that can occur at the end of the term. In reality, there are many possible outcomes because volatility occurs continuously, not discretely. The possibility of many outcomes can be considered, however, by expanding the binomial with additional iterations of expected prices and adjusting volatility to correspond with the number of iterations selected. For example, if the value of the underlying security could increase or decrease at the end of 45 days, and that value could increase or decrease at the end of the next 45 days, the binomial would have to be expanded to include the possibility of a different value for each possible outcome. Such expansion is illustrated as follows, assuming a volatility of 5.66 percent and a risk-free interest rate of 1.00 percent for a 45-day period:

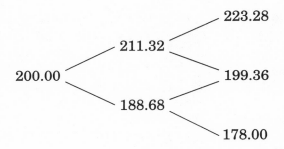

As can be observed from the example, the formula is derived on an exit pricing relationship. Because the value of the underlying indexed instrument can be computed at maturity based on its volatility, the process requires that the value of the underlying indexed instrument at maturity be used to compute the value of the option by working backward. The value of the option is then computed for each binomial, starting with the immediate expiration binomials and working backward in time, solving for the option price of each binomial by using the computed option price of the succeeding binomial until the option value is determined for the initial iteration. This procedure is illustrated as follows using the data from the above example. The value of the call option is computed using the same methodology explained previously.

Binomial	Value of Alternative Investment
223.28	$223.28S - (D + D \times I) = 25.28$
211.32	
199.36	$199.36S - (D + D \times I) = 1.36$
	Result: Call = 15.28
199.36	$199.36S - (D + D \times \sim = 1.36$
188.68	
178.00	$178.00S - (D + D \times A = 0$
	Result: Call = 0.79

Having solved the value of the call option for each of the expiring binomials, the results are used in the computation of the value of the call option for the preceding binomial, which in this example is the first iteration and, therefore, results in the value of the call option as follows:

Binomial	**Value of Alternative Investment**
211.32	$211.32S - (D + D \times 1) = 15.28$
200.00	
188.68	$188.68S - (D + D \times \sim = 0.79$
	Result: Call = 9.22

The accuracy of the valuation increases with the number of iterations used in the model. As the number of iterations increases, the binomial model performs more like the Black–Scholes continuous time model, but it has the advantage of being able to consider events, such as dividend payments and early exercise, that can occur at discrete points in time.

There is no standard or convention that specifies the number of iterations that should be used for a specific period of time. One approach that could be used to make this determination is to expand the binomial until the results of the expansion show little or no difference from the previous iteration. Such a procedure will result generally in the use of 25 to 50 iterations within one year.

The procedure for valuing options that is described above can be used to value call options as well as put options, and it can be extended to any number of future periods. A number of modifications can be made to the basic model to improve its theoretical accuracy to comprehend different types of instruments without fundamentally changing the technique for valuing the option. Valuing dividend-paying equity options, for example, requires a modification of the model to comprehend the possibility of early exercise. Valuing options on fixed-income securities, as another example, would require a number of adjustments to the basic binomial model. Interest rates would be varied along the yield curve to correspond with the cash flows that will occur at various points in time, and such rates would be adjusted to eliminate arbitrage opportunities. A discussion of different refinements that must be considered for different types of options is contained in Chapter 8, Valuation—Specific Types of Instruments.

Some instruments are considered to have "path-dependent" payoffs, which means that the impact of a change in the value of the instrument in one period will continue to affect the value in future periods even though the factor that caused the change is reversed. Mortgage-backed securities, for example, are path-dependent because prepayments resulting from a downturn in interest rates cannot be reversed in future periods even if interest rates subsequently increase to their prior level. The binomial lattice may not be practical for path-dependent instruments because it requires many more nodes in the expansion of the binomial than for instruments that are not path-dependent. As a result, a Monte Carlo simulation of the binomial expansion may be a more practical approach to modeling the value of this type of instrument. However, Monte Carlo simulations require that the sample be large enough to provide reliable results.

Volatility

Volatility is one of the most subjective variables used to price options. Although it is difficult to get quotations of estimated volatility, sources for such estimates include investment bankers, data services, and pricing sources. It can also be computed using historical data or by reference to comparable options that are traded. The latter computation is referred to as *implied volatility*.

There is no standard convention for computing volatility. It can be computed for a number for hours, days, weeks, months, or years, and it can be annualized in a number of ways including the use of the actual number of days in a year or the number of work days in a year. It is generally quoted as an annualized standard deviation, however; and it is usually based on annualized daily observations of changes in prices or yields, as applicable. Annual volatility quotations can be converted to shorter periods of time by dividing the annual amount by the square root of the number of periods to be used within a year. For example, if annual volatility equals 12 percent, quarterly volatility equals 6 percent, which is 12 percent divided by 2, with the 2 equal to the square root of 4 periods.

Because there is no standard for computing expected volatility, any number of approaches can be used and would be considered appropriate. However, to be valid as a predictor of future changes, the price or rate changes that occurred during the time period used to compute volatility should be considered to reasonably represent the changes that are likely to occur in the future. Because it is difficult to assess the reasonableness of historical volatility as a predictor of the long-term behavior of future volatility, options pricing models are effective generally for rather small changes in volatility during short periods of time.

Other Considerations

Although the binomial model can value certain options more precisely than the Black–Scholes model, it is also more costly to apply because it requires a large number of computations. However, the cost-benefit may not be sufficient to require the use of the binomial method for financial reporting. A paragraph entitled "Option Pricing Theory" in Appendix B of the FASB's *Recognition and Measurement of Financial Instruments* discussion memorandum referred to previously states in part: "The research suggests that the imprecisions may be very important to traders seeking arbitrage profits but are apparently not that large by the standards of materiality in financial reporting—that, even with its limitations, the modified Black–Scholes technique appears to have an absolute precision over 90 percent and a relative precision even higher." As mentioned previously, no model is a perfect substitute for market values evidenced by exchanges on an active market. There is a tradeoff, and in many instances it is necessary only to provide reasonable indications of value.

There are many books and publications about options, option pricing, and the economic characteristics of options. A more thorough overview of options is contained in the FASB's discussion memorandum referred to above, complete with a bibliography of additional reading material. A number of concepts described in this chapter were obtained from the publications listed in the bibliography of this chapter, and a much fuller understanding of these areas can be obtained by referring to such publications.

PREPAYMENT RISK

Financial instruments that give the issuer a call option or an option to prepay will generally require a higher than ordinary interest rate (expressed as an additional spread over the risk-free Treasury rate) for this right to prepay. To the holder of the financial instrument, the potential of an early principal payment is an uncertainty known as *prepayment* or *call risk*. Financial instruments that are identical in every respect, except for the presence of prepayment risk, will be valued differently by the market because the risk of prepayment (and the resultant reinvestment risk) commands a premium.

Factors Causing Prepayments

Because mortgages generally may be prepaid by the issuer (borrower) at any time prior to maturity, holders of such instruments, including mortgage securities and derivative products, are subject to prepayment risk. Prepayments occur for a variety of reasons. The most common cause for mortgage prepayments is declining interest rates. As rates fall, it becomes increasingly advantageous for borrowers to incur prepayment costs such as penalties, legal fees, and closing costs to refinance their mortgage at a lower rate. Obviously, the higher the coupon rate a mortgage bears, the more sensitive it will be to prepayments when interest rates decline. In periods of drastically falling interest rates, prepayments become more pronounced with each decline in the discount rate. In these instances, prepayment risk exposes the investor to reinvestment risk—the risk that the proceeds returned will have to be reinvested at yields that are below the yield of the security that was prepaid. Other factors affecting prepayment levels include relocations, new home purchases, and demographic considerations.

Regardless of the underlying interest rate, mortgages and mortgage securities are affected by individuals who choose (or are forced to) relocate. Mortgages will be prepaid by individuals who choose to buy larger (in the case of growing families) or smaller (in the case of older homeowners who will eventually retire and possibly relocate) homes at different stages of their lives. The risk of prepayment due to relocation will vary depending upon the geographical profile of the mortgage or pool of mortgages. Mortgages drawn from areas that are more prone to migration (such as New York or California) will be much more sensitive to prepayment resulting from relocation than those from areas that have more stable mortgage lives.

The age of a mortgage can also be an important factor in estimating prepayments. The probability of prepayments occurring is low during the first few years after the mortgage is created, but such probability will increase up to a point after which it levels off or declines as the mortgage matures. Modeling prepayment experience is relatively more difficult for generic than for specific mortgage pools because the characteristics of the generic pool are not known. In such instances, the historical prepayment record becomes an important factor in estimating prepayments.

In a world where perfect information existed, demographic data—such as age, education, income, and social status—about individual borrowers in a pool of mortgages would be particularly helpful. Although this data is pertinent and certainly affects prepayment experience irrespective of interest rate environment, it is often unavailable in the detail that would be useful and must therefore be estimated and extrapolated.

Forecasting Prepayments

The possibility of prepayments makes it extremely difficult to determine the ultimate return on an investment and to evaluate it against alternative investments, even against other instruments that have prepayment risk but whose underlying collateral has qualitative differences that would give rise to different prepayment streams. However, investors in financial instruments that are subject to prepayment risk must attempt to forecast future prepayments accurately in order to evaluate future cash flows and investment returns.

Any attempt to forecast future behavior should begin with a careful analysis of past experience, from which standard estimates can be derived and used in a model to determine anticipated prepayments and resultant yield to maturity. The word *standard* is crucial because it is important that all market participants be using like terminology in communicating their estimates in order for rational decisions to be made regarding alternative courses of action. Toward this end, several conventional approaches have been developed to measure and express the rate of prepayment anticipated.

One of the first widely used conventions for estimating future prepayments and assigning a mathematical value to them was based on data accumulated by the Federal Housing Administration (FHA) pertaining to FHA-insured mortgages. This data provided the investor with an estimate of FHA-insured prepayment experience in each month an FHA series mortgage was outstanding. Using this as a benchmark (100 percent of FHA experience, 200 percent of FHA experience, and so on), investors were able to estimate the distribution of cash flows over the life of various mortgage pools and express this estimation in a manner that was understood and commonly used by other market participants. Although this represented a great improvement over previous methods, there were significant limitations that had to be addressed when attempting to apply this methodology to any non-FHA mortgage pools. Because only FHA-insured mortgages (which are subsidized by the federal government and are assumable upon transfer of the underlying property) are included in the database from which the prepayment estimates are drawn, it is inappropriate to apply those results to estimate prepayments of non-FHA pools, including Government National Mortgage Association (GNMA) or Federal National Mortgage Association (FNMA) pools. Also, because the data applies only to series with like maturities (such as all 30 years), it is not particularly useful when applied to mortgage pools with loans of varying maturities.

CPR and PSA Methods

Forecasting limitations led to the development of additional methodologies to estimate and quantify prepayment activity. The two most commonly used at this time are the conditional prepayment rate (CPR) approach and the Public Securities Association (PSA) rate approach.

The CPR approach assumes that a constant percentage of the remaining principal is prepaid each period, which is generally expressed as a yearly rate and then translated into a monthly rate for purposes of applying the formula. It is based on the historical experience, geographical constitution, and other characteristics of the particular pool and on the economic environment. This implies that the amount of pre-payment is related to the principal balance at the beginning of each month. The advantage of using a CPR approach is that it relates prepayments to particular economic and financial variables of the pool in question.

The PSA standard was introduced by the Public Securities Association to replace the FHA standard. The PSA standard is expressed as a monthly series of annual prepayment rates beginning at 0.2 percent per month in the first month and increasing by 0.2 percent each month until month 30 when the rate levels off at 6.0 percent per annum. These percentages are applied to the principal balance outstanding at the beginning of a month. This progression would be referred to as 100 percent PSA. A slightly faster-paying pool might be expressed as a 150 percent PSA, which would begin at 0.3 percent and level off at 9.0 percent per annum in month 30; a slower-paying PSA would be the inverse at, for example, 50 percent PSA. Implicit in this methodology is the assumption that prepayments occur relatively infrequently for new mortgages and speed up as they season. After month 30, the PSA standard is essentially the same as a CPR methodology.

Although CPR and PSA standards are expressed differently, they are generally modeled as a percentage applied to unpaid mortgage balances on a monthly basis.

To convert the annual CPR figures to monthly prepayment rates (a single monthly mortality rate or SMM), the following formula is used:

$$SMM = 1 - (1 - CPR)^{1/12}$$

In the case of PSA figures being applied prior to the thirtieth month, the PSA benchmark being used is expressed as a fraction of the months passed to date. For example, in the case of a 100 percent PSA in the twenty-fifth month, $^{25}/_{30}$ths of 6 percent would be substituted for the CPR in the above formula.

The use of CPR and PSA to model prepayment estimates is fairly standard. However, there is no standard approach for determining the prepayment speed itself, and many different models are used to estimate prepayment speeds. Differences in the models relate not only to the estimated impact of interest rates, relocations, new home purchases, and demographic considerations, but also to the timing of the impact relating to these factors. For example, some models give immediate effect to changes in interest rates; other models lag such effects. Because there is no standard for estimating prepayments, estimates will differ for the same instrument, resulting in a range of values. Many entities consider their prepayment models proprietary, and many entities use more than one model at a particular time.

For instruments that are not traded, prepayment estimates can be obtained by reference to comparable instruments that are traded, for which prepayment estimates are quoted. Estimates can also be obtained by reference to industry statistics and by tracking the history of the portfolio or using the history of similar portfolios.

Once prepayment speeds are obtained, they can be incorporated into the models discussed above to generate anticipated cash flows. To the extent that an options adjusted spread (OAS) approach is used to value the instruments, an estimate of current prepayment speed will not be sufficient to generate an estimate of cash flows. The options adjusted spread approach produces different interest rate scenarios based on some level of interest rate volatility. Prepayment speeds will be different at different interest rate levels. Accordingly, it will be necessary to use a model to estimate prepayment speeds over a range of interest rate scenarios comprehended by the simulation.

CREDIT RISK

Credit risk refers to the possibility that a borrower or obligor may default in whole, or in part, on an obligation. The consideration of credit risk is an important factor in assessing the fair value of receivables and various other financial instruments. Depending on the particular financial instrument, it could be the most difficult and subjective factor to assess for purposes of estimating the fair value of a financial instrument.

Reserves for Credit Losses

All entities manage credit risk in some fashion. Most entities that have large receivables balances have established rather elaborate systems and procedures to identify the problem receivables early and to monitor and manage them to minimize losses. Such systems and procedures also encompass a methodology for estimating losses and assessing the adequacy of credit allowances to be reported for financial statement purposes. Even with the sophistication of these systems and procedures, the process of estimating losses for financial statement purposes is extremely subjective.

If the subjectivity could be removed from the process of establishing and maintaining reserves for loan losses, such reserves would not necessarily be equivalent to the reduction in value that the marketplace would assign to a particular receivable or portfolio of receivables. For financial statement purposes under SFAS No. 5, *Accounting for Contingencies,* only probable losses that have been incurred and can be reasonably estimated are recorded. This definition suggests that reasonably possible losses and losses that have not been incurred at a financial statement date are not recorded for financial statement purposes. A buyer of loans—a "market participant"—however, would make adjustments to the value of loans and receivables for these additional items, even though they are not considered under SFAS No. 5. Therefore, the fact that the allowance for losses is considered adequate for financial statement purposes prepared on a historical-cost basis of accounting does not necessarily mean that the loan carrying amounts approximate market value, even if all other factors affecting value (such as interest rates) remain unchanged since the loans were originated.

Problem and Delinquent Accounts

Classification of loans to reflect credit risk is a subjective process. For purposes of this discussion, consider problem loans as those in which there is cause for concern that the debtor will not collect all contractual principal and interest due under the terms of the loan agreement, but the loan is not considered to be "insubstance" foreclosed. Delinquent loans include those that have overdue interest and/or principal payments but are not necessarily considered to be problem loans.

Once a receivable becomes delinquent, or is otherwise identified as having some loss potential, the assessment of the fair value of the receivable becomes extremely difficult and sometimes perhaps impossible, particularly if the receivables are not collateralized. If the receivables are collateralized, very frequently the collateral can be used as a basis for assessing fair value. However, if the value of the collateral cannot be reasonably assessed, or if it is not clear if or when the collateral can be secured, it may not be appropriate to use it as a basis for assessing the fair value of the receivable.

The fact that a receivable is past due does not necessarily mean that its fair value cannot be assessed reasonably. In such instances, a risk adjustment may be estimable. However, the loan or receivable might be delinquent for a long period of time (for example, more than three months), or there may be a known financial or other problem relating to the borrower that indicates a serious concern over collectability. The fair value of such problem and delinquent receivables is extremely difficult to assess. Because the problem loans are infrequently sold except in forced sales, it may be difficult to establish a reliable exit value for them. Because lenders do not make loans when there is any indication that they will not be repaid in the normal course, there is no known entry value for them. As a result, there is no single solution to the difficulty of determining the fair value of problem and delinquent receivables. However, there are a number of alternatives that can be considered to comply with SFAS No. 5.

Practicability Exemption under SFAS No. 107

The estimated fair value of problem and delinquent receivables is best assessed on an individual basis because the specific characteristics and assumptions used in the calculation may vary greatly from receivable to receivable, even though certain receivables may be considered homogeneous. Such an approach, however, may be impracticable. Furthermore, because of the extreme subjectivity involved in the assessment of the market value adjustment relating to the credit component of a troubled receivable, it may not be considered practicable to assess the fair value for such receivables, even on a portfolio basis. If fair value determinations are solely for the purpose of disclosure under SFAS No. 107, instead of making a disclosure of the estimated fair value of such receivables, the entity may conclude that it was not considered practicable to make such estimates.[5]

Portfolio Entry Value under SFAS No. 107

A market assessment might be possible on an entry-value basis for the portfolio as a whole as an alternative. An entity might conclude that, even for a commercial loan portfolio, a level of losses can be anticipated with some reasonable degree

---

5. The practicability exemption under SFAS No. 107 is discussed further in Chapter 6.

of accuracy on a portfolio basis. If that were not the case, the entity would not be able to continue to originate such loans. From this perspective, the interest rate charged when the loans are originated comprehends both the position of the yield curve and an adjustment for credit. To the extent that the entity's system for monitoring credit exposure has not identified any unusual or abnormal loss and/or exposure trends and ratios, the entity may conclude that the fair value of the portfolio can be estimated on an entry-value basis and that fair value is determined primarily as a function of current lending rates and ultimately by reducing the preliminary amount by the specific and general loss allowances of the portfolio. The entity might then be able to conclude that it believes that the balances net of reserves reasonably approximate an entry value, given the nature of such receivables and expectations of portfolio losses.

AGGREGATION

Theoretically, the most precise measurement of value would be based on estimates of periodic cash flows for each investment to be valued, discounted at the market rate applicable for the period. SFAS No. 107 suggests the use of aggregation in computing estimated fair values. Paragraph 15 of that statement, which deals with practicability, states in part: "Practicability, that is, cost considerations, also may affect the required precision of the estimate; for example, while in many cases it might seem impracticable to estimate fair value on an individual instrument basis, it may be practicable for a class of financial instruments in a portfolio or on a portfolio basis. In those cases, the fair value of that class or of the portfolio should be disclosed." There could be some disagreement, however, over the selection of the items that could be appropriately aggregated. Although aggregation facilitates computation, it also distorts results. The greater the level of aggregation, the more likely it is that the distortion could be significant. Fair value measurements would be distorted by:

- Estimating portfolio prepayments and computing portfolio cash flows based on weighted-average maturities and weighted-average coupons when maturities differ significantly and/or when coupons differ significantly.

- Combining instruments with different payment characteristics and applying a single discount rate (such as combining zero coupon instruments with amortizing bonds).

- Combining seasoned instruments with new issues, which may distort results because new issues are generally more liquid than seasoned issues, suggesting a lower discount rate for the new issues. For financial instruments that are subject to prepayments, seasoned portfolios generally have different prepayment characteristics because they have been through interest rate cycles and borrowers have already had an opportunity to prepay.

- Using a single discount rate for all periods to discount cash flows whenever the yield curve is not flat.

The FASB provides no guidance concerning the levels of aggregation that are appropriate or the methods that may be used to facilitate fair value estimates on a portfolio basis. As a result, in practice there is considerable flexibility in aggregating financial instruments. This does not mean that all financial instruments can be aggregated without limitation. The impact of distortion must be balanced against the ease of making computations when aggregation is used.

There are a number of factors to consider when aggregating financial instruments to estimate fair value. Some of these factors are as follows:

- Financial instruments generally should be aggregated by type of instrument because similar instruments generally have similar credit risk and cash-flow terms. Junk bonds, for example, generally should not be aggregated because their value is influenced primarily by credit concerns that will differ from issuer to issuer, unless the investor has a reliable system for classifying and differentiating credit risk.

- Similar instruments with different coupons can be aggregated, but the coupons should be within some range of acceptability. For instruments that are subject to prepayment, the acceptable range should be rather narrow, perhaps within 100 basis points. As higher coupons tend to prepay faster than lower coupons, a wide range would suggest significantly different possible cash flows.

- Different maturities are indicative of different interest rate and risk characteristics, which affect value. The greater these differences are, the higher the level of distortion. Distortion resulting from the use of a weighted average maturity will generally be within an acceptable level, providing the maturity dates of the individual instruments being valued are within the following ranges:

Average Maturity	Range of Individual Instruments
Less than 5 years	± 6 months
6 to 10 years	± 1 year
10 to 25 years	± 2 years
Greater than 25 years	± 5 years

Because no standards are specified by the FASB, an entity can choose the parameters it considers to be reasonable. If an entity is outside of the parameters referred to above or the parameters it establishes, it may consider the desirability or necessity of testing its results under different scenarios to ensure that such results reasonably approximate fair value. Entities may wish to disclose their aggregation methods and recognize the potential for imprecision resulting from such aggregation.

Bibliography

Bierawag, Gerald O. *Duration Analysis (Managing Interest Rate Risk)*. Cambridge, MA: Ballinger Publishing, 1987.

Bodie, Zvi; Alex Kane; and Alan J. Marcus. *Investments*. 2nd ed. Boston, MA: Richard D. Irwin, 1993.

Bookstaber, Richard M. *Option Pricing and Investment Strategies*. 3rd ed. Chicago, IL: Probus, 1991.

Cox, John C.; and Mark Rubenstein. *Option Markets*. Englewood Cliffs, NJ: Prentice-Hall, 1985.

Douglas, Livingston G. *Yield Curve Analysis: The Fundamentals of Risk and Return*. New York: New York Institute of Finance, 1988.

Dubofsky, David A. *Options and Financial Futures: Valuations and Uses*. New York: McGraw-Hill, 1992.

Edwards, Franklin R.; and Cindy W. Ma. *Futures and Options*. New York: McGraw-Hill, 1992.

Fabozzi, Frank J. *The Handbook of Fixed Income Options (Pricing Strategies & Applications)*. Chicago, IL: Probus, 1989.

Fabozzi, Frank J.; and T. Dessa Fabozzi. *Bond Markets, Analysis and Strategies*. Englewood Cliffs, NJ: Prentice-Hall, 1989.

Figlewski, Stephen; William L. Silber; and Marti G. Subrahmanyam, eds. *Financial Options: From Theory to Practice*. Homewood, IL: Business One Irwin, 1990.

Financial Accounting Standards Board. *An Analysis of Issues Related to Recognition and Measurement of Financial Instruments (Discussion Memorandum)*. Norwalk, CT: FASB, November 18, 1991.

Gibson, Rajna. *Options Valuation: Analyzing and Pricing Standardized Option Contracts*. New York: McGraw-Hill, 1991.

Hull, John. *Options, Futures and Other Derivative Securities*. 2nd ed. Englewood Cliffs, NJ: Prentice-Hall, 1993.

Kapner, Kenneth R.; and John F. Marshall. *The Swaps Handbook (Swaps and Related Risk Management Instruments)*. New York: New York Institute of Finance, 1990.

Luskin, Donald L. *Index Options & Futures: The Complete Guide*. New York: John Wiley & Sons, 1987.

Powers, Mark J.; and David Vogel. *Inside Financial Futures Markets*. 2nd ed. New York: John Wiley & Sons, 1984.

Van Horne, James C. *Financial Markets Rates & Flows*. 4th ed. Englewood Cliffs, NJ: Prentice-Hall, 1994.

Windas, Tom. *An Introduction to Option-Adjusted Spread Analysis*. New York: Bloomberg L.P., 1993.

CHAPTER 8

Valuation—Specific Types of Instruments[1]

John T. Smith

Different valuation techniques will be required for different financial instruments, and variations of such techniques will be required for variations of similar instruments. A number of broad categories of financial instruments are presented in this chapter along with specific instruments within each category to provide an understanding of the primary characteristics of the various instruments, the sources for obtaining estimates of fair value, and an overview of the related pricing and valuation methods and conventions. A large number of financial instruments are not presented and discussed in this chapter because market quotations can be obtained for them from established markets and exchanges. There should be no difficulty, for example, in obtaining market quotes on U.S. Treasury instruments. Also, short-term financial instruments are not presented because their fair values are generally equal to their book values (such as commercial paper and

1. This chapter is adapted with permission from *Financial Instruments: Fair Value Considerations* (Wilton, CT: Deloitte & Touche, LLP, 1992).

repurchase transactions). Credit factors, however, would be required to be assessed separately.

Whole loans and long-term corporate debt are discussed in this chapter even though they are not derivatives because valuation of those instruments is required in accounting for some transactions that involve derivatives.

WHOLE LOANS

Loans represent a receivable for the use of funds or the transfer of assets or services. There are many different types of loans, each having different terms and characteristics. In addition to borrowing and lending activities, purchase and sales transactions may give rise to loans. Loans can be secured or unsecured. Whole loans refer to individual loans in a portfolio of loans.

Consumer Loans

Consumer loans are generally made to individuals to finance household, family, or other personal expenditures. Consumer loans might be made to finance purchases of consumer goods, such as automobiles, boats, mobile homes, household goods, and vacations. Other types of consumer loans include student loans, property improvement loans, loans collateralized by savings accounts, credit cards, overdraft protection, and other lines of credit. Consumer loans may be collateralized by the goods purchased, as in the case of an automobile or boat loan. The principal form of payment is through installment. However, many different repayment structures are used.

Real Estate Loans

Real estate loans are collateralized by residential or commercial property or vacant land. Real estate loan repayments vary considerably, and interest may accrue at a fixed rate or at a variable rate. The loans are typically subject to credit (default) risk, prepayment risk, and interest rate risk. Residential real estate loans are typically repaid on an installment basis with terms ranging from 15 to 30 years. The terms of commercial real estate loans vary depending primarily on the type of property being financed. Construction loans are typically made on a short-term basis. Loans for operating properties, such as hotels and shopping centers, are typically made on a medium-term and long-term basis.

Commercial Loans

Commercial loans are generally made to businesses to provide working capital, to finance the purchase of inventory or equipment, and for other general business purposes. Commercial loans may be due on an installment basis with fixed payments, on a demand basis, or may be subject to "balloon" payments. The loans may have fixed or variable terms of interest and may be unsecured, collateralized by specific assets of the company, or guaranteed by a third party.

Valuation Considerations for Whole Loans

An active market for the sale and purchase of whole loans exists, but the transactions are private. Fair value will generally fluctuate depending on changes in interest rates, economic conditions, the value of collateral if applicable, and on the borrower's creditworthiness.

An active market exists for packages of residential real estate loans that conform to certain Government National Mortgage Association (GNMA), Federal National Mortgage Association (FNMA), or Federal Home Loan Mortgage Association (FHLMC) guidelines and are used as collateral for mortgage-backed securities and for certain consumer loans sold as securities, which are discussed in the next section of this chapter. The securitization of credit card and certain other loan receivables is becoming more common. An estimate of fair value for these types of whole loans can be made by reference to the securitization transactions with appropriate adjustment for credit risk, seasoning, interest rates, and collateral. (See Chapter 5 on accounting for securitization transactions.)

For whole loans, valuation estimates may be obtained from investment bankers, who have experience with the securitization or sale of these types of loans and receivables. For residential loans or pools of such loans, dealer quotes may be available if underwritten by quasi-governmental agencies (such as FNMA, GNMA, FHLMC).

Fair value may also be estimated by comparison to mortgage-backed securities collateralized by similar loans. Fair value may be assessed by estimating the future cash flows to be received from the loan and discounting such cash flows to the present value by using a discount rate appropriate for similar loans (for example, in regard to maturity, interest, and liquidity) made to similar borrowers (such as in regard to credit risk). Estimates for prepayments and defaults should be incorporated in the valuation of a group of loans. This approach is particularly useful when valuing commercial loans for which no trading markets exist. Credit defaults and prepayment speeds are often estimated based on past history. Under SFAS No. 107, discount rates may be based on entry values (interest rates being charged currently by the entity valuing the loans or its competition). Discount rates generally can be derived by reference to packaged loans sold as securities. For large portfolios of consumer loans, homogeneous loans may be grouped together and discounted using average terms to maturity and other characteristics. The use of aggregation may be more difficult for commercial loans, however, because their terms and credit characteristics are not homogeneous; therefore, such items are not predictable.

ASSET-BACKED SECURITIES

Asset-backed securities consist of receivables that have been pooled and converted into a form that can be easily sold. Principal and interest payments received by the servicer are passed directly to the investor or to a special purpose entity that passes the cash flows on to the security holders. The originator of the underlying receivables may be obligated to compensate the purchaser of securities for certain credit losses in the portfolio or reductions in yield resulting from prepayments underlying asset-backed securities.

Mortgage-Backed Securities (MBS)

Mortgage-backed securities (MBS) are participations in pools of mortgage loans that are sold as a unit. The securities can have fixed or variable rates and are subject to prepayments and, in some instances, to credit losses. *Fixed-rate securities* generally have original terms of 15 or 30 years. *Adjustable-rate securities* may have original terms that are less than 15 years. The individual mortgages are subject to price (interest rate) risk, prepayment risk, and default risk. Securities issued by quasi-governmental agencies are guaranteed by the agencies against credit loss. GNMA is explicitly backed by the U.S. government.

Interest-Only (IO) and Principal-Only (PO) Securities

Interest-only and *principal-only securities* (also known as *strips*) are created by splitting a traditional mortgage-backed security or pool of loans into an interest-only portion and a principal-only portion. This is done to better match investor needs with product attributes. IO securities may have fixed or variable interest rates. Both IO and PO securities are subject to prepayments. They can be stripped from fixed- or adjustable-rate loans or a pool of fixed-rate loans containing a range of different mortgage rates. The individual mortgages are subject to prepayment and default risk. PO securities issued by quasi-governmental agencies are guaranteed or partially guaranteed against credit loss.

An IOette is an IO with a relatively low principal amount and high coupon rate. The principal and interest components of mortgage-backed securities are sometimes separated and recombined in varying proportions to create "synthetic coupon" securities.

Other Securitized Loans and Receivables

Other securitized loans and receivables consist of pools of receivables and loans that have been packaged and sold as a security. Many different types of loans and receivables are pooled and sold as securities, including credit card receivables, student loans, and consumer loans such as auto loans, boat loans, mobile home loans, and various types of loans for installment purchases.

Subordinated Loan Interests

Subordinated loans and receivables represent a portion of a pool of loans that is retained by the seller, usually a subordinated interest in the pool or a subordinated portion of a pool of loans that was purchased by the investor.

Valuation Considerations for Asset-Backed Securities

Prices generally move with changes in interest rates and are influenced by prepayments. Credit is generally not a significant factor in estimating value for securities that are either guaranteed or have a senior interest in the underlying collateral pool. Credit is, however, an important valuation consideration for investors in the subordinated portion of the collateral pool.

There are active markets for many of these securities. Price quotations for representative issues of MBS can be obtained from the *Wall Street Journal,* the *New York Times,* and other financial media. Quotations also can be obtained from investment bankers for less liquid issues. Price quotations for some issues can be obtained from one of several pricing services that specialize in matrix pricing.

Quotations may not be available for older issues and for certain other issues in which there is no active market. In these instances, fair values can be computed by reference to comparable instruments that are traded or by computing a present value based on estimated prepayments, credit losses if applicable, and a discount rate based on a spread to Treasury rates. Cash flow estimates also should consider the effect of any yield maintenance and clean-up call provisions.

COLLATERALIZED MORTGAGE OBLIGATIONS (CMOS)

There are many different types of collateralized mortgage obligation (CMO) structures, each having very different cash-flow characteristics. The broad categories of CMO bonds and CMO residuals are discussed below.

CMO Bonds

A *CMO bond* is a bond that is collateralized by mortgage-backed securities and issued in several classes of securities (referred to as *traunches*). CMOs are frequently issued by Real Estate Mortgage Investment Conduits (REMICs) as a result of the Tax Reform Act of 1986. The traunches typically have different maturity and interest rates such that the cash flows from the underlying mortgage-backed securities are applied to the different traunches at specified rates, allowing certain traunches to be retired earlier than other traunches. The sequence of payments is "deal specific" and is generally modeled by the issuer. Initial CMO structures consisted primarily of several fixed-rate traunches with different maturities. Recent innovations to the CMO structure include floating-rate traunches and a Planned Amortization Class (PAC) traunche. PACs typically provide investors with a relatively certain paydown schedule, except under extreme prepayment conditions.

CMO Residuals

CMO residuals represent the excess cash flows from the underlying collateral on mortgage-backed securities or a pool of loans and include reinvestment income thereon after paying the debt service on the CMO and the related administrative expenses. Generally, most CMO structures have residuals due to the conservative structuring requirements necessary to achieve the highest rating by the rating agency. Generally, cash flows are generated from (1) interest differential between the collateral for the CMOs and the CMO itself; (2) interest differential between the various classes of bonds (generally, the highest bond coupon will be utilized to discount cash flows in the pricing of CMOs); (3) reinvestment income; and (4) overcollateralization income. There are a number of different types of CMO residuals, including floating-rate residuals, inverse floating residuals (interest rates vary inversely with floating rates), and PAC residuals.

Valuation Considerations for CMOs

There is an active market for some CMO bond issues. Some CMO dealers offer valuation services, while other pricing services specialize in matrix pricing to determine price and yield calculations. Dealer quotes are readily available for CMOs that are actively traded. CMOs that are not actively traded can be compared to similar instruments that are actively traded.

CMO residuals may have high returns due to the risk of the investment. Significant changes in prepayments, however, can cause a residual's yield to decline in value or to become negative.

There is generally no active market for CMO residuals. CMO dealers can utilize modeling techniques to price residuals by calculating their yields, taking into account the prior payment experience of the underlying loans and an estimate of future payments. The computed yields are then compared to the yields of similar instruments to determine whether the residual should be priced at a discount or premium to par.

LONG-TERM CORPORATE DEBT

There are many different types of long-term corporate debt. Issues can be collateralized or unsecured, rated or unrated. Repayment terms are varied. Several of the more common types of long-term corporate debt are discussed below. Debt with embedded options characteristics is discussed in a separate section.

Investment Grade Debt

Investment grade debt is corporate debt that has received an investment grade rating of BBB or Baa or better from a rating agency. The value of such debt generally fluctuates with U.S. Treasury rates. Credit is generally not a significant factor affecting value unless the issuer is in danger of losing its credit rating.

High-Yield Debt

High-yield debt, also known as *junk bonds,* consists of high-yielding bonds judged to be below investment grade by the bond rating agencies. Issuers have often borrowed heavily as a result of a highly leveraged transaction such as a leveraged buyout or a major recapitalization. Issuers may have experienced a significant economic hardship; for example, dramatic declines in sales and/or income, adverse product liability claims, or regulatory and political changes that have affected the issuer's debt-service ability. The simplest type of junk bond is a *plain vanilla* cash-bearing instrument that obligates the issuer to pay current interest in cash. Interest rates may be fixed or floating. Other types of junk bonds typically fall into the categories of either deferred interest securities or payment-in-kind securities. *Deferred interest securities* consist of zero coupon bonds, in which all accrued interest is paid at maturity, and bonds whose interest is deferred for an initial period—usually two to four years. *Payment-in-kind* securities are securities that "pay" the required interest in more of the same (or sometimes different) securities for a specified period of time.

Subordinated Debt

Subordinated debt is generally unsecured corporate debt that has a claim that is secondary to other corporate issues. It generally pays a high interest rate because of its inferior credit position.

Valuation Considerations for Long-Term Corporate Debt

There is an established market for investment grade debt and a secondary market for many junk bond and subordinated debt issues.

Prices for investment grade debt generally move with U.S. Treasury rates, but they are affected by the investment grading on the bonds, which is an indication of the general creditworthiness of the issuer. Price quotations for many issues can be obtained from the *Wall Street Journal,* the *New York Times,* and other financial media, as well as from investment bankers.

Quotations may not be available for most unrated corporate debt issues. If a specific issue does not have an active market, value may be obtained from broker-dealers who make markets in similar securities. However, because many unrated debt issues are thinly traded, any estimate of value is subject to significant bid/ask differences and significant differences from broker to broker.

Estimates of fair value can also be obtained by computing a present value based on estimated cash flows and risk-adjusted interest rates. These estimates should, generally, be based on an evaluation of appropriate factors, primarily credit quality but also institution-size, trading in similar securities, coupon rate, maturity, type of issue, and other available data. Because of the sensitivity of high-yield bonds, subordinated debt, and other unrated corporate debt to credit concerns, their values will fluctuate more with changes in credit than with changes in interest rates.

INDEXED DEBT

Indexed debt is debt with a contingent "interest" payment based on a specific commodity or index. The contingent payments made on the debt may be based on changes in the price of a specific commodity, such as gold, silver, or oil, or a specific index such as the S&P 500. In some cases, the right to receive the contingent payment may be separable from the debt.

The debt, which has a fixed maturity date, will generally pay guaranteed periodic interest at a fixed rate. However, the guaranteed interest rate on the debt will be lower than interest rates on comparable debt without the contingent interest feature. The contingent interest index can have a significant impact on effective yield ultimately paid on the debt and on the value of the debt at any given point in time.

The pricing of indexed debt is based on expected cash flows. Prices generally move with interest rates and the commodity or index on which the contingent payment is based. Prices are also influenced by the creditworthiness of the issuer.

If the indexed debt is traded, price quotations can be obtained from investment bankers. However, this type of debt is largely issue-specific, and accordingly, price quotations are generally not readily available. Fair value can be estimated by splitting the indexed debt between the guaranteed and contingent portions and valuing each piece separately. The value of the guaranteed interest can be estimated using a discounted cash-flow model, adjusted as necessary for the creditworthiness of the issuer. The contingent portion, if based on some of the more common commodities or indexes (such as gold or silver, or S&P 100 or 500), can be valued by reference to index trading option quotations. If the contingent portion is not based on a commodity or index with an active option trading market, value may be estimated by a qualified investment banker, from an appraisal, or by use of an options pricing model based on the value of the underlying commodity, the applicable index, the volatility of such index, appropriate discount rates, and general credit quality of the debt issuer.

FUTURES AND FORWARD CONTRACTS

Futures Contracts

Futures contracts are standardized, transferable forward contracts to buy or sell a predetermined quantity of a commodity or financial instrument on a specified future date at a specified price. Futures contracts are actively traded on organized exchanges that set and enforce trading rules. There are two principal differences between futures contracts and forward contracts. First, futures are standardized agreements where all terms are dictated by the exchanges on which they trade. The only item that is not fixed is the final price, which fluctuates as the underlying economics change. Second, the exchange clearinghouse interposes itself as a counterparty to both sides of the contract, thus guaranteeing the performance of both parties. These two characteristics allow trading to be conducted by turning an exchange contract between two parties into a fungible financial instrument. Unlike forward contracts, futures contracts are generally settled in cash prior to expiration. Because all exchanges have margin requirements, all positions are marked-to-market on a daily basis as traders settle up by collecting gains or delivering shortfalls. This is another key distinction between futures contracts and forward contracts.

Forward Contracts

Forward contracts are agreements for the purchase or sale of a predetermined quantity of either commodities or financial instruments at the contracted forward price with a future delivery and settlement date specified in the terms of the agreement. Forward contracts are generally tailored to meet the specifications of the parties to the transaction; they are not standardized in any fashion and are neither transferable nor cancelable without the consent of both parties. Forward contracts are not traded on exchanges or in any common market. Forward contracts are similar to futures contracts except that physical delivery is generally required for settlement, and forward contracts are not traded on an exchange. Because forward contracts are not traded on commodities exchanges, they lack the flexibility and protection provided by these exchanges. Credit risk becomes a primary concern because a company is dealing directly with the counterparty and is directly at risk in the event of default by that counterparty.

Forward Rate Agreements (FRAs)

A *forward rate agreement* is a contract between two parties
to exchange short-term interest rate payments based on a
notional principal amount over a predetermined period. The
short-term interest rate payment is based on the difference
between an agreed-upon interest rate and a reference rate
(LIBOR, Treasury bills, or other) at a specified future date.
The FRA is generally settled on this specified date. The investor in a FRA locks into a fixed rate of interest while the
seller locks into a floating rate for the predetermined period.
FRAs can be used to hedge transactions of any size or maturity and offer an alternative to interest rate futures for
hedging purposes.

FRAs are not traded on commodities exchanges and
therefore do not offer the liquidity or protection provided by
these exchanges. Credit risk is a primary concern because the
entity usually deals directly with the counterparty and is
directly at risk in the event of default by that counterparty.

Valuation Considerations for Futures and Forward Contracts

Prices of futures, forwards, and FRAs generally move with
changes in the underlying indexed commodity, foreign currency, or other financial instrument. Forward and FRA prices
are influenced by the creditworthiness of the counterparty.
Credit is generally not a concern for futures contracts traded
on established exchanges.

Price quotations for specific futures contracts can be
obtained from the *Wall Street Journal,* the *New York Times,*
and other financial media. Quotations are generally not available for forward contracts and FRAs.

To estimate fair value, the terms of the forward contracts
and FRAs should be compared with the terms of similar
futures contracts, securities for delivery in comparable months,

and interest rate structures, as applicable. Because value is derived from the underlying indexed instrument or commodity, price quotations for representative reference rates, which can be obtained from the *Wall Street Journal,* the *New York Times,* and other financial media, can be used as a basis for calculating value. Estimated fair values of forward contracts and FRAs can be calculated using the method described for futures and forward contracts in the section of Chapter 7, Futures, Forwards, and Foreign Exchange Valuation.

INTEREST RATE AND CURRENCY SWAPS

There are numerous variations of interest rate and currency swaps. Swaps can be linked to any number of underlying instruments and indices, and swap terms can vary greatly.

Interest Rate Swaps

Interest rate swaps represent an agreement between counterparties to exchange interest cash flows on a notional principal amount for a specified period. The most common type of interest rate swap involves the exchange of fixed-rate interest cash flows for variable-rate cash flows. Interest rate swaps do not involve the exchange of principal between the parties. Swaps range in maturities, generally from 3 to 10 years. The greatest risk of swaps is default by the counterparty. This risk is usually minimized by requiring the counterparty to post collateral if there is any indication of credit risk. Swaps may be structured so that the notional principal amount is adjusted up or down during the term of the swap. Floating rate reset periods range from daily to yearly.

Currency Swaps

A *currency swap* is an agreement between two parties to exchange two different currencies with an agreement to reverse the exchange at a later date at specified exchange rates. The exchange of currencies at the inception date of the contract generally takes place at the current spot rate. The reexchange at maturity may take place at the same exchange rate, a specified rate, or the then-current spot rate. Interest payments, if applicable, are generally made between the parties based on interest rates available in the two currencies at the inception of the contract. The term of currency swap contracts may extend for many years. Currency swaps are usually negotiated with commercial and investment banks. Contracts are subject to risk of default by the counterparty and, depending on their terms, may be subject to exchange rate risk. Some currency swaps may not provide for exchange of principal; they will only provide for the exchange of interest cash flows.

Valuation Considerations for Interest Rate and Currency Swaps

Interest rate swaps and currency swaps are not traded on exchanges. However, because there is such a large volume of interest rate swap and currency swap transactions, fair value estimates can generally be obtained. Estimated fair values might be based directly on dealer quotations or on dealer quotations for similar interest rate and currency swaps such as forward exchange contracts, adjusted for any differences in contract terms. If reliable prices cannot be obtained from dealers, fair values can be computed.

Prices for interest rate swaps generally move with changes in interest rates. Prices for currency swaps move with changes in interest rates in each country and with changes in the spot currency rate.

For interest rate swaps, both the variable-rate and fixed-rate sides of the swap must be considered in their valuation. The variable-rate side of a swap is adjusted to market by adding to or subtracting from the fixed-rate side of the swap any spread on the variable-rate side of the swap. For example, if an entity was paying a fixed rate of 9.00 percent and receiving LIBOR minus 0.50 percent, the fixed-rate side of the swap would be adjusted to 9.50 percent. An additional adjustment is required if the market rate for the variable index has changed before the variable rate is repriced. For example, if the variable-rate side of the swap is a six-month LIBOR and the LIBOR rate changes, an adjustment would be necessary until the LIBOR side of the swap reprices at the new LIBOR rate. After making any adjustments to the variable-rate side of the swap, the fixed-rate side of the swap is then valued by comparing the adjusted rate with the current market interest rates and discounting the effect of the difference, if any, on the notional amount over the term of the swap. Discount rates should be based on an interest rate swap yield curve, which can be developed from current swap prices over a series of maturities.

For currency swaps, fair values can also be computed based on a present value approach. A currency swap's market price can be determined by comparing current exchange rates and relative market interest rates in each country over the term of the swap with the terms of the currency swap, with any differences discounted to the present value. Again, the discount rates should consider the term structure of the relative interest rates in each country.

FINANCIAL OPTIONS

There are many different types of options, each having unique characteristics. Many options are traded on active exchanges; however, liquidity can vary for over-the-counter (OTC) options and for many foreign currency options. Pricing is primarily a function of the option term, the exercise price relative to forward rates, and the probability that the option will expire "in-the-money." Price quotes for many exchange traded options can be obtained directly from brokers and from the

Wall Street Journal, the *New York Times,* and other financial media. Quotations can also be obtained from options writers and traders such as major money center banks.

Option pricing for OTC, illiquid, and nontraded options, as previously explained, is complex, and the methods used can vary. For this reason, no single model can be used to value all types of options. The fundamental methods for valuing options are discussed and illustrated in Chapter 7 under "Options Pricing." However, a number of modifications can be made to the basic options pricing methodology in order to comprehend the unique characteristics of different option instruments. A number of the more typical options are presented below along with a brief discussion of the related valuation modifications that must be considered.

Valuation Considerations for Different Types of Options

Options on Stocks

The basic binomial model assumes that prices are distributed in a log-normal fashion. Historical data may suggest, however, that stock prices are expected to move differently. The basic binomial model can be adjusted for these differences and for the nonstationary variance of stock returns by altering the normal volatility factor. For example, instead of assuming an equal probability of an increase or decrease in price, volatility could be set at 10 percent for increases and 5 percent for decreases, and these percentages could be altered over time.

Options on Bonds

Although the basic binomial model remains the same, a number of modifications must be made to value options on bonds. Coupon payments are comprehended in the same manner as dividend payments for stocks, and the value of the option on a bond is based on the higher of the holding value or the exercise value. The basic model assumes a constant interest rate, usually the risk-free interest rate. Bonds are priced, however, based on the yield curve, which means that rates are different at different points on the curve. A theoretically correct bond option pricing model must comprehend the term structure of interest rates and preclude arbitrage opportunities along the yield curve. This requires that the yield curve be included in the options pricing model. It should be included in such a way as to ensure that arbitrage is not possible but without significantly adjusting the volatility assumption and the shape of the distribution. A technique for modeling options on bonds is discussed rather thoroughly in F. Fabozzi's *The Handbook of Fixed Income Options* (Probus, 1989).

The basic model also assumes that volatility is constant over time. However, the price volatility of a bond decreases as time passes, and it falls toward zero as the bond reaches maturity. An additional adjustment is not required for the change in volatility, however, because it is comprehended through discounting along the yield curve in the model. The bond values at each node are discounted back to the prior node, and such discounted amounts are averaged to arrive at the value of the preceding node.

Options on MBS

Path-dependent instruments can be valued by using simulation methods. However, such methods are much more difficult to use if the option is an American option because it requires many more nodes to be evaluated with each binomial step. However, options on mortgage-backed securities can be valued using simulation methods without too much difficulty because the optionality of the underlying instruments is evaluated independently by means of a prepayment model that recognizes that not all borrowers respond rationally to interest rate movements.

Options on Futures

The value of an option on a futures contract is determined using the basic options pricing model. However, estimated changes in value resulting from applying the volatility factor are based on the cash price of the indexed instrument, not the futures price, because the futures price will eventually converge with the cash price at expiration. In addition, in relating the expected payoff to an equivalent investment, the investment includes only the cost of or profit from investing in the futures contract; that is, the expected cash price minus the futures price. As a result, the borrowing cost is less than it otherwise would have been for an option on a cash instrument because the underlying instrument is not purchased until a future date.

Options on Foreign Currencies

The basic model assumes a risk-free interest rate. For foreign currency options, however, an adjustment to the basic model must be made to comprehend the relationship between foreign and domestic interest rates. This relationship, which is explained in Chapter 7, under "Futures, Forwards, and Foreign Exchange Valuation," determines whether the currency will be at a forward premium or discount. For European options, an adjustment is made based on the relative forward rates. For an American option, an adjustment is made depending on the relative interest rates in each country, which determine whether or not the option will be exercised early.

Warrants

Warrants are similar to call options except that, unlike a call option, the exercise of a warrant results in the issuance of new shares of stock, and the proceeds from the warrant are included in and thereby increase equity. In computing the estimated fair value of warrants, it is necessary to reduce the market price per share of the common stock by the dilutive effect of the increased number of shares that would be outstanding as a result of the exercise of the warrant and to reduce the amount to be paid upon exercise by the proportionate interest in such amount as a result of acquiring the common stock. In most instances, the effect of these refinements will not significantly affect the resulting valuation of the warrant.

Caps, Collars, Floors

Caps, collars, floors, and variations of these instruments are options. However, instead of being indexed to an underlying security, such options are linked to a notional principal and an underlying indexed interest rate.

The buyer of a *cap* has the right to receive the excess of a reference interest rate over a given rate based upon a specified notional amount. The buyer pays a premium to receive this right. A cap is analogous to a put option on debt securities. Caps allow a variable rate borrower to limit the risk associated with an increase in interest rates; if interest rates move down, the buyer has only lost the premium paid, which may be partially offset by reduced interest costs. Cap writers (normally variable-rate lenders) limit their ability to profit from increases in interest rates in return for premium income, and bear the risk of an unfavorable change in interest rates.

Cap variations include the *corridor,* which is composed of the simultaneous purchase and sale of a cap whereby the cap sold is for a higher rate than the one purchased, and the *deferred cap,* in which the cap has a delayed start date.

The buyer of a *floor* has the right to receive the excess of a given rate, known as the strike price, over a reference rate. The buyer pays a premium to receive this right. A floor is analogous to a call option on debt securities. Floors allow a variable-rate lender to limit the risk associated with a decline in interest rates; if interest rates move up, the buyer has only lost the premium paid, which may be partially offset by increased interest earnings. Floor writers (normally variable-rate borrowers) limit their ability to profit from decreases in interest rates in return for premium income and bear the risk of an unfavorable change in interest rates. Both buyers and writers are at risk if the interest rate being hedged does not precisely correlate with movements in the rate subject to the floor.

A *collar* combines the strategies of a cap and a floor. The buyer of a collar buys a cap and writes a floor; the writer of a collar writes a cap and buys a floor. When the premium received equals the premium paid, the collar is known as a *zero-cost collar*. Collars fix the rate a lender will receive or a borrower will pay between two levels (the cap and floor levels). Collars also serve to reduce the cost of buying outright a cap or floor. Because a borrower or lender is usually only interested in protecting against movements in interest rates in one direction, the premium earned by writing a cap or floor serves to reduce the cost of the cap or floor purchased. The maximum exposure under a collar is the difference between the strike price of the cap and floor.

There are variations of the basic collar that may be utilized. The *participating interest rate agreement* is a collar that has different notional amounts for the cap and floor. There are also *path-dependent caps and floors* that are indexed to an average of interest rates for a given period of time rather than at a specific time. This may be advantageous for corporate treasurers who are translating income statement accounts at average rates over a period of time.

The value of a cap, collar, or floor will decrease as time passes (as it nears maturity) and will change as interest rates change. Although there is a certain amount of credit risk relating to these instruments because the contracts are not insured or guaranteed, such risk is generally not significant because brokers and counterparties usually require collateral to be pledged whenever there is any perception of risk.

The market value of caps, collars, and floors is generally based on the expected cash flows and is not readily determinable by quoted market prices. However, other valuations based on derived values or value quotations from the writer of the agreement may be acceptable. Market values may also be obtained from dealer quotes or options pricing models. Generally, a plain vanilla quote that assumes full creditworthiness of the counterparty may be received from a dealer.

From a valuation perspective, caps, collars, and floors are a series of options with each option expiring on each interest reset date. For example, a three-year cap with quarterly payment dates can be valued as the sum of the values of the related 12 call options, each expiring at the end of each quarter over the next three years. As the value of a cap, collar, or floor is linked to interest rates, these instruments can be valued using the binomial model used for bonds because it comprehends the forward interest rates.

Swaptions

Swaptions are options on swaps that provide the holder with the right to enter into a swap at a specified future date at specified terms or to extend or terminate the life of an existing swap. As indicated by the name, a swaption has characteristics of an option and an interest rate swap. Swaptions may be exercisable on only one date in the future, exercisable at any date in the future, or exercisable at any date after an initial exercise "lockout" period. As with all options, the purchaser of an option is at risk only for the premium paid to enter into the contract. Although swaptions are generally structured as interest rate swaps, they may also be structured as other types of swaps, such as currency or commodity swaps.

A *caption* is a variation of the swaption except that it is an option to purchase or sell a cap at some point or period in the future.

There is no active market for funding swaptions. Similar to interest-rate swaps, prices of swaptions move with changes in interest rates.

The method of estimating the fair value of swaptions and captions is similar to that for any option. However, because the option is on a swap that starts or terminates at a future date, it must be valued based on the forward interest rates in effect during the life of the new swap or what would have been the remaining life of the existing swap if it could be terminated under the swap option. The principle is the same for a caption, which is an option on an option that starts or terminates at a future date. It also must be valued based on the forward interest rates.

DEBT WITH EMBEDDED OPTIONS CHARACTERISTICS

There are many different types of debt with embedded option characteristics and variations thereof. Typically the debt features are rather easy to understand and value. However, the option features complicate the instrument. In many instances, even the marketplace does not fully appreciate the characteristics of the compound debt instrument and, as a result, will tend to misprice, from a theoretical point of view, the option features.

There is an active market for many different issues of debt with embedded option characteristics. Prices, generally, move with changes in interest rates and are influenced by the terms of the embedded option features. Price quotations for representative publicly traded issues can be obtained from the *Wall Street Journal,* the *New York Times,* and other financial media. Quotations can also be obtained from brokers and dealers who make a market for certain issues.

Quotations may not be available for older issues and for issues with no active market. In these instances values can be estimated based on the current market yields for similar issues of similar credit standing and by computing fair values based on the characteristics of the debt and the option. Different option features require a different approach to valuation. For this reason, a number of the more common types of debt with embedded options are discussed below along with the valuation considerations unique to each category of debt.

Valuation Considerations for Different Types of Debt with Embedded Options Characteristics

Callable Bonds

Callable bonds contain a provision permitting the issuer to buy back the bond at a specified price (call price) on a specified date, or after a specified period of time, prior to the maturity of the bond. The call price is, generally, in excess of the bond par value. A call provision in a bond issue works to the benefit of the issuer and to the detriment of the investor and, therefore, tends to increase the yield on the bonds. These bonds are subject to prepayment risk because as interest rates decline and market prices exceed the call price the issuer is likely to call the bond. The result of the call provision is that it places a price ceiling on the bond. Individual bonds are also subject to the credit risk of the issuer. Callable debt issued or guaranteed by governmental agencies is guaranteed or partially guaranteed against credit loss.

The value of a callable bond is equivalent to the value of straight debt or a noncallable bond minus the value of the call feature. In order to value a callable bond, it is first necessary to value the underlying debt as straight debt, which is normally valued using a discounted cash flow approach. However, because the call feature permits exercise at some future period, the straight debt must also be valued at each node or option valuation date in the future. The option model must measure the benefit of holding or exercising the option based on the value of the debt at each node.

Putable Bonds

Putable bonds are like floating-rate or short-term instruments because they are effectively payable on demand once the deferment period expires. The principles of valuation of a putable bond are similar to those for callable bonds.

Convertible Bonds

A *convertible bond* is a debt security that is convertible, at a specified price, into stock of the issuer or of another company in which the issuer has an investment. Some securities also allow the holder to convert the security into cash equal to the fair value of a base number of shares of the issuer's stock. The securities are generally convertible at the option of the holder or at maturity. The securities are usually callable at a premium at the option of the issuer. Convertible debt can have an initial principal amount with a fixed or variable rate of interest. Some issues have no stated rate of interest but are sold to an investor at a discount (similar to a zero coupon bond). Maturities vary in length, although the terms normally range from 5 to 20 years. The *equity note* is a variation of convertible debt that is redeemable at maturity either into shares of the issuer's stock or cash generated from the sale of such stock.

Convertible debt is typically issued at a lower rate of interest than nonconvertible debt and has an initial conversion price greater than the market value of the issuer's stock at the time of issuance. The debt is subject to default risk and is usually subordinated to nonconvertible debt. The reduced yield of a convertible bond represents the price of an embedded call option the corporation has written.

Convertible bonds frequently sell at a premium over both conversion value and bond value because of the potential to obtain the benefit of any increase in the value of the stock or in the value of the bond. The bond value usually establishes a floor on the price of the convertible instrument. It is not constant, however, and will change with changes in interest rates and credit risk. The common stock will establish the ceiling when the price of the common stock is high relative to the value of the bond because the instrument will be priced only on its common stock feature.

The value of a convertible bond is equivalent to the value of the straight debt plus the value of the conversion option. The conversion feature can be valued based on the binomial options pricing model. The model should comprehend the value and volatility of the stock relative to the value of the bond at each node. A two-factor binomial lattice should be used for convertible bonds to comprehend the volatility of the bond and the volatility of the stock. However, the expansion of the binomial using a two-factor approach cannot be accomplished efficiently without the use of a very powerful computer. As a result, bonds with embedded options are usually valued using one-factor models. A simpler approach is to value each component separately. However, when using this approach, the option valuation should consider both the number of shares to be issued upon exercise of the option and the transfer of the debt amount to equity in assessing the value of the stock.

To complicate this valuation process even further, most convertible bonds also have a call provision. The valuation, then, is a function of the underlying debt instrument, the call option, and the option to convert. Each of these features requires some refinement in the valuation process. In many instances, however, refinements to the basic model can be ignored because they do not significantly affect the value of the option.

A number of variations of convertible debt contain features that make the valuation process more difficult than for ordinary convertible debt. The *zero coupon convertible note* is issued at a premium or discount which is convertible into the issuer's stock. Sometimes the terms of the conversion require the holder to forfeit all accrued and unpaid interest. The securities may also include a put whereby the holder can put the note back to the issuer on specified dates at an accreted value. The issuer, at its option, may elect to settle the put with cash, stock, or subordinated notes. The zero coupon convertible bond is issued at a discount, with no periodic interest coupon payments. The bond is redeemable at face value at maturity or convertible into the issuer's stock or cash equal to the fair value of the issuer's stock into which the bond is convertible. Some bonds can be redeemed at periodic intervals instead of only at maturity.

A *convertible bond with a premium put* is usually issued at par and allows the holder to redeem the bond at a premium at a specified future date or dates prior to maturity. Convertible bonds with a premium put have the same characteristics as conventional convertible debt except that investors can put the bonds to the issuer at a premium above face value. Accordingly, the risk of the security is somewhat less than for convertible debt; therefore, the security usually has a lower coupon rate than a typical convertible bond. The securities are subject to the same default and credit risks as convertible debt securities.

The *carrot-and-stick bond* is a convertible bond with a carrot-and-stick provision. The carrot provision is a lower than normal conversion premium to encourage investors to exercise their conversion right earlier than normal. The stick provision gives the issuer the right to call the bond at a specified premium if the issuer's stock is trading at a certain percentage rate above the conversion price.

Exchangeable Bonds

Exchangeable bonds are debt instruments issued with a warrant allowing the holder to exchange the debt for an equity interest in a third party. Exchangeable debt allows the investor to participate in the appreciation of the third party's equity security while receiving a constant return from the debt instrument. However, if the stock fails to appreciate, the investor has received a lower yield than could have been obtained from conventional debt.

The warrants may be detachable or nondetachable. Detachable warrants are often traded separately from the debt instrument and thus should be assigned a fair value separate from the debt instrument. Nondetachable warrants are an inseparable component of the debt instrument, thus requiring both instruments to be traded together. Consequently, a fair value should be calculated in conjunction with the debt instrument with no separate value assigned to the warrant.

Exchangeable bonds are similar to convertible bonds, except that they are converted into the stock of another corporation. They are valued, generally, as a convertible bond. However, because the value of the bond and the value of the stock are not linked with each other, risk is diversified. Accordingly, the value of the exchangeable bond may be greater than the value of a similar convertible bond. This advantage, however, is offset somewhat by the tax impact associated with the exercise of the exchangeable feature, which is not present with the exercise of the conversion feature.

Pay-in-Kind Debt

Pay-in-kind (PIK) debentures are bonds that provide the issuers with the option to pay interest with additional PIK debentures ("baby bonds") rather than in cash. These instruments are often used in leveraged buyouts and corporate restructurings because they preserve cash flows that may be needed to reduce debt and finance operations. PIK debentures generally have a fixed rate and are subject to prepayments. These instruments generally limit the time period during which interest can be satisfied with additional PIK debentures. Typically, these instruments are issued by entities that either through asset sales or equity offerings raise funds to retire the debt. Like most corporate bonds, PIK bonds are generally callable by the issuer.

Investors in PIK debentures are provided a high yield due to the risky nature of the investments. If interest rates increase, the issuer will exercise its option and pay with additional bonds, which results effectively in the issuance of new debt at a below market interest rate. If interest rates decline, however, the issuer may call the bond and issue new debt at lower interest rates. As a result, from the investor's perspective, the instrument generally loses value for both increases and decreases in interest rates.

COMMITMENTS AND GUARANTEES

Financial commitments and guarantees can have many different characteristics. *Commitments* may be conditional or unconditional. Commitments may be one-sided obligations, whereby a single party or entity agrees to be obligated under the commitment, or two-sided obligations, whereby both parties are bound by the commitment. *Guarantees* usually are conditional one-sided obligations, whereby only the guarantor is obligated upon the occurrence of a future event.

Unconditional two-sided financial commitments that convey the right or obligation to purchase or sell a financial instrument in the future are equivalent to and should be valued like forward exchange contracts. The value should be based on the difference between the forward price of the goods or services to be purchased or sold and the commitment price. The forward price contemplates the interest that could be earned on an alternative investment less any cash flows, such as dividends, that are foregone by not investing in the underlying indexed item today.

Conditional commitments usually are one-sided obligations requiring an entity to perform at the option of another entity or person or upon the occurrence of a future event. A bank, for example, may make a commitment to make a mortgage loan to a customer. The customer, however, is not obligated to borrow from the bank. As another example, an entity that sells a cap has made a conditional commitment to make a payment to the buyer of the cap if interest rates move above a specified interest rate in the future. A conditional commitment is economically equivalent to an option and should be valued like an option. The value of a conditional commit-ment to purchase or sell a financial instrument, for example, should be based on an options pricing model considering the value and volatility of the underlying financial instrument.

A financial guarantee also is similar to an option, but the exercise of the option requiring performance under the guar-antee is usually beyond the control of the guarantor or the guaranteed party. The value of a guarantee should be based on the amount of the exposure under the guarantee, which in theory is then valued like an option. However, its value is based on the volatility of the possible occurrence of the event that gives rise to the guarantee and the volatility of the value of any applicable collateral. More practically, guarantees are valued based on the amount of exposure under the guarantee and the likelihood of performance being required.

EQUITY INVESTMENTS

Equity investments include equity securities, such as common and preferred stock, and equity interests, such as joint ven-ture interests. There are many variations of each. For pur-poses of SFAS No. 107, joint venture interests include, for example, an investment in a real estate entity, such as a real estate limited partnership or real estate investment trust, accounted for on the cost basis of accounting.

Nonmarketable equity securities represent ownership interests in shares of stock that are not traded on a national securities exchange or on an over-the-counter market. Enti-ties whose stock, equity units, or other forms of ownership rights are not traded on an organized exchange are usually referred to as private companies or privately held companies.

Market quotations can be obtained rather easily for publicly traded companies but generally are not available for private companies. As a result, the valuation of a private com-pany is extremely subjective. Sales of stock, if any, tend to be limited, and the terms of the sales are generally not known.

Appraisals can sometimes be obtained from entities that specialize in the valuation of privately held companies or from investment bankers, but appraisals tend to be expensive.

There is no uniform approach to estimating the fair value of an entity whose stock is not traded. For entities that have significant, stable operations, a valuation could be based on expected cash flows from future operations. For entities with limited assets and liabilities, a valuation could be based on the value of the individual components. Regardless of the type of entity or the valuation approach that is used, the assumptions will typically be very subjective.

CHAPTER 9

Management Control of Derivative Operations

Michael A. Moran

This chapter discusses control issues for the management of derivative activities. The control concepts that apply to derivative activities are the same as those that apply to other areas of an organization's activities. However, because derivative activities are often conducted through an electronic medium (by telephone or through computer terminals) and, more importantly, because derivative contracts often contain a high degree of leverage, internal controls over derivative activities must be specific and constantly monitored. Some organizations might conclude that because they currently have entered into only a small number of derivative transactions the control concepts discussed in this chapter go far beyond what they need. It should be noted, however, that as organizations continue to expand their markets both domestically and internationally their need for new and additional derivative transactions will grow. As a result, control procedures that may have been considered effective when an organization had only a handful of simple derivative contracts will be quickly overwhelmed with increased derivative transaction complexity and volume.

By the passage of the Foreign Corrupt Practices Act of 1977, the Securities Exchange Act of 1934 was amended to require companies that have securities registered under Section 12 of the Act or who are required to file reports under Section 15(d) of the Act to

(A) Make and keep books, records, and accounts which, in reasonable detail, accurately and fairly reflect the transactions and dispositions of the assets of the issuer; and

(B) Devise and maintain a system of internal accounting controls sufficient to provide reasonable assurance that:

(i) Transactions are executed in accordance with management's general or specific authorizations;

(ii) Transactions are recorded as necessary (a) to permit preparation of financial statements in conformity with generally accepted accounting principles or any other criteria applicable to such statements, and (b) to maintain accountability for assets;

(iii) Access to assets is permitted only in accordance with management's general or specific authorization; and

(iv) The recorded accountability for assets is compared with the existing assets at reasonable intervals and appropriate action is taken with respect to any differences.

A comparison of the above requirements to the published reports of significant losses incurred in derivative activities will identify at least some of the reasons why losses of such a magnitude could continue to be undetected.

CONTROL OVERVIEW

Derivatives are important tools to assist management in the control of certain risks. Derivatives, however, can create far more risks than their benefits if the derivative activities themselves are not carefully controlled. Derivative activities are trading activities that often involve significant financial amounts and that are conducted without much of the individual transaction paperwork and prior written approvals and authorizations that accompany many business transactions.

There are five key reasons why derivative operations require active management control:

1. Derivatives are financial instruments that involve very high leverage. The dollar amounts recorded at the inception of a transaction (if any) represent only a small fraction of the financial risk in the transaction.

2. The notional amounts of derivative transactions are usually very large. The size of these transactions, when combined with their leverage, represents potentially significant financial risk to rapid changes in market values.

3. Derivative operations are conducted in an electronic environment. Transactions are often agreed to by telephone or through computer terminals between two individuals. As a result there is little paper trail until well after a transaction has been agreed to.

4. Derivative transactions are executed very quickly and without prolonged negotiation. As a result many transactions can be agreed to in the course of a trading day and sizable long or short positions can be created in a brief period of time.

5. Derivative transactions are very dependent upon individuals. As most transactions are agreed to by two individuals representing the counterparties to the transaction, an organization can be committed to a significant transaction before anyone else in the organization knows about that transaction.

The most critical difference between derivative trading activities and cash trading activities (such as securities trading) is the inherent leverage in derivatives transactions.

Management control and risk management of derivative activities requires the following:

1. A strong control environment
2. An organizational understanding of derivatives activities risks
3. The establishment of a "risk appetite" for derivative activities
4. Documentation of policies and procedures that address the risk appetite
5. Maintenance of risk management monitoring activities
6. Ongoing reevaluation of the derivatives risk management process

THE CONTROL ENVIRONMENT

The control environment reflects an organization's approach to controlling its activities. The control environment includes the organization's attitude toward controls, the manner in which it assesses risks, how it communicates control matters throughout the organization, and how it monitors its activities and resolves errors and omissions. Because of the leverage risks that are inherent in derivative operations, it is imperative that an organization's management establish and maintain control processes and procedures that prevent errors and omissions or that quickly detect and correct them. The most critical control component is processes and procedures that operate to prevent errors and omissions. The second most critical control component is the speed with which control processes and procedures detect and correct errors and omissions because any delay in detection and correction can result in catastrophic loss to the organization.

There are four elements that comprise the control environment:

1. The commitment to control
2. The risk assessment process

3. The information and communication systems
4. The monitoring and control activities

Commitment to Control

An organization's commitment is the single most important element of its control environment. If the board of directors and senior management have a strong commitment to control, then processes and procedures will be designed and implemented to provide effective control. If the board of directors and senior management have a weak commitment, then regardless of the control policies and procedures that may be documented in its records, significant errors and omissions will continue to occur because the control policies and procedures will only exist on paper and not in the mindset of the organization and its officers and employees.

The commitment to control is evident in the manner in which the board of directors and senior management instill and enforce integrity and high ethical values. It is evident in written codes of conduct, in policies and procedures related to conflicts of interest, and in the manner in which the company sets performance goals and rewards its managers. Most important, an organization's commitment to control is evident in the manner in which the organization resolves the occasional ethical issues that confront it. Indicators of a commitment to control can be found in the activities of the board of directors and key board committees, such as the audit committee and the compensation committee. The frequency of meetings, the quality and completeness of information provided to the board and its committees, the independence of their deliberations, and the nature of the questions that they raise to management about the organization's activities are all indicators of the audit committee's effectiveness.

An organization with a strong commitment to control will maintain an organizational structure that is appropriate for its size and complexity. It will define and assign authorities and responsibilities so that key managers will clearly understand their duties and will take responsibility for the activities assigned to them. In addition, an organization with a strong commitment to control will have hiring and training policies and procedures that assure that personnel are adequately trained to perform their duties and that a sufficient number of properly trained personnel will be assigned to provide control support. Finally, an organization with a strong commitment to control will exhibit an absolute intolerance for intentional violations of policies and procedures. Nowhere is an intolerance for intentional violations of policies and procedures more critical than in trading activities such as with derivatives. When an individual knows that, regardless of the outcome to the organization, his or her employment will be terminated if controls are intentionally violated, the temptation to cut corners to try to make additional profit, suppress a loss, or save costs will be sharply reduced.

For derivative operations, the key components of the control commitment are not different from those that should exist in other parts of the organization. The difference between derivative operations and many other corporate activities is the speed at which material errors can occur and accumulate if controls are poorly designed or fail to function properly.

Risk Assessment Process

The second element of the control environment of an organization is its risk assessment process. Every organization encounters both internal and external risks and these risks are constantly changing as the organization evolves over time. Some organizations react to risks as those risks become apparent in losses, either in that organization or in other organizations—the problem is how to not be the first one to experience the loss! Successful organizations, however, establish and maintain processes to assess and address risks as the organization's activities evolve. The assessment process serves not only to identify situations where controls should be created or modified, but also to consider the impact of the risks on the pricing and profitability of the activity. Successful organizations occasionally terminate an activity or decide not to engage in an activity based upon their assessment that the risks involved outweighed the potential profitability of that activity. In regard to derivative activities, a thorough risk assessment process is crucial. Several notable publicly disclosed losses from derivative activities were accompanied by statements that the organization did not understand the risks involved. Without a thorough understanding of the risks, the losses were inevitable.

The risk assessment process begins with the establishment of objectives for an activity that are:

1. Consistent with the overall strategies and business plans of the organization.

2. Internally consistent within the activity.

3. Developed by and committed to by all levels of management.

Those objectives must be clear and unambiguous enough to assure that they will be understood and must be communicated effectively to both employees and the board of directors.

Once an activity's objectives are established and understood, mechanisms to identify risks should be established and maintained. Risks from both external sources and internal sources should be identified and stratified in order of significance. In addition, the likelihood of the risks' occurrence and their potential impact should also be assessed so as to provide a basis for determining the actions needed to address those risks.

Finally, the risk assessment process should be an ongoing activity because risks are constantly changing. The uses for derivative transactions are continuing to evolve and this evolution not only modifies existing risks (and in certain cases reduces previously significant risks to minor risks), but also can create new risks. Of particular importance are risks that arise because of concentrations of transactions that can alter credit risks perceived in individual transactions. Concentrations of transactions can also create additional market risk and will alter liquidity risks.

Information and Communication Systems

An organization's commitment to control and to its risk assessment process are highly dependent upon the quality of its information and communication systems. It is the quality and timeliness of the information that an organization receives, from both external and internal sources, that enables it to assess changes in opportunities and changes in risks and to communicate the results quickly and efficiently of any changes in the organization's risk assessments to the appropriate activities throughout the organization. In decades past, it was often possible for a successful organization to rely on a current risk assessment at the individual transaction level and to consider portfolio and concentration risks on a much less frequent basis. However, advances in computer technologies and telecommunication have resulted in an ability to process a significantly greater number of transactions and to do so much more quickly than in the past. Technology has thus changed the rules of the game. Because of the ever increasing number and velocity of transactions, including individually significant transactions, "real time" risk-management information has become a crucial element of many organization's management processes. Trading activities and especially derivative activities (because of their leverage) are classic examples of the need for accurate and timely risk management information.

Well-designed information systems meet the following criteria:

1. They are focused on obtaining adequate external and internal information that enable management to assess the performance of an activity relative to the stated objectives.

2. They provide the appropriate reports (and *only* the appropriate reports) in a sufficient, but not excessive, level of detail to the proper personnel to enable them to carry out their responsibilities.

3. They are fully supported by management which dedicates both the human and technological resources so that the information systems provide an integral support for the organization's strategies and objectives.

As important as well-designed information systems is management's ability to clearly communicate to the appropriate personnel in a clear and concise manner and to receive feedback from subordinates. Effective communication is what determines the effectiveness of an organization's risk management activities. Effective communication systems fulfill these functions:

1. They clearly communicate the duties and responsibilities of each of the organization's personnel.

2. They provide a well-understood process for approvals of "overlimit" transactions and for resolution of exceptions.

3. They have a well-understood process for the resolution of disagreements regarding the conduct of the organization's activities (and encourage the use of the process).

4. They include channels of communication for personnel to report suspected improprieties or unethical behavior.

5. They have channels of communication that encourage personnel and customer suggestions to improve organizational performance.

Communication from the point of view of the receiver (not the sender) is a continuing issue for many organizations. At times, the information that management thinks it is communicating to its personnel and the information that the personnel think that management is communicating to them are vastly different. When the information being communicated to personnel relates to control issues surrounding trading activities such as derivative activities, any ambiguity or imprecision in that information can result in increased (not decreased) risks.

Monitoring and Control Activities

The final element in an organization's control environment is its monitoring and control activities. It is these activities that demonstrate whether an organization's control environment is truly functional. The manner in which control exceptions and deficiencies are identified, communicated, and resolved either confirms that the control environment is strong—or confirms that it exists only on paper.

There are five key elements of effective monitoring and control activities:

1. The organization's processes include routine procedures that identify whether the system of internal control is functioning.

2. Periodic comparisons are made between detail records and physical assets.

3. Access to assets and sensitive records and information are appropriately restricted.

4. Internal audit activities are conducted by qualified personnel and those activities focus on appropriate risks.

5. Control errors and deficiencies are raised to the appropriate level of attention and are addressed from both an individual and systemic risk perspective.

An effective monitoring and control process achieves continuous improvement by actively seeking to identify control exceptions and deficiencies, not only to address the specific exceptions and deficiencies but also to assess whether they indicate a systemic problem or impact other control areas. An effective monitoring and control process also regularly reevaluates whether risks that were previously considered to be significant continue to be significant and whether control procedures that were previously considered to be effective continue to be effective. The constant reevaluation of risks and the related control procedures is an important activity, because continuing to focus on risks that are no longer significant is costly and can divert the attention of personnel from new or increased risks. Similarly, risk control procedures that are no longer effective in controlling specified risks are wasteful.

Derivative activities risks can change very quickly. Derivative activities also demand a constant monitoring of control exceptions and deficiencies as the size, velocity, and leverage in derivative transactions can result in what appears to be a relatively small exception or deficiency causing a significant loss.

Derivative activities should not be undertaken unless an organization institutes a strong control environment for that activity and the organization is committed to a process of continuous reevaluation of the derivative activity control environment.

UNDERSTANDING ORGANIZATIONAL DERIVATIVE RISKS

Before an organization decides to engage in derivative activities it should satisfy itself that it has a sufficient organizational understanding of the risks involved. This means that not only should the managers and other personnel who are directly involved in the activity have a thorough understanding of derivatives and their risks, but also that the monitoring and control activities such as the internal audit function, the controllership function, the treasury function, and chief financial officer should be fully knowledgeable about the risks and rewards of the derivatives. In addition, other members of senior management and the board of directors should have a sufficient knowledge about derivatives to be able to assess the portfolio risks involved, to evaluate the performance of the managers and other personnel engaged in the derivative activities, and to assess the issues related to the derivative activities that are raised by the monitoring and control functions.

In many organizations, the organizational understanding of risks is achieved by the activities of a *risk management committee*. A risk management committee should include members of senior management and a broad representation from the various risk disciplines (operations, internal audit, treasury, controllership, and so on) in the organization. Collectively, the members of the risk management committee can ensure that the organization has sufficient understanding of the various risks involved in any activity and that the appropriate policies and procedures are in place to monitor and control those risks. Derivative activities must be clearly understood by all the members of the risk management committee.

As with any other type of trading activity, certain derivative transactions are mechanically simple and easily understood. Certain other derivative transactions, however, are highly complex. In addition, within the derivative transaction groups that are considered mechanically simple and easily understood, the terms of a particular derivative transaction could still present a significant risk to an organization. For example, a simple interest rate swap contract (often called a plain vanilla swap) provides for the exchange of cash flows related to a notional amount of principal where one party pays a fixed rate of interest and the other party pays a floating rate of interest (such as LIBOR). Other interest rate swap contracts contain option features or other conditional terms that make their operation much more complex. Further, some interest rate swap contracts contain terms that result in extreme leverage. For example, interest rate swap contracts have been written whereby one party paid a fixed rate of interest and the other party paid a specified market floating interest rate *cubed!* In other words, the party that was obligated to pay the floating rate of interest had accepted exponential interest rate risk: If the specified market floating interest rate increased from two to three percent, the floating rate of interest applicable to the derivative transaction would increase from 8 to 27 percent.

Creating the policies and procedures that would establish a risk management program for derivative activities requires a sufficient understanding of the mechanics of the risks involved to be able to decide what types of derivative transactions will be permitted to be entered into, to establish trading limits, and to design and implement the monitoring and control procedures. Thus if a derivative financial instrument is too complex to be well understood by either management or the functions that provide monitoring and control for the organization, then that type of derivative financial instrument should be avoided.

Several risks must be understood in connection with derivative activities. Although each is discussed herein as a separate risk, they are all interrelated. For example, interest rate and credit risks can both affect liquidity and market risks

The following are the risks that need to be understood in connection with derivative activities:

1. Hedging risks (including economic hedges versus accounting hedges)
2. Interest rate risks
3. Credit risks
4. Liquidity risks
5. Market risks
6. Operational risks
7. Information risks

Hedging Risks

Hedging risk is the risk that transactions entered into to hedge perceived risks do not effectively hedge those risks and/or cannot be reflected in the financial statements as accounting hedges. Many organizations initially enter into derivative transactions to hedge perceived financial risks. In doing so, some believe that the derivative transactions will eliminate the perceived risks for the life of the derivatives transactions. Unfortunately, this is not true. To function effectively as a hedge, an inverse correlation must exist between changes in value of the hedging instrument and the changes in the value of the item hedged. Further, to qualify as an accounting hedge, the inverse correlation must be both mathematical and economic. The higher the degree of inverse correlation, the more effective the hedge. The problem is that the inverse correlation is rarely 100 percent so some of the risk will be retained.

Understanding how much risk is retained is an important part of understanding hedging risks. Further, regardless of how effective the inverse correlation may be initially, the effectiveness of a hedge can deteriorate and can even be eliminated by events. The inverse correlation may break down only for a brief period of time; however, if the inverse correlation breaks down for an extended period of time, the hedge is ineffective and the derivative transaction could actually increase the risk that was intended to be hedged. For example, during the 1980s some depository financial institutions entered into interest rate swap contracts whereby they agreed to pay interest on a significant notional amount at fixed interest rates and to receive interest on that notional amount at variable interest rates. Their intention was to fix the funding costs of their interest-sensitive assets because they believed that interest rates would rise. However, when interest rates instead fell, the depository financial institutions were trapped with the falling interest rates on their interest-sensitive assets while their funding costs remained at a fixed higher level. Management who understand that the risk that inverse correlation can break down will establish the necessary procedures to constantly monitor hedged positions and will take effective action to adjust hedged positions if the inverse correlation breaks down for more than a temporary period.

Hedges that qualify as accounting hedges require not only that a high degree of inverse mathematical and economic correlation exists, but also that the hedging instrument is specifically identified with the hedged item (or at least with a group of hedged items that function as though they were a single item). Effectively, this means that the notional of a hedging instrument cannot exceed the recorded amount of the hedged item, and that the maturity of the hedging instrument cannot be greater than the maturity of the hedged item. The contractual maturity hedging requirement sometimes creates problems with accounting for transactions as hedges in financial statements.

Asset/liability managers often assert that requiring individual assets, liabilities, or fixed commitments to be hedged over their contractual lives is very inefficient, and that a much more effective and efficient hedge of a risk (of market, interest rate, liquidity, and so on) can be created by hedging that risk on a portfolio basis (not an individual item basis) and over the duration of the portfolio (not the individual contractual maturities of the items in that portfolio). The problem is that while either of the two methods of hedging may have the economic effect on the organization, only accounting hedges may be reflected as such in the financial statements. Hedging instruments that may be economically effective but do not qualify as accounting hedges must be reflected at their market value in the financial statements. As a result, the period-to-period income statements might show dramatically different results based solely on whether the hedging instruments qualify as accounting hedges. It is important that an organization understand whether a hedge being entered into qualifies as an accounting hedge and what the effect on the financial statements will be if a hedge does not qualify as an accounting hedge.

Interest Rate Risks

Interest rate risk is the risk that changes in interest rates will affect the value of portfolios and that such changes will affect cash flows. Managing interest rate risks is an important activity in financial services organizations and especially in depository financial institutions whose primary source of income is the "spread" between interest income and interest expense. Derivative financial instruments are often used to manage interest rate risk when the interest rate risk cannot be managed naturally by recording interest-bearing assets and interest-bearing liabilities whose interest rate calculations and maturities reduce interest rate risk. In addition, while the general level of interest rates rise and fall from time to time, interest rates do not always rise and fall to the same degree for financial instruments having different maturities. This is often described in terms such as "a flattening of the yield curve," or "a steepening of the yield curve," or "an inverse yield curve." These conditions occur because short-term interest rates and long-term interest rates do not always rise and fall in unison. For example, if interest rates are declining, long-term interest rates could fall faster than short-term interest rates, Similarly, when interest rates are rising, short-term interest rates could rise faster or slower than long-term interest rates. Situations can also occur where short-term and long-term interest rates rise or fall to a similar degree, but intermediate-term interest rates rise or fall to a different degree, thus creating a "bulge" in the yield curve. Before engaging in derivative activities, an organization should understand the effect that changes in interest rates will have on the financial instruments it holds or has issued and the effect on these financial instruments if changes in interest rates do not occur uniformly across the yield curve. The changes in interest rate patterns in recent periods can assist in this understanding, but an organization should also understand which changes in interest rates would most negatively affect the organization and the likelihood that such changes will occur.

Credit Risks

Whenever an organization holds a financial instrument (an amount receivable from, or evidence of an ownership interest in, another organization), it has assumed a *credit risk*. Credit risk is normally thought of as the risk that the debtor or equity issuer will be unable to pay the principal and interest or dividends associated with the financial instrument. When a debtor or equity issuer has agreed to pay a variable amount of interest calculated on market rates or a dividend amount calculated on market rates, the credit risk changes whenever the reference market rate changes. In addition, if the debtor or equity issuer has several issues outstanding with variable interest or dividend amounts calculated on market rates, changes in reference market rates can cause the credit risk of the debtor or equity issuer to change dramatically. Credit risk can also be assumed in the timing of the receipt and delivery of payments related to financial instruments. Therefore, an organization must be concerned not only about the credit risk in the debtor or equity issuer, but also the credit risk in the counterparty from which a financial instrument is acquired or to which a financial instrument is sold. Thus, when an organization purchases or sells a financial instrument there is a risk that the counterparty will be unable to deliver the financial instrument after payment has been made or will be unable to deliver the payment after the financial instrument has been delivered.

Credit risk inherent in the timing of receipt and delivery of payments is exacerbated when the parties involved in the transaction are separated be several time zones. In the early 1970s the bankruptcy of a German bank caused losses to U.S. banks because the German bank had issued payment orders to the U.S. banks during its business day, which was before the U.S. banks had opened for the day. Unfortunately, the German bank was closed by the German Central Bank at the end of the business day in Germany (which was late morning in New York) before the German bank had transmitted the funds to cover its payment orders. Many of the U.S. banks had already made the payments that the German bank had instructed them to make and thus incurred credit losses as a result of the timing of delivery and receipt of payments.

Because of the leverage inherent in derivatives, credit risks can change much more quickly than they would in many other financial instruments. Therefore, it is important that an organization that chooses to engage in derivative activities should establish and maintain credit risk evaluation processes that can respond to the more rapid and more significant changes in derivative financial instruments' credit risks.

Liquidity Risks

Liquidity risk involves the ability of an organization to meet its financial obligations as they mature. Liquidity risks also involve the ability of a market to assure a routine and efficient resolution of transactions among the market participants. For an individual financial instrument, liquidity is often a function of the duration of that financial instrument. Generally, the longer the maturity of a financial instrument, the less liquid it becomes. Liquidity can also be a function of the complexity of a financial instrument: The more complex the terms of a financial instrument, the less liquid it becomes. The reason why a longer duration or more complex financial instrument is less liquid is because there are fewer potential purchasers who are willing to take the longer or more complex risk.

When financial instruments are traded on a securities exchange, the liquidity risk is reduced because the exchanges have established procedures to ensure that transactions can be routinely resolved. In regard to derivative financial instruments, the exchanges require that cash (or near cash) collateral be deposited to collateralize unrealized depreciation in those financial instruments. However, if an organization enters into derivative financial instrument contracts directly with another organization (and not through a securities exchange) liquidity risk must be given more serious consideration. To the extent that the derivative financial instrument is widely held and traded (such as a short-term plain vanilla interest rate swap) liquidity risk is lower. However, as stated above, if a derivative financial instrument contains complex terms, or has a very long life, or includes other unique features, then the number of potential alternative counterparties who would be willing to bid will decrease and, therefore, the liquidity of that derivative financial instrument will also decrease. The liquidity risk of an "over-the-counter" (non–exchange-traded) derivative financial instrument is often much greater than for exchange-traded derivative financial instruments. Thus, if the original counterparty cannot perform under the terms of the derivative financial instrument, the holder of the derivative financial instrument may have to maintain (or obtain) the funding to support the derivative financial instrument held until the original counterparty is able to perform or a substitute counterparty can be located. An organization that plans to engage in derivative financial instrument activities should carefully evaluate the liquidity risks related to the types of derivative financial instruments it plans to use.

Market Risks

Market risk is the risk that changes in market values could have an adverse effect on an organization's portfolios. Market risk is closely related to liquidity risk. If derivative transactions are planned to be entered into for trading profit, then an understanding must be obtained of the depth and breadth of the markets for the various types of derivatives intended to be traded. A very liquid market usually results in very narrow bid and ask spreads, so the trading risk decision must consider both the potential for profit and the liquidity of the market. If the complexity or the duration of a derivative financial instrument significantly reduces the number of market participants who regularly trade that derivative financial instrument, then changes in general market conditions generally will require a more significant adjustment to the value of the derivative financial instrument to induce a market participant to acquire that derivative financial instrument. Should markets conditions become adverse, they are likely to become even more adverse for less liquid financial instruments, especially derivatives. If an organization intends to trade derivative financial instruments for a profit (as opposed to using derivatives solely for hedging purposes), it must understand the depth and breadth of the markets for those types of derivatives and, as a result, it must assess how quickly the market value of those derivative financial instruments could change in a significant amount. Only then can an organization effectively establish trading procedures to protect itself from a significant decline in the value of those derivatives.

Being able to liquidate a position quickly is often very important in a rapidly changing market. As with any other trading activity, an organization must set maximum loss limits beyond which derivatives traders must take action to limit the organization's losses. The more liquid the market is for a particular derivative financial instrument, the easier it will be for the derivatives traders to limit their losses. The less liquid the market is for a particular derivative financial instrument, the more narrow and stringent the "stop loss" procedures must be.

One of the methods to assess the potential effect of holding various financial instruments is to perform a "value-at-risk" or a similar estimation. Value-at-risk and similar estimation methodologies attempt to quantify the impact on the value of various financial instrument portfolios if the market were to move adversely to a defined degree. The defined degree of adverse market movement varies among various calculation models but all are generally designed to estimate the most adverse market movement that could be expected to occur. Value-at-risk and similar methodologies do not guarantee the maximum amount of loss that an organization could incur; they calculate the loss based upon an adverse market movement to a defined degree, but an actual adverse market movement could exceed that defined degree. Nonetheless, a value-at-risk estimation does assist an organization in setting limits on the amount of risk it is willing to accept in its various financial instrument portfolios and in defining conditions under which actions would be undertaken to reduce or eliminate the effects of adverse market movements. Because market movements are not absolutely predictable and can be caused by psychological as well as fundamental factors, it is imperative that an organization involved with derivative financial instruments understand the market risks and the processes necessary to properly manage those risks.

Operational Risks

Operational risk management involves the ability of an organization's systems to process transactions accurately and on a timely basis. With financial instruments, the ability to process transactions accurately and on a timely basis impacts not only the presentation of the financial statements, but also the ability of the traders to know what the organization's positions are in the various financial instruments it holds. In volatile market conditions, such information is crucial. Accurate transactional records are also crucial to effectively monitor the activities of the traders and the organization's risk position. These transactional records must not only be accurate in total, but must accurately segregate (1) transactions entered into for the purpose of hedging an organization's own assets, liabilities, and firm commitments, as separate from (2) transactions entered into to accommodate customers' needs (with part or all of the market risk hedged in the market), and further as separate from (3) transactions entered into for proprietary trading purposes. Obviously, such segregation must be prepared by type of financial instrument.

An organization that plans to engage in derivative activities must assure that its systems and procedures are adequate to provide the necessary transactional records not only for the level of trading initially planned, but also for the potential of substantially higher levels of trading. Organizations sometimes encounter problems even after they have successfully managed a limited trading operation because they quickly expanded their trading activities beyond the capability of the operating systems to process the increased volumes of transactions. Such an unsupported expansion of derivative activities not only results in losses from errors, processing differences, and compensation for failed transactions, but also in trading losses incurred because traders do not know what the organization's positions are in the various derivative financial instruments it trades. Therefore, an organization that plans to engage in derivative activities must know how many transactions and positions its systems can adequately control and must plan for the actions that will have to be taken (as well as the cost and time to implement those actions) to support substantially higher levels of trading.

Information Risks

Information risk relates to the risk that an organization will make business decisions based on inaccurate or incomplete portfolio information. The hedging, interest rate, credit, liquidity, and market risks discussed above cannot be effectively managed without accurate information about the organization's positions in the financial instruments it holds, the cost of those positions, the creditworthiness of the counterparties, and the current market value of those positions. Assessing these risks based on an infrequent (such as weekly or monthly) manual analysis is simply unacceptable in today's rapidly changing trading environments. More importantly, as technology continues to improve the processing capabilities of trading environments, the volume of transactions will continue to increase and thus risk and profitability analysis at the portfolio level will become much more important. Similarly, portfolio concentration risks will continue to grow as transactional volumes grow. Information capabilities, not mere processing capabilities, will be a key success driver in trading activities in the future. Again, because of the leverage inherent in derivative financial instruments, the information risk relative to derivatives is greater than for other financial instruments.

The Importance of an Organizational Understanding of Risks

Risk management must be an organizational activity if it is to be effective, and organizational risk management is absolutely necessary in regard to derivative activities. In several recently disclosed cases of significant losses connected with derivatives, individuals were engaged in trading without the effective supervision of others in the organization. In some instances the individual allegedly took actions to deliberately conceal the trading losses; but in others, it appeared that the individual simply was not properly supervised. Unless derivative transactions are minor, isolated, and infrequent, the leverage and risk involved in derivatives activities make it almost impossible for one individual to keep abreast of all of the potential risks. In addition, one or a few individuals can become too focused on the derivative activities and may not be anticipating any new or modified risks that could impact those activities. Further, the very basic internal control feature of separation of key duties is rendered totally ineffective if the individuals involved in performing those duties do not have an understanding of the activity's risks. Thus, before engaging in any new activity—and especially in derivative activities—an organization should satisfy itself that a sufficient number of key personnel possess a firm understanding of the derivative activities from a portfolio level, a process level, and an individual account level to enable the organization to properly manage those activities.

ESTABLISHING A RISK APPETITE

When an organization enters into a new activity, it normally does not set a limit on the maximum amount of profit that it is willing to earn on that activity. However, it *must* establish a limit on the amount that it is willing to *lose* on that activity. Establishing the maximum amount of loss that an organization is willing to accept in the conduct of an activity is referred to as establishing *risk appetite*. The maximum amount of acceptable loss should be estimated based on the anticipated frequency of the loss, the amount of the loss by each occurrence, and the income that the organization expects to earn in the conduct of that activity. When the total amount of the loss—either from a high number of loss occurrences or from a fewer number of larger losses—reduces the profit from that activity to an unacceptable level, policies and procedures must be put into place to reduce those losses.

Inherent in the risk appetite estimation process are the costs of the policies and procedures that the organization intends to put into place to assure that losses remain within acceptable limits. For example, in the extension of credit an organization should know what interest rate it can charge for a particular type of credit and, based upon that interest rate and its credit underwriting, operating, and funding costs, how much credit loss it can incur and still remain acceptably profitable in extending credit. The organization will then establish credit underwriting standards to identify the type of entity to whom it can afford to extend credit. It would also establish monitoring and collection procedures to ensure that the losses resulting from the credit extensions do not exceed the established limits. If an organization is extending several different types of credit to several different types of debtors, loss limits would be established for each type of lending and each type of debtor.

The process by which a risk appetite is established for derivative activities is no different from the establishment of a risk appetite in any other activities. An understanding of the various risks involved in the various types of derivatives will enable an organization to establish loss limits for each type of derivative financial instrument in which it intends to trade, as well as the loss limits for each type of counterparty with whom it intends to trade. The process of establishing loss limits will ultimately translate into both intra-day and end-of-day trading and position limits for each type of financial instrument and for each counterparty. It will also result in establishing currency, maturity, and concentration limits.

The establishment of risk appetites for derivative activities is not a one-time matter because risks are constantly changing. Thus, effective risk management of derivative activities requires an ongoing reevaluation of the various risks and, when necessary, an adjustment of the individual and total risk appetites and the resultant risk limits.

DOCUMENTING RISK MANAGEMENT POLICIES AND PROCEDURES

Once an organization has achieved an understanding of the risks involved in the derivative activities that it plans to undertake and an overall risk appetite has been agreed on, policies and procedures must be created to communicate the organizational decisions to the affected personnel. If the organization already has a risk management committee, then the overall risk management policies and objectives will probably have already been decided and disseminated to the organization's personnel. It then only remains for more specific policies and procedures to be created to address the particular risk issues of derivative activities. However, if the organization does not have a risk management committee, it may be necessary first to define the broad risk management policies and objectives as well as the structure of the risk management process, and then to define both the risk management policies and objectives as they relate to derivative activities and the structure of the derivative activities' risk management process.

The derivatives risk management policies and procedures should be simply stated but very direct. They should establish very clearly defined limits and parameters and, while permitting a wide latitude of decision, they should specify an absolute intolerance for intentional violations of those limits and parameters.

Clearly Defined Lines of Authority and Responsibility

A lack of clearly defined lines of authority and responsibility is certain to cause internal control risks. For derivative activities, a lack of definition can cause significant risks. In a financial organization, derivative activities might be established to enter into derivative transactions to hedge the organization's own financial risks as well as derivative transactions to accommodate customers' needs. At the same time it could also enter into derivative transactions as a proprietary trading activity for profit. If each of these three functions reports to a different officer in the organization, there is a risk that changes in control needs which occur as the activity grows and evolves will not be adequately addressed in all three control flows. Similarly, in a nonfinancial organization derivative activities might be established to hedge certain identified financial risks, but because the derivative activities are not a part of a "core" business they might not be formally assigned to a line of business and thus might not be subject to the same approval and authorization processes as other core business activities. Proper management of derivative activities requires that the chain of command for approvals and authorizations be clearly defined so that personnel who are engaged in derivative activities know whose approvals must be obtained and in what circumstances. As important, the managers and officers who provide such approvals must know when their approvals are required.

Clear Segregation of Key Duties

A recurring theme in many surprise losses from trading activities is the lack of proper segregation of duties. In several of the significant derivative activities losses reported during the 1990s, the lack of separation of duties between those who entered into the transactions (traders) and those who recorded the transactions and resolved trade differences (operations) enabled unauthorized trades to be entered into and enabled losses to remain undetected for extended periods of time.

As part of the control procedures traders should be required to record their trades (either on written tickets or through computer terminals) at the time that a trade is entered into. After that time traders should not have the authority or the ability to unilaterally make changes to the terms of re-corded trades. If a trader wishes to change or make corrections to the terms of a recorded trade a request should be submitted to the appropriate operations activity for review and approval by a designated person or group that is not involved in the trading function. In addition, the terms of all trades should be automatically confirmed with the counterparties by a function that is independent of the traders. Finally, the operations functions that record trades should be segregated from the functions that receive or deliver the payments, and both of these activities should be segregated from the reconcilement and control activities. Segregation of key duties is essential to accomplishing the basic purpose of internal control—preventing errors and omissions or detecting and correcting them quickly.

Clearly Defined Trading and Position Limits

Derivative activities' risk management policies and procedures should set both transactional and position limits that reflect the risk appetite specified by the organization. Simply stating an overall dollar exposure limit (either in total or by trader) is insufficient. Exposure limits should be set for both individual transactions and for intra-day and end-of-day positions for:

- each type of derivative
- each counterparty
- various maturity periods
- each currency
- the overall positions

In addition, depending on the circumstances limits might be established to reduce other risks such as the maximum size of an individual transaction, concentrations in counterparty industries, or cash settlement intervals.

The purpose of setting so many different types of limits is to prevent unintended concentrations of transactions greater than the sum of the individual risk considerations. The limits should be set high enough to permit normal trading activities, but should be reasonable enough to alert traders and risk managers to changing concentrations of risks. However, the most important objective of setting clearly defined limits is so that each of the traders knows the maximum amounts that can be transacted without the required approval of another individual.

Overlimit Approvals and Authorizations

Certain set limits may be prohibited from being overridden, but market conditions and customer requests will occasionally require that many established limits be temporarily exceeded. However, the conditions under which limits may be exceeded and the process by which required approvals and authorizations for exceeding limits are to be obtained and documented must be clearly defined. Required approvals and authorizations should be obtained prior to or at the time that a transaction is entered into, not only to confirm that the proposed transaction is allowed, but also so that risk managers can assess the impact of the transaction (as well as other overlimit transactions) on the organization's overall risk position. In addition, the nature and number of overlimit approvals must be monitored to identify patterns that should be brought to the attention of the risk management committee for consideration of changes in individual established limits. Monitoring also serves as an early warning system for a market (or a portion of a market) becoming "overheated," a signal that even closer monitoring of positions should be undertaken.

Coordination of Risk Management Activities

Risk management policies and procedures should be designed to assure that separate risk management activities and techniques are coordinated to achieve maximum benefit. Often when a significant derivative activities loss is uncovered the indicators that a problem existed were present in separate areas of the organization that incurred the loss, but the problem was not addressed soon enough because of uncoordinated risk management efforts. Thus, the loss was not prevented or detected and corrected quickly. The leverage and potential volatility of derivative activities require that risk management functions stay as current as possible about changes in the various risks identified in the derivative activities. An organization should link the risk management function in the trading activity with the organization's credit function and its operations function. In addition, parallel sources of risk management information, such as internal audit and regulatory examination reports, should be provided to the risk management committee as soon as the issues are identified.

The two most important criteria necessary for effective risk management policies and procedures are that they should be very clearly stated and that they should be widely disseminated and communicated. The more personnel who are aware of the policies and procedures (whether or not the personnel are directly involved in derivative activities), the more likely that violations of policies or procedures will be reported. In that connection, the policy statements should be brief and to the point. Policy statements that contain explanatory language or other "background" information are considerably less useful than a policy that states the organization's policies simply and clearly. Poorly written or overlong policy statements can make a policy ambiguous. Similarly, the procedure documents that are issued to implement the policies should be clear and concise. For the policies and procedures to be effective, the personnel whose activities will be governed by them should be able to understand them and quickly refer to them for guidance when necessary. Finally, periodic training to reinforce the policies and resolve any questions that might arise will assure that the personnel whose activities are governed by the policies and procedures clearly understand them.

MONITORING RISK MANAGEMENT ACTIVITIES

All controls must be regularly monitored to identify errors and omissions, to assess whether the controls in place continue to function properly, and to identify any emerging systemic problems. When risks are not significant or when the effects of the risks would be slow to result in material losses, the monitoring of the controls can be performed on a infrequent basis. However, when derivative activities are involved the risks can be individually significant and errors and omissions can result in material losses very quickly. As a result control monitoring activities should be performed continuously and, in some cases, on a real-time basis.

The substantial advances in information and processing technology during the past decade have been both a problem and a benefit to risk management activities. These technological advances have enabled organizations to process significantly higher volumes of transactions with the same or fewer personnel and in many cases with vastly increased speed. As a result, an individual review of transactions in trading activities, and even an individual review of significant transactions, becomes very difficult to accomplish prior to the execution of the transactions. So to ensure that transactions are proper and are properly executed, organizations increasingly rely on computerized risk management techniques to identify transactions or patterns of transactions that do not conform to predetermined criteria. As the technological advances continue organizations will become even more reliant upon computerized real-time monitoring of their activities, especially trading activities such as in derivatives, to achieve their risk management objectives.

An organization that intends to engage in derivative activities should design its risk management monitoring activities not only for its initial planned level of derivative activities, but also for any possible intermediate-term growth in those activities. An organization may initiate a new activity and monitor the activity's risks carefully, but then may permit the activity to expand its transactional volume without considering whether the risk management monitoring activities then in place can function effectively in that environment. In many cases, the risk management monitoring activity becomes overwhelmed and losses (sometimes significant losses) occur.

When designing its risk management monitoring activities, an organization should identify the control risks and limits that it believes should be monitored:

1. Before a transaction is executed, such as individual transaction limits.

2. Throughout the day, such as concentrations and counterparty credit limits.

3. After the close of trading for a day or by the next business morning, such as unusual trading patterns and the frequency of trader requests for overlimit approvals.

Risk management monitoring activities accomplish four goals. First, they identify transactions and situations that require immediate attention in order to prevent or correct identified errors and omissions. Secondly, they serve as an information source to enable the organization to reassess whether the control processes and the limits that the organization has put in place are continuing to identify the appropriate situations or whether controls and limits should be changed. Thirdly, risk management monitoring activities can identify situations where additional training is needed or clarifications of existing policies and procedures should be issued. Finally, the existence of an effective risk management monitoring activity contributes to a strong control environment because personnel will be regularly reminded that control procedures and established limits are being checked regularly.

ONGOING REEVALUATION OF THE DERIVATIVE RISK MANAGEMENT PROCESS

It usually takes more than one business cycle to experience the effects of the risks in any new financial instrument because those risks might be more or less significant at different times. Derivative financial instruments are still relatively new for many organizations although their use is becoming more commonplace. New purposes for existing derivative financial instruments are being tested by market participants, and new types of derivative financial instruments are regularly being introduced into the marketplace. As a result, all of the risks in the existing derivative financial instruments may not yet have been identified, and many of the risks related to the new types of derivative financial instruments have not been learned. In addition, as more and more organizations become familiar with particular derivative financial instruments, their use of them will likely increase. Increasing volume and/or size of derivative transactions changes those activities' risk profile.

For all of these reasons an organization engaged in derivative activities should ensure that its risk management committee conducts a regular review of those derivative activities and the risks associated with them as the nature and size of the derivative activities evolve. All of the risk appetite assessments that are made at any point in time and the policies and procedures that were put into place to control those identified risks should be reevaluated whenever changes in the risks have been identified. Risk assessments should also be reevaluated at regular intervals to assure that no changes need to be made to the existing risk appetite assessments in light of recent events. In addition, the policies and procedures that are in place to control risks should be reevaluated to ensure that they are still necessary and effective. It might become beneficial to computerize a manual monitoring procedure related to an identified risk when there are increases in volumes of transactions and advances in technology. Similarly, a risk previously identified as a significant risk might become less significant as the market for a particular derivative financial instrument matures and becomes more liquid. Further, information obtained about derivative activities problems, losses in other organizations, and new or different techniques to monitor and control risks should be evaluated regularly.

Finally, whenever an organization intends to begin entering into a new type of derivative financial instrument or any new activity that will require the use of derivatives, a complete risk review should be conducted—not only on the risks involved in that new derivative or activity but to ascertain the probable affect that it will have on the existing identified risks in the organization's derivative activities.

A SUGGESTED APPROACH FOR MANAGEMENT CONTROL OF DERIVATIVE ACTIVITIES

To summarize the points discussed in this chapter, an organization that intends to engage in derivative activities should consider at least the following among its risk management activities:

Establish a Risk Management Committee or Group to Assess Risks, Set Risk Appetites, and Create the Policies and Procedures to Control Those Risks

1. It should be a senior management activity.

2. All significant organizational functions should be represented.

3. It should be charged with the responsibility of overseeing the identification and evaluation of risks related to derivative activities and the necessary policies and procedures to control those risks.

4. It should approve the risk appetites set for derivative activities.

Identify and Understand the Risks Involved in Derivative Activities

1. Hedging Risks
   - Identification of individual items to be hedged
   - A high degree of inverse mathematical and economic correlation
   - Economic versus accounting hedges

2. Interest Rate Risks
   - Yield curve shifts
   - Yield curve slope changes
   - Rate volatility

3. Credit Risks
   - Direct extensions of credit
   - Indirect extensions of credit in the timing of funds flows
   - Time zone differences

4. Liquidity Risks
   - Depth of markets
   - Complexity of the terms of the derivative
   - Duration of the contract
   - Differences in currencies

5. Market Risks
   - Volatility of the market
   - Depth of the market
   - Delays in the settlement process
   - Time zone differences
   - Differences in currencies
   - Legal restrictions on funds flows
6. Operational Risks
   - Transactional accuracy and timelines
   - Disaster recovery capabilities
   - Technological age of systems
   - Quality of internal controls
7. Information Risks
   - Information accuracy
   - Quality and depth of information
   - Timeliness of delivery to key risk managers

Set a Risk Appetite for All Levels of Identified Risk

1. Overall Financial Limits
   - Total positions at end of day and intra-day
   - Cash versus forward positions
   - By type of transaction
   - By type of derivative financial instrument
   - By currency
   - By counterparty industry
   - By settlement delay
2. Individual Counterparty Limits
   - Total positions at end of day and intra-day
   - Cash versus forward positions
   - By type of transaction

- By type of derivative financial instrument
- By currency
- By settlement delay

Document and Communicate Risk Management Policies and Procedures

1. Overall objectives and policies
2. Structure of the risk management process
3. Approval and authorization chain of command
4. Limit-setting process and limits set
5. Required referrals (especially overlimit approvals)
6. Coordination of risk management techniques

Establish and Maintain Risk Monitoring Activities

1. Computerized monitoring (as much as possible)
2. Transactions that require prior approval
3. Intra-day transactional and position information
4. End of day or next-morning information
5. Detailed information for transactional review
6. Summarized reports for position portfolio and trends review
7. Use to evaluate current limits, policies, and procedures
8. Use to consider policy, procedure, and training revisions

Ongoing Reevaluation of the Derivative Risk Management Process

1. The maturation of the market
2. Effect of newly identified risks in existing derivative financial instruments

3. Effect of new derivative financial instruments
4. Current experiences and personnel development
5. Effect of new activities that use derivative financial instruments
6. Experiences of other organizations
7. New risk management technologies and techniques

MANAGEMENT CONTROL OVER DERIVATIVE ACTIVITIES

Establishing and maintaining management control over derivative activities requires an organization to understand the risk issues involved in derivative activities, to set appropriate risk appetites related to those risks, to create and enforce policies and procedures to monitor and control those risks, and to regularly reevaluate the risks and the organization's approach to controlling those risks.

Risk management can be considered a business activity that reduces uncertainty to identifiable risks and then monitors and controls those risks in order to achieve the organization's objectives. When an organization intends to engage in derivative activities it is imperative that it address the uncertainties related to derivative financial instruments and take steps to reduce those uncertainties to measurable risks and to understand how risks can be monitored and controlled. If an organization does not do so, it subjects itself to the laws of probability and will, sooner or later, incur a significant loss.

INDEX

A

Accounting for Debt and Equity Securities; SFAS No. 115, 27
Accrual, 54
Aggregation, 321–24
American Institute of Certified Public Accountants (AICPA), 27, 30
Statements of Position, 27
Asset-backed securities, 129, 180–81
  interest-only (IO) securities, 331–32
  principal-only (PO) securities, 331–32
  subordinated loans interests, 332
  valuation, 331–32

B

Black, Fischer, 10, 18–19
Black-Scholes model, 302–4, 311–12
Bonds
  callable, 351
  carrot-and-stick bond, 354

Bonds *(Continued)*
  CMO bonds, 333–34
  convertible bond, 104–6, 110–11, 352–54
  dual currency bonds, 113–14
  exchangeable, 354–55
  fixed-pay, 141
  junk bonds, 335–36
  options on, 344–45
  payment-in-kind debentures, 355–56
  pay-through, 141
  putable, 351–52
  synthetic callable bond asset, 120
Brokered markets, 270

C

Callable bonds, 351
Call bull spreads, 46, 48
Call options, 3, 16–22, 47–48
  call bull spreads, 46
  call writer, 18
  conventional issuer, embedded in debt instruments, 99–100
  defined, 301